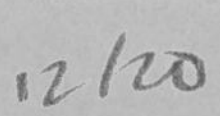

"What a role model Harriet the Spy was for a kid: whip-smart, curious, and bold. It turns out her creator, Louise Fitzhugh, was just as daring. *Sometimes You Have to Lie* is a rollicking and insightful biography about a modern literary heroine."

—Anne Zimmerman, author of *An Extravagant Hunger: The Passionate Years of M. F. K. Fisher*

SOMETIMES YOU HAVE TO LIE

THE LIFE AND TIMES OF LOUISE FITZHUGH, RENEGADE AUTHOR OF *HARRIET THE SPY*

LESLIE BRODY

SEAL PRESS
NEW YORK

Cover design by Chin-Yee Lai
Cover image used with permission from Julie Ann Johnson: Lilyan Chauvin, photographer, from the collection of France Burke, by permission of Sam Shea

Seal Press
Hachette Book Group
1290 Avenue of the Americas, New York, NY 10104
www.sealpress.com
@sealpress

Printed in the United States of America

First Edition: December 2020

Published by Seal Press, an imprint of Perseus Books, LLC, a subsidiary of Hachette Book Group, Inc. The Seal Press name and logo is a trademark of the Hachette Book Group.

Print book interior design by Trish Wilkinson

Library of Congress Cataloging-in-Publication Data
Names: Brody, Leslie, 1952– author.
Title: Sometimes you have to lie : the life and times of Louise Fitzhugh, renegade author of Harriet the spy / Leslie Brody.
Description: First edition. | New York : Seal Press, 2020. | Includes bibliographical references and index.
Identifiers: LCCN 2020022922 | ISBN 9781580057691 (hardcover) | ISBN 9781580057707 (ebook)
Subjects: LCSH: Fitzhugh, Louise. | Authors, American—20th century—Biography. | Illustrators—United States—Biography.
Classification: LCC PS3556.I8554 Z54 2020 | DDC 813/.54 [B]—dc23
LC record available at https://lccn.loc.gov/2020022922

ISBNs: 978-1-58005-769-1 (hardcover), 978-1-58005-770-7 (ebook)

LSC-C

1 2020

For Gary

CONTENTS

PART THREE

INTRODUCTION

A Nasty Girl and Horrid Example

> When I grow up I'm going to find out everything about everybody and put it all in a book.
>
> —*Harriet the Spy*[1]

Harriet the Spy is—in the coolest sixties slang—*an experience.* From its publication in 1964, readers recognized author Louise Fitzhugh's heroine, eleven-year-old Harriet M. Welsch, as an entirely new and radically different version of the American girl: unnerving, unsentimental, nosy, sometimes anxious, extremely funny, rather shrewd, and brutally frank. Some children's books critics simply couldn't get over how "nasty" they thought she was, and what "a horrid example" she set. Children, unsurprisingly, loved the many ways in which Harriet defied authority. When Harriet says, "I'll be damned if I'll go to dancing school," she sends up a howl as staggering—in its way—as Allen

Ginsberg's poem by that name.[2] Harriet is raucous, unruly, and unwilling to compromise with phonies and finks. She's a pint-size harbinger whose schoolroom battles for respect and understanding look in microcosm like the battles for equality many women and girls would wage over the coming years.

Louise Fitzhugh began writing *Harriet the Spy* in 1963, the same year Betty Friedan in *The Feminine Mystique* denounced postwar male chauvinism in America, identifying and rethinking social relations in family and society.[3] As Friedan's manifesto exhorted girls and women to wake themselves up and demand equal rights, radical notions of female empowerment and self-determination were sweeping through popular culture. That was the year seventeen-year-old pop singer Lesley Gore recorded "You Don't Own Me," with the lyrics *Don't tell me what to do / Don't tell me what to say*—and Gloria Steinem published "A Bunny's Tale," an undercover exposé about sexism and working conditions for waitresses at the Playboy Club.[4] Into this heady world Harriet sprang, ready to fight for her independence.

As a child of the fifties, Harriet was a Baby Boomer original. She was a girl spy and practicing writer who dressed in boys' clothes. Her friend and fellow sixth-grader Janie Gibbs was an amateur scientist whose experiments were on track to "blow up the world."[5] Both were budding Upper East Side Manhattan career girls, ambitious, assertive, and coming of age in a time when children were taught, in Friedan's words, "To pity the neurotic, unfeminine, unhappy women who wanted to be poets or physicists or presidents."[6] And while some adults consider Harriet's stalking, peeping, eavesdropping, and occasional breaking and entering a nasty business, betrayal is never Harriet's intention. She doesn't spy to extort or to blackmail or to abuse the secrets she collects; she is an apprentice writer gathering *material*. It is all in service of her craft.

In those bad old days when many women still couldn't get a credit card without a male cosigner, and advertisements entreated wives to make "husband-pleasing coffee," *Harriet the Spy* gave children countercultural *ideas*. She did things that kids weren't supposed to do—and things they may not have considered before reading about them: Harriet quaffed egg creams; she rode three to a motorcycle; she saw a therapist. She wore a tool belt with a flashlight and a knife and ate cake every day after school. She eavesdropped (through a skylight, or in a dumbwaiter) and kept notes on strangers and friends. *Harriet the Spy* inspired the many enterprising children who formed spy clubs and took their notebooks on expeditions around their neighborhoods. Kids saw themselves in her flawed, fearless image.

The book's distracted, comic adults were also new to modern children's literature. Harriet's mother and father are busy, worldly New Yorkers, affectionate but unreliable. Fortunately, they leave care of their daughter to a learned nanny named Ole Golly, magical in her erudition. When Harriet's independence is pressured by the demands of conformity, Ole Golly helps her find the means to resist, and even to subvert situations to her advantage. For instance, Harriet understands that learning to foxtrot and waltz is a rite of passage in her upper-crust society, and she dreads dancing school as a place where preteen girls are sent to learn all the correct steps and to follow a boy's lead. Ole Golly helps Harriet reimagine the ballroom floor as a field of operation where agents like Mata Hari, a great dancer *and* a great spy, triumphed undercover. Harriet's tradecraft takes a dangerous turn when her school friends discover one of the notebooks in which she has recorded her truthful and unflattering impressions of them. In short order, they form a gang of spy catchers to expose and shun her. Again, Ole Golly offers counsel. If Harriet wants her friends back, she is going to have to apologize, and she is going to have to lie—in effect, to publicly repudiate her own writing. This is terrifying medicine that comes with its own antidote: "Writing is to put love into the world, not to use against your friends," Harriet learns. "But to yourself you must always tell the truth."[7]

Baby Boomers made *Harriet the Spy* a success, but it was with later generations that it became a phenomenon. Its influence became more pervasive among the future women of Gen X: girls who were between eight and ten years old in the late 1970s and early 1980s. Within a decade of publication, *Harriet the Spy* was recognized by the librarians who shelved it, the educators who taught it, and the scholars who memorialized it as one of the first books for children written in a modern, realist style. Over time, those supporters and legions of readers have made *Harriet the Spy* one of the most popular books of children's literature and propelled its eleven-year-old protagonist into the company of other brainy girl heroines, such as Scout in *To Kill a Mockingbird* and Jo in *Little Women*. In its first five years, the book sold around 2.5 million copies.[8] By 2019, it had sold nearly 5 million copies worldwide.

Although the book was in many ways a product of its newly liberated time, it has lasting appeal. There is, in particular, much to be said for the self-reliance and self-respect that the gleeful Harriet has gained by the end of the book. Ever since, she has shown free-thinking children they can be happy as *themselves*, and her truth-telling has launched a million journal-keepers. That's the legacy for which so many readers love her—and why they fondly remember their Harriet Experience.

Like Harriet, Louise Fitzhugh was used to being underestimated. As a young woman, Louise's smallness—she was four feet, eleven inches—"made many people mistake her for a child and completely misjudge her."[9] She tried not to misjudge or delude herself. If a decade of therapy left Louise with any particular theme, it was that lying to herself only made matters worse. She adhered to this principle more or less successfully (depending on whether she'd been drinking heavily). The letters she wrote to friends reflect repeatedly, and above all things, her belief that artists have a sacred charge to be completely honest with themselves and with one another about their work.

But a reader of *Harriet the Spy* who wanted to learn about Louise Fitzhugh would have had precious little to go on. Most of her readers never knew that she was the only progeny of a Jazz Age marriage that ended in rancorous divorce. Her father was a lawyer from a wealthy and powerful Memphis family, her mother a dancing teacher from Clarksdale, Mississippi. Louise grew up in a world where well-educated but unemployed women were tracked to become the wives and hostesses of prominent businessmen and politicians. She felt trapped in the Memphis high society of her father and despised the violence and prejudice of the Jim Crow South. By the time she graduated from high school in 1946, she was already planning an escape to Paris, where she hoped to study art and be a painter.

By 1950, Louise was living in Greenwich Village, part of a bohemian enclave. There, she socialized with, among others, modernist artist and writer Djuna Barnes, photographer Berenice Abbott, literary critic Anatole Broyard, playwright Lorraine Hansberry, and her close friends Marijane Meaker (whose many pen names included M. E. Kerr), and Sandra Scoppettone. The first time Louise ate a macadamia nut, it was in abstract expressionist Helen Frankenthaler's Manhattan apartment. Through the 1950s and 1960s, Louise continued to paint, draw, and write plays. She mostly wrote autobiographical comedies of manners, satires, and farces meant to expose inequities and injustices in what she called

"This lousy world."[10] In 1963, after a disappointing gallery show, she began to write a children's book, which she said would feature "a nasty little girl who keeps a notebook on all her friends."[11]

In the literary marketplace before Stonewall and for years after, secrecy was the de facto position for a children's book writer who was also a lesbian. For Louise, exposure could have caused real trouble—not just for herself, but also for her agent, editor, and publisher, all of whom might be publicly hounded, censored, and boycotted and suffer humiliating personal attacks. Louise was a popular and successful children's author who gave no lectures, interviews, or readings to promote herself in the public sphere. There was only one canned biography on the flaps of her books, relating only that she had been born in Memphis in 1928 and lived in New York City. And there were her author's photos—two in circulation, both taken by her friend Susanne Singer. In one, she's seated on a playground swing, smiling with a sweet, childlike demeanor. In the other, she's more introspective, holding her female Yorkshire terrier, Peter.

When Louise died in 1974, a *New York Times* obituary described her as single; as survived by her mother; as an artist of lively and funny drawings as well as realist paintings; and as the innovator of a new realism in children's fiction.[12] Over the following decades, biographical articles and a scholarly book added tantalizing details: her parents divorced when she was an infant; she spent over a decade in psychoanalysis; she swore off wearing women's clothing in 1950; she told droll stories about her beloved cats and dogs; and she suffered from wanderlust.

After her death, Louise's friends were understandably protective of her reputation. The common view was that outing her would be detrimental to her legacy and to the sales of her books. By the 1980s, as the culture inclined slightly more toward tolerance, some of Louise's friends were beginning to give interviews about the author of *Harriet the Spy*. One such friend was Alixe Gordin, to whom Louise had considered herself married for almost a decade. Alixe and Louise had been part of a social circle of high-flying career women who in their youth had crashed through literary and artistic ceilings at a rip-roaring velocity: they included not just writers of children's books, but also writers of mysteries and crime thrillers; editors at glossy magazines and book publishing companies; copywriters, photographers, and illustrators at advertising agencies; theatrical producers and literary agents and casting directors; and professors, painters, and actors. One of their friends, the playwright and author Jane Wagner, characterized this extensive network as a collection of "successful, creative, pleasure loving, ambitious, knowledgeable lesbians."[13] It was a world of downtown gay bars and uptown house parties, and in the summer, shared Hampton rentals.

Louise's many friends often relied on the language of myth and folklore to describe her. She was a sprite, a fairy, a tomboy. She was like Tom Thumb, Peter Pan, or a Victorian boy, and when she was older, a little man, or a little elf. She was tiny—even her teeth were tiny.[14] With such petite stature came a certain swagger. She was deeply sensitive and hated to be underestimated. She was impatient, often quarrelsome, mischievous, and intolerant of stupidity at home and in the world. She could tell a heartrending, spellbinding tale. She welcomed a battle: she had a trial lawyer's perspicacity and wore out several sparring partners on the subjects of politics and literature. She defended weaker friends but could be a bully to snobs. Sometimes she'd assume a sort of Baby Snooks–style speech and vocabulary, catching friends off guard by the "bizarre" infantile voice she'd adopt out of nowhere. She sang beautifully, played multiple instruments, and spoke excellent French. Nobody ever called Louise sunny, but she was certainly funny and gifted and good company. Asked to characterize the woman she'd lived with for five years—and who had left her a fortune—Louise's last girlfriend, Lois Morehead, said Louise was "intense."[15] Her moods could swing in a matter of seconds from cheerfulness to anger. When she was angry, she could be vicious, and when she was good, she was passionate. She believed in love, hard as it might be to preserve, and was always falling in and out of love with women and men, with cars and musical instruments, with dogs and cats. Sandra Scoppettone, coauthor with Louise of their picture book *Bang Bang You're Dead* and author of *Suzuki Beane*, which Louise illustrated, had some "tremendous feuds" with her, but they always made up because, said Sandra, their friendship was "so worth it."[16]

In 1995, an article in the *Village Voice* by the journalist Karen Cook revealed Louise at last to be the multidimensional person Alixe Gordin and other friends knew. It included a previously unpublished photograph of Louise in her mid-forties with a lived-in complexion and cropped hair, smoking a cigarette. She looks smart, skeptical, and real. She had, her friends agreed, a childlike quality, "but she was no child."[17]

Louise felt a great sympathy for eleven-year-olds. She considered her reading public to be open-minded individuals, not people to be talked down to, patronized, or palmed off with fairy tales. She didn't write many books and published only two novels and two picture books during her lifetime. Two more novels came out posthumously. Her books are full of resistance—to liars, to conformity, to authority, and even (radically, for a children's author) to make-believe. The children she invented were engaged in the zeitgeist as beatniks and cool cats; they were antiwar and civil rights advocates; and they were children's liberationists. That Louise wrote *Harriet the Spy* for middle-school readers, catching children before they settled into the powerful grooves of gender that would keep many of them on conventional tracks through adolescence, was radical. Kids who felt they were different could read parts of their secret selves in Harriet, relate to her refusal to be pigeonholed or feminized, and cheer her instinct for self-preservation.

Although she is best remembered today for a commercial children's book, Louise Fitzhugh was a serious artist. She wrote *Harriet the Spy*, and all her work, to influence hearts and minds. But she was often insecure about whether what she wrote or painted would ever be found truly meaningful. She waged a gallant battle against her own doubt, her shyness, and a sneaky streak of misanthropy. Toward the end of her life, she wrote to a friend that the state of the world in the mid-1970s had left her with her mouth "open in horror all the time" at social injustice, prejudice, and poverty.[18] In particular, children were—as they always had been—hostages to the ideological winds. For Louise Fitzhugh, change was what was needed, and her writing for children was the best way to put a little love back into this lousy world.

PART ONE

I'm going to be a writer. And when I say that's a mountain, that's a mountain.

—*Harriet the Spy*

PROLOGUE

In the summer of 1948, Louise Fitzhugh was nineteen years old and just about five feet tall. She'd cut her hair short and still fit into the bib overalls she'd worn as a tomboy in grade school. She was a smart, funny, and sometimes reckless girl, who had lately become particularly quarrelsome. Louise was bored in Memphis, sick to death of bigots and phonies, fed up with the way her more forward-looking ideals were routinely dismissed, and done with pretending to heed her father. In September, she would escape to Bard College in New York State to study poetry and painting.

For part of that summer, Louise worked for the local newspaper, the *Memphis Commercial Appeal*, answering the phone and filing articles in the newspaper morgue, where all the issues of years past were indexed. For as long as she could remember, Louise had wanted to know more about her divorced parents' early life and marriage, a secret subject that was hushed up at home. On her own in the newspaper morgue, she privately investigated.

Among the archives, Louise found announcements of generations of her family's births, graduations, and marriages along with records of their travels, land purchases, garden club leadership, Methodist affiliation, and history as benefactors of hospitals and colleges. Finally, among the many boosterish articles recording her family's tireless dedication to social uplift, she found a thick folder of clippings, photographs, and articles dedicated to her mismatched parents' scandalous breakup in 1927—as lurid as the rest was dull.

Halfway through that hot afternoon, Louise slammed out of the newspaper offices and went straight to see her close friend Joan Williams. They'd known each other since childhood, but Joan had never seen her friend so angry and upset. Louise wouldn't sit down, Joan later said. "She just kept repeating, 'I was a baby and they threw me on the couch.'"[1]

one

CLASSIFIED

In 1916, when Louise Fitzhugh's father, Millsaps Fitzhugh, was thirteen years old, his mother inherited her parent's immense fortune—the twenty-first-century equivalent of $17 million. Millsaps enjoyed a privileged youth in Memphis, Tennessee—or, as his divorce lawyer would later say, he was "brought up in a gentle home under cheerful home influences." His parents were Captain Guston Taylor Fitzhugh, a veteran of the Spanish-American War, and Josephine Buie Millsaps Fitzhugh, who had graduated from the Belhaven College for Young Ladies with a degree in piano and voice. In 1897, a local society columnist had declared her one of the "rare rosebuds" of the Jackson, Mississippi, debutante season.[1]

Josephine and the Captain (as he was called) raised Millsaps, their eldest son, to be the very model of a southern gentleman.[2] Millsaps, full of zip and animal spirits, was well read (with a preference for the Russian masters, favoring Tolstoy in particular), well turned out (in bespoke suits, monogrammed handkerchiefs, and handmade Italian shoes), and well educated (at Emory University in Atlanta, and then at Emory's law school). He belonged to the best clubs and fraternities, was an avid tennis player and an expert rider, and was appreciated for his quick wit, amusing conversation, and social savvy. Through Millsaps's self-possession there also ran a seam of menace, an impulse to violence that was never seriously confronted, criticized, or curbed. As a child he had a temper, which those who had reason to fear it hoped he'd outgrow. In young manhood, the less savory bits of his character seemed to add a rakish charm. He was considered far more charming than "bad." He was ferociously ambitious and had high political aspirations. Millsaps told his friends he would be president one day.

Louise Fitzhugh's mother, Mary Louise Perkins, was born December 18, 1904. She was a gentle, intelligent girl who at the age of six—with an unshakable sense of destiny—declared her ambition to become a dancer when she grew up, and later a dance *teacher*. Not every child's wish can come true, but Mary Louise was passionate and dedicated and became a hometown prodigy. Wearing ballet slippers and gauzy angel's wings, she began her career as star of her Clarksdale, Mississippi, middle school's May Festival.

By the age of fifteen, Mary Louise had branched out from ballet to more popular dance forms, including tap, which, although it had its own tradition among her Black neighbors, she learned mainly from the movies. Mary Louise would have seen tango demonstrators dance at local pageants, and as a devoted moviegoer, she copied Vernon and Irene Castle's "Castle Walk" from films like *The Whirl of Life*. Perhaps even more influential were the Ruth St. Denis dancers in the movie *Intolerance* by D. W. Griffith, men and women who—among its cast of thousands—expressed themselves with sensual abandon on the steps of a back-lot Babylonian temple.

When she was eighteen, Marie Louise's parents, Walter Baird and Josie Naylor Perkins, purchased the Sunflower Lumber Company, where they had met and worked side by side for ten years. Aspiring to equip their children with the education and social skills equal to their rising status, they sent Mary Louise to Washington, DC, to study dramatic arts and interpretive dance at the Marjorie Webster School of Expression and Physical Education, a well-regarded teacher-training college for women. After two years, Mary Louise continued her education at Goucher College in Baltimore, but left in March 1924, when her beloved father died unexpectedly of nephritis. After his death, the Perkinses struggled to save the family lumber business and pay off debts. Mary Louise, no longer able to justify an expensive Goucher education, packed up her tap shoes and ballet slippers and went home to Clarksdale to find a job.

In 1925, the state of Mississippi was in the throes of a changing culture and shifting population. A post-Reconstruction caste system of Supreme Court–approved "separate but equal" facilities and rules had divided white and Black. African American residents were departing in record numbers, escaping the iniquitous Jim Crow laws that insulted and demeaned them. Harsh state laws demanded segregation of all public schools, railroads, streetcars, hotels, libraries, and museums; even zoos and playgrounds were segregated. Marriage between people of different races was outlawed, with severe penalties for transgressors.[3] Eventually, over a million Black southerners would join the Great Migration to the North's urban centers, looking for better work and education for themselves and their children.

In Clarksdale, as elsewhere, Jazz Age generational battles were simmering. The future was announcing itself in new, lurid billboards and in the jumble of telephone wires that crisscrossed farmers' fields. A welter of new voices and images conspired to irritate religious and civic leaders. Young people were driving their roadsters at maddening speeds, dancing the Charleston to the Black-inspired jazz music spilling from home radios, drinking illicit cocktails, and reading in new movie magazines about the lewd, rich, and famous. Ladies exposing their kneecaps, sarcastic pilots hanging upside down from airplanes, and Charles Darwin's nineteenth-century evolutionary theory seemed to some of the more conservative citizens to be all of a piece, commensurate with atheism, anarchism, and the sexual temptations that lured youngsters away from family farms.

In 1925, the summer before Louise Fitzhugh's parents met, and around four hundred miles from Millsaps Fitzhugh's Memphis home, the small Tennessee town of Dayton became internationally famous when a high school teacher, John Thomas Scopes, confessed to flouting the Butler Act, which made it illegal to teach evolution in a public school. The trial, otherwise known as the Scopes Monkey Trial, became a showpiece of the Roaring Twenties culture wars when William Jennings Bryan, a popular champion of fundamentalism, argued for the prosecution against civil libertarian Clarence Darrow, who defended Scopes, science, and enlightenment. Scores of reporters and tourists flooded the town until every hotel room was full; every restaurant, café, and drugstore with edible food was jam-packed, and gift shops sold out of souvenir merchandise.

H. L. Mencken, who covered the trial for the *Baltimore Sun*, asked where the other Tennessee intellectuals who could come to the aid of Scopes and his legal team were. He decried their failure to challenge the "obscene buffoonery" on display and mocked Tennessee mercilessly as a circus of holy-rollers.[4]

Millsaps Fitzhugh, who had just returned to Memphis with his newly minted law degree from Emory, was outraged by the premise of the trial—and by the bad publicity Tennessee received from it. He and his circle of college friends advocated progress and championed female suffrage, industry, and free enterprise. Most of them considered the Monkey trial a hill-country aberration. When it was over, they saw the departure of the reporters and politicians and all the associated razzmatazz as their chance to get to the real business of building a new South.

Back in Clarksdale, Mary Louise Perkins was busy applying her own entrepreneurial expertise. Fulfilling her prodigious childhood ambition, she was building a dance studio in her mother's house. She taught classes and choreographed dances for local festivals and musical events. In February, a local columnist reported, "The Eliza Clark School's Better Books for Children program will feature Little Miss Evelyn Rosenberg, a talented member of Miss Louise Perkins' junior dancing class." Her dancers were also invited to perform at the town's amateur Musical Circus, and at the Exhibition and Industrial Pageant of 1926.[5]

By the following summer, Mary Louise had saved enough from teaching to take time off for a once-in-a-lifetime package tour of Europe with a group of her friends from Clarksdale and Goucher. The other girls may have had wild romantic fantasies about meeting young men on board their ship or in Venice, beneath a full moon, but not Mary Louise. While not opposed on principle to romance, she was a practical girl with other ambitions. She'd left Clarksdale with her mother's blessing and never forgot her obligation to help support her mother and younger siblings. She thought about auditioning for a place in the corps of a Parisian ballet company, or in the chorus of a Broadway play. She packed her steamer trunk with her chiffon party dress, her strappy heels, several hats in summer cotton, at least one beaded hairband, her compact and cigarette case, some swim attire, and, in their boxes, wrapped in tissue paper, her gleaming tap shoes and satin ballet slippers.

Their ocean liner, the Cunard RMS *Carmania*, sailed from New York on its way to Plymouth, England, on June 11, 1926. Afterward, the young ladies planned to go by ferry and train through some of the most glamorous places in Europe: Paris, Marseille, Nice, Monte Carlo, Venice, Genoa, Rome, and Naples. On board, the Clarksdalians met another party of young southerners—including the recent Emory law school graduate Millsaps Fitzhugh. He was twenty-three, Mary Louise twenty-two. They were instantly attracted to one another. Mary Louise had met rich boys before, in Washington and Baltimore. But Millsaps was of a different order. He had no qualms about spending lavishly. Such self-assurance was impressive. She found him sexy and charismatic.

They spent their time dancing to the ship's orchestra, drinking champagne, gin rickeys, and sidecar cocktails in the ship's bar and walking on the ship's deck at all hours. Neither had been abroad before, and both were too young to have had many legal drinks before Prohibition was declared. The very idea of ordering whichever cocktail they desired, whenever they wanted it, made them lightheaded. The atmosphere on the ship was superheated with romance, like something from the movies. On starry nights with ocean breezes, they Charlestoned and rumbaed. It was seductive, intoxicating, combustible. Millsaps was a courteous and dedicated beau, whose friends let her know two important details: he had a sweetheart back home in Memphis, and he was the son of a millionaire. By the time they arrived in England, Millsaps didn't want to say goodbye. He changed his own itinerary to tag along on the young ladies' package tour. Louise, flattered, was encouraging but still cautious.

After about a month of touring France and Monte Carlo together, the young couple found themselves in Venice on the Lido under a full moon. Millsaps would be leaving for Tennessee in the morning. They shared a bottle of dark red wine, which was more available then the champagne they preferred, but they'd grown used to guzzling it after months of practice. The gondoliers yodeled in the distance as Millsaps told Mary Louise he loved her. She found his rakish charm alluring, but she didn't lose her head; too much was at stake. They'd only known each other for a short time, and a holiday was not real life. She thought that once he returned home, back to his wealthy friends and family, he'd change his mind; as she later testified in court, she also didn't want to be hurt. If he was going to make promises, she told him, "be very sure that you love me."

"Mary Louise," he said, "If I ever write to you or put it on paper that I love you, you may consider that a proposal."

"You certainly are being a lawyer now," she replied, thinking, and later testifying, that it was "a very peculiar statement."

And so they parted, Millsaps to Memphis, and Mary Louise with her persevering group to Switzerland, Holland, Belgium, England, and Scotland. She made her own return crossing via Montreal, drawing it out through New England to New York. Then, just before boarding the boat for a trip through Lake George and Lake Champlain, she received a cablegram from Millsaps that read, simply, "I LOVE YOU."

They had known each other for less than three months. As her shipboard friends scattered to their families and schools, Mary Louise booked a New York hotel room and enrolled at the Alviene School of Dance (whose alumni included Fred and Adele Astaire). Not even a serious proposal from the son of a millionaire was going to stop her from pursuing her cherished dream of becoming a dancer in New York City.

In the fall of 1926, Broadway was the center of the hoofer's universe. Musicals such as *Lady Be Good*, *Rhapsody in Blue*, and *The Ziegfeld Follies* had an insatiable appetite for fresh chorines. If, like Mary Louise, a young woman was beautiful and agile, and could learn her routines quickly, she might, given time, persistence, and luck, find something. The downside was that it meant low wages, unpredictable and sudden show closings, absurd working conditions, and scarce sleep. Cheap bootleg liquor flowed, the lodging was dodgy, and the men in power often predatory. It took moxie and a little bit of a hard-boiled shell to tough it out, but the rewards must have seemed worthwhile to the gypsy moths flitting from show to show in that Golden Age of Broadway. They were given the chance to dance onstage every night to wonderful music with lots of friends in the same boat. After all, why couldn't it be Mary Louise Perkins who went out there a chorus girl and came back a star?

Suffice to say, no such dream came true. Mary Louise wasn't offered any reliable work from Broadway producers, and by that time, all the money she'd saved was gone. Millsaps had written her several ardent letters, which she later said "thrilled me a great deal." But she was still hesitant. "I didn't think he was serious. I did not know that he was *that* interested in me," she would later testify.

Millsaps was besotted. After returning to Memphis on August 13, 1926, to join his father's law practice, he announced to his parents and friends that Mary Louise Perkins was his ideal match, a cultivated and intelligent girl, not the least pretentious but natural and graceful in her manners and taste. She wore beautiful clothes and loved books as he did. His mother and father had never heard of the girl but were inclined to give him the benefit of the doubt. It was no grand match, but their son said she was a lovely, sweet girl, and anyone could see he was deeply in love. Meanwhile, Mary Louise, out of time and money, was drawn in. She might not have been head over heels in love, but Millsaps was passionate and romantic, and his persistence either turned her head or wore her down.

Millsaps's friends were not as cautious or responsible in their appraisal. Memphis society also had a word for girls like Mary Louise Perkins, "who came visiting in Memphis from Mississippi or Arkansas [and] did not bother to abide by the usual rules of civilized warfare. They were *marauders*."[6]

When Mary Louise said she was going to marry the son of a millionaire, her mother replied that she was prepared to overlook his shortcomings and love him for the sake of her darling daughter. Through her work in the lumberyards, Josie Perkins had met many rogues, but her only experience with millionaires was reading about Daddy Warbucks, Little Orphan Annie's guardian in the funny papers, and seeing some old men in the movies with top hats who twirled canes. This fellow Mary Louise had met on her European tour sounded like he was a soft young lawyer from a snooty family, but she prayed he would be worthy. Josie hadn't expected Mary Louise to ever give up her deep-rooted ambition to be a dancer, even for a rich husband, but she supposed that her daughter knew her own mind.

Mary Louise barely knew her future husband when she agreed to marry him, and she soon discovered that with his intensity and high spirits came their opposite: depression and insecurity. Millsaps was possessive; he sulked if he didn't get his way; and he couldn't help showing off. During Prohibition, when liquor of any sort was illegal, Mary Louise said, he "spent worlds of money on whiskey." He had many friends who appreciated his generosity and hospitality, but Mary Louise's friends were divided over her fiancé's character. Some were attracted to Millsaps's commanding presence and keen intellect, while others thought him a snob with a short fuse. When he drank he could be aggressive, and on Christmas Eve in 1926, at a Revelers Ball reception in Memphis, the couple had a public argument. Millsaps's excessive drinking embarrassed Mary Louise. Perhaps she thought she could change him or that he'd eventually settle down. Millsaps was strong willed, but Mary Louise was no pushover, and optimistic besides.

The newspaper announcement of their engagement came on January 31, 1927. In the hectic buildup to their April wedding, there were luncheons, bridge parties, evening dances—sometimes with full orchestras—and roadhouse excursions, with abundant bootleg whiskey and a lot of drunk stumbling and fumbling. Millsaps erupted on several occasions leading up to the happy event. At one luncheon held in honor of the couple, he flew into a rage because some flowers he had ordered had not yet been delivered. Another time, he threatened loudly to sue the *Memphis Commercial Appeal* because it had reported, underwhelmingly, that their wedding would be "one of" the most important social events of the coming week. On a visit to Memphis, Mary Louise's friend Georgia Peacock was dismayed when Millsaps barked at his fiancée because she was a few minutes late to lunch. Another friend, John T. Jones, later testified that he didn't think Millsaps "was as kind to Louise as a fiancé should have been."

But despite such fits of pique, on April 28, 1927, Mary Louise Perkins and Webster Millsaps Fitzhugh were married at seven o'clock in the evening. The church was decorated to a fare-thee-well, with chandeliers at each pew and the altar banked with lilies and violets. There was a choir, an organist, and a soloist who sang "O Promise Me." The society columnist at the Memphis paper swooned over the bride's gown, calling it "an exquisite old-fashioned model, designed with a tight bodice and long full hoop skirt . . . of crêpe minor satin, richly embroidered in crystals. On either side of the skirt a huge silver flower basket of ribbons was embroidered, with white satin roses and foliage. . . . [The] skirt was finished with filmy lace, studded with rhinestones. . . . The bridal veil of tulle was fastened with real orange blossoms sent to the bride by friends from California and Florida."[7]

In addition to seven bridesmaids (all, according to the newspaper, "popular and attractive young girls"), a maid and matron of honor, and a phalanx of groomsmen, the large wedding party included ring bearers, train bearers, and a flower girl. Millsaps's younger brother, Little Gus (still called this nickname despite being twenty-two), was his best man, and Mary Louise's brother gave her away. The ring ceremony was read by the Reverend Walter E. Dakin, the maternal grandfather of then sixteen-year-old Tennessee Williams. On the Fitzhugh side of the aisle, Josephine Millsaps Fitzhugh was in a pink satin gown trimmed with rhinestones; on the bride's side, Josie Perkins wore a white chiffon gown, also with rhinestones. She may have been partly distracted by thoughts of the lavish reception to be held at her home on Yazoo Avenue in Clarksdale. They'd hired an orchestra to play on the lawn and hung baskets of lilies of the valley from the chandeliers.

There may have been some Cassandras in the pews who could have objected, but nobody did. Mary Louise would have been determined—in that fog of orange blossom and tulle—having likely steeled herself with a gulp of corn liquor. She couldn't know that in less than a year, her groom would file for divorce, and she would endure a two-state, multiyear, lowdown, no-holds-barred trial to defame and degrade her and her family, and that this would be followed by her hospitalization for a complete mental breakdown. Worst of all, her infant daughter, Louise, would be taken from her.

As no one spoke, on they processed, the bride and groom making their way down the aisle as the organist performed the inspirational fanfare to Felix Mendelssohn's *Midsummer's Night Dream*.[8] Almost any other music would have been more honest—perhaps something like that year's hit song by Bessie Smith, "A Good Man Is Hard to Find." But the Perkins-Fitzhugh nuptials was not an occasion to which African American blues singers were invited, or where reason prevailed.

two

CLEAR AND PRESENT DANGER

The Captain and Josephine Fitzhugh's wedding gift to the newlyweds was a large down payment on a renovated, fully furnished home at 1660 Central Avenue, next door to their own. It was, from the Fitzhughs' point of view, an extravagant, expensive gift offered out of love. To Mary Louise, it looked like her in-laws wanted to keep their eyes on her. As an additional nuptial gift, Millsaps's parents gave the couple a check for $5,000, to be used for household expenses or to pay off the remaining mortgage on their house.

Millsaps and his parents recognized that Mary Louise was used to a physical life. They imagined that membership in their country club, where she might swim and play golf, would compensate. Instead, Mary Louise wanted to practice dance in her own studio, and asked for a car so she could visit Clarksdale, a ninety-minute drive away. It irritated Millsaps that she wanted a sleek new Packard speedster instead of a less expensive model, but he acquiesced. Mary Louise felt she could persuade Millsaps to indulge her if she convinced him she was acting under his influence—but it only worked so long as she played the charade of enjoying his company. Not long after their wedding, she confided to her mother that she'd made a terrible mistake. She didn't respect her new husband. He was a thin-skinned blowhard with a "sense of self-importance and false pride."[1]

Millsaps was possessive of his beautiful wife, whom he wanted both to keep to himself and to show off. She wasn't the clingy type, and according to one observer spent "as much time with the other men in their set as with Millsaps." Occasionally, he would prod her to dance for him in public, a party trick of which she soon tired. On one such occasion, Mary Louise's friend Anona Jenkins observed that Millsaps, again having had too much to drink, insisted that his wife dance for the company. Mary Louise did not wish to do so. She said she felt unwell, and they quarreled. He said that by defying him, she'd publicly humiliated him. Mary Louise said he'd embarrassed her again. At home afterward, their quarrel grew more intense. He accused her of deception and adultery, then cursed her, as she would later tell the court in their divorce trial: "Damn you to hell!" he yelled.

Millsaps responded to Mary Louise's increasing lethargy with energetic pedantry. He said that since she didn't know how to budget or run a household, he would get in experts to teach her—like his mother. When she did try her hand at interior decoration or cookery, he criticized the results. Mary Louise felt offended that he only gave her an $80 monthly allowance, out of which she had to buy all her clothes and food for their meals. It irked her that Millsaps complained of her extravagance while spending freely on his own expensive clothing and liquor cabinet. During Prohibition, Millsaps had collected a lavish cellar full of bootleg liquor. He proudly served only the best Scottish whiskey instead of the inexpensive corn liquor made locally.

Millsaps certainly thought he knew best. When the couple went shopping together, he ridiculed many of her choices as *common*. He believed he could influence and shape her taste, which, according to a college friend, "was not to be trusted until it had been trained by his aesthetic guidance." Mary Louise found these arrangements mortifying. When she said so, he sharpened his offensive. She was from ignorant folk, uncouth and provincial, whereas his big ambitions could take them places. One night he told her, "If you play your cards right, stick with me, you'll land in the White House. That's right, the White House. If, however, you think of leaving me, you'll be left high and dry. All of your fair-weather friends will reject you, because you won't have a dime of your own. I won't give you one dime. You won't get very far in a divorce. Because I have the courts sewed up."

By Christmas of 1928, after a year and a half of marriage, Mary Louise had stopped eating meals with Millsaps. For weeks, she would not speak to him. She often drove herself to Clarksdale and rarely said when she would return. The hostility in their home was eroding both their spirits, and the stress was making Millsaps ill. His doctor diagnosed him with hypertension and advised him to take some time off to recuperate. During Prohibition, when whiskey was often considered a versatile treatment for influenza, snakebite, and matters of the heart, his doctor prescribed at least three to four glasses of whiskey every day as a valuable strengthening agent.

In a last-ditch effort to patch up their marriage, Millsaps asked Mary Louise to accompany him on a vacation to San Antonio, where he hoped she might come around to feeling some kind of affection for him again. Millsaps believed Clarksdale to be a place where Mary Louise was a prisoner of her mother's domination, while Mary Louise considered her mother's house a refuge. She felt like the San Antonio trip would only prolong the inevitable breakup of their marriage rather than offering any long-term fix. She suspected that, with a prescription for whiskey, Millsaps would stay drunk all week. Still, she agreed to accompany him. It was during this trip that she became pregnant with Louise.

As future grandparents, the Fitzhughs were at once solicitous. That summer on hot nights, they invited Mary Louise to sleep on their spacious porch, where she might catch a passing breeze. As always, she preferred to stay in Clarksdale, and when she wasn't there, her family visited her in Memphis. Millsaps found this situation intolerable. He deplored his wife's relations as a "mob" taking advantage of his hospitality. He complained of their country accents and about how they liked to sleep on mattresses on the floor. They were hicks who only ever ordered steak—the most expensive meal on the menu—when he treated them to dinner at the Peabody Hotel.

In August, two months before baby Louise's birth, Mary Louise told Millsaps she was leaving to visit her mother, who had just had her tonsils removed. He shook his fist in her face. "If it weren't for your condition, I'd knock your damn head off," he said. She didn't go, and with her pregnancy almost full term, felt isolated and unhappy in Memphis.

One hot September afternoon, while Mary Louise was alone at home on Central Avenue, Millsaps's younger brother, Gus Jr., came over from next door to visit. She could tell he had been drinking and thought he may have been suffering from the DTs (delirium tremens). He told her he felt like he was dying. Unlike Millsaps, Little Gus was inward, distracted, and socially clumsy in a way that gave him a reputation for not being all there. On his visit to Mary Louise, in addition to disturbing symptoms of withdrawal from alcohol, he may have also been suffering the pangs of a frustrated poet. Indeed, being a poet was Little Gus's only work, an occupation much indulged and admired by his protective mother for its delicacy and spirituality—and much discounted by his father and brother.

Little Gus wrote hundreds of rhyming verses, many of them odes to nature, to the gallant South, and to motherhood.[2] Titles included "Could Man Forget His Mother," or, for his party piece, "My Old Black Mammy," which began, "Around the hearth we used to sit / And listen to her sparkling wit / Or hear her tales, about the war / And all the generals she once saw / It thrilled me when I learned from her— / She cooked for many a Southerner."

Mary Louise didn't have a lot of sympathy for Little Gus or his oeuvre. She made him coffee to be kind, then called for a doctor, an act of betrayal that outraged the Fitzhughs. They paid nurses to give Little Gus private care; by calling for outside help, Mary Louise had risked exposing their family and Gus's alcoholism to public scrutiny. For her part, Mary Louise was outraged that Little Gus had come to her house while she was alone and subjected her, while pregnant, to that kind of "excitement," as she called it. Later, in her court testimony, she would confirm that Little Gus hadn't frightened her. She'd felt sorry for him, but had grown angry afterward that the Fitzhughs had been more concerned about their reputation and keeping Gus's behavior a secret than about her health and safety.

In the early morning hours of October 5, 1928, there was a temporary cessation of hostilities when Louise Perkins Fitzhugh was born, a beautiful healthy baby, in Memphis at the Methodist Hospital. With their child's arrival, Millsaps was able to keep Mary Louise in Memphis, but he also had Josie Perkins around full time. Millsaps hired a baby nurse, Jane Moore, known as Aunt Jane, who had cared for a number of children born to prestigious Memphis families. From the first, Josie and Mary Louise distrusted Aunt Jane as a Fitzhugh loyalist and spy—and they were absolutely right. Aunt Jane had nursed some of Millsaps's childhood friends. More importantly, Millsaps raised her salary and took the time to compliment and thank her, whereas Josie Perkins, Aunt Jane said, was often rude and criticized her care of the newborn. One day, Mary Louise snapped at Aunt Jane when the nurse happened to say the baby looked like Millsaps. "Never say that again!" she warned the nurse.

Millsaps had prepared for fatherhood by reading about modern child-rearing, and he intended to apply his theories. He adamantly refused to let the baby sleep in the master bedroom instead of the nursery. Mary Louise believed he was acting from pure spite, just to separate her from her child. Years later she would tell her niece, Regina Inez Ragland, that when the baby came, Millsaps had increased his demands on her attention. "It was as if he were jealous of his own child," Mary Louise said.[3]

One evening in November 1928, when Josie Perkins was helping to care for little Louise, Millsaps, irritated by his baby's crying and his mother-in-law's presence, snapped. He berated Josie, shouting that she was "ignorant" and "common." And then, seeing one-month-old Louise sucking her thumb, he slapped the baby's hand. Mary Louise lost her temper, shouting that he was a cad, unworthy, and dishonorable. Millsaps first tried to justify this violence, saying he had read that thumb sucking led to children developing "sexual organs that should not be developed."

"You read too much!" Mary Louise shouted at him. To her, this was another crackpot theory—like when her visiting sisters had shared a bed and he'd complained that it was "improper" for young girls to sleep together. She'd had enough, she said, and would no longer suffer his insults. He called her a whore and said her mother was trash.

After this catastrophic fight, Millsaps moved out of the house and into the Peabody Hotel. He left some money, including wages for their servants, and a note to say that he would return only if his wife phoned and agreed to treat him fondly. Aunt Jane tried to persuade Mary Louise to ask her husband to come back, but Mary Louise was glad he was gone and hoped he'd stay gone. Josie Perkins returned to Clarksdale. And on her own in Memphis, according to Aunt Jane, Mary Louise turned to fortune-telling and folk magic. She repeatedly "ran the cards" to learn her future, hoping to see a successful divorce and alimony ahead. One night, Aunt Jane opened the door to a fortune-teller whom Mary Louise had invited over for a consultation. The fortune-teller, known locally for her gifts, told Mary Louise that if she would "sleep with a buffalo nickel under her head for nine nights," then her wish—that Millsaps would file for divorce, so that she would appear the injured party—would come true.

On March 10, 1929, Millsaps finally did file for divorce, and he moved into his parents' home next door. To Mary Louise, it must have seemed that luck was with her—until the next day's *Memphis Commercial Appeal* came out, with a headline revealing Millsaps's strategy. "Fitzhugh Strife Laid to Mother of Wife," the headline read. His lawyers would try to prove that under Josie's influence, Mary Louise had changed from a wonderful girl to a mercenary gold digger who showed "reckless extravagance and total disregard for the size of his income": "At no time," the article said, "did she ever show for him the affection ordinarily expected from a wife."[4]

On April 4, Mary Louise Perkins Fitzhugh filed countercharges of cruelty and inhuman treatment. She asked for a divorce in her own right, together with custody of her infant daughter. The *Greenwood Commonwealth* in Mississippi boasted on its front page the next day that Mary Louise's filing was one of the longest ever submitted in the State of Tennessee up to that point.[5]

During the two months leading up to the divorce trial, which was set for June 24, Mary Louise was instructed by the court to share custody with Millsaps. She was required to send baby Louise next door to be with her father's family between 5:00 and 7:00 p.m. every evening. Mary Louise said it was often hard for her "to get the baby over there." She also said that she was fearful that when she did send the baby to Millsaps, he and his friends "would make fun of the poor little thing." The Fitzhughs, unmoved by her excuses, would phone or send staff emissaries to remind her to meet her obligation.

One evening in May, around 7:30, Mary Louise arrived at the Fitzhughs' house with baby Louise in her arms. She came through the kitchen unannounced, surprising Millsaps, Captain Gus, and her estranged husband's sister, Mary Holmes, in the living room. Mary Louise tried to give the baby to Millsaps, who would not accept her. According to the Captain's deposition, Millsaps replied, "It is rather late now. I do not want it." Mary Louise then turned to the Captain to say, "You take it."

"No, not now," he said, indicating that without nurses and nannies, he would not know what to do with a baby. Frustrated by their replies, Mary Louise, in Captain Gus's version, threw the baby on the divan. Then, turning to leave, she said, "I have never got anything out of this marriage but a baby, but I am going to get all you have got on June 24th."

In his testimony, Millsaps told the same story, emphasizing that Mary Louise threw their baby on the divan. Mary Holmes added a few colorful details. She thought Mary Louise "was white in the face and cold looking," and that her insolent sister-in-law had first looked Millsaps up and down before speaking in defiance. Meanwhile, the poor baby had been crying inconsolably.

Mary Louise's version is different, of course. She said that when she tried to hand the baby to Millsaps, "he kept his arms behind his back and didn't say a word, not a sound." She then placed little Louise on the divan. "I sat my baby down. I did not throw my baby down, but I kissed my baby twice," she later claimed. As she spun around to face them, she reminded them that it was the court that had ordered they take the baby at this hour. "I didn't say anything," she insisted, "about what was going to happen on the 24th."

three

INTERROGATION

Scandal sold a lot of papers, and it looked like this trial had everything—embarrassing revelations of the rich and powerful, country people versus city folk, a dancing flapper girl taking on old-money lawyers, forbidden liquor, and a little baby's future hanging in the balance. Front-page articles on the divorce jumped to columns surrounded by ads for "Tasty, Delicious Cans of Devil Crabs," "Special Spot Dry Cleaning!" and "Tasty Tea Rolls, New, New!"

A heat wave didn't reduce the long lines of curiosity-seekers thronging the courthouse at nine in the morning for the grand spectacle of the Fitzhugh divorce. There were whole families making a day of the visit and tourists from out of town trying to catch a glimpse of the proceedings. In the sweltering, crowded courtroom—especially thick with press from around the region—the judge, called a "chancellor," made several attempts to thin the crowd. He eventually ordered that whenever a reporter stood up, a court steward could take the reporter's chair away. The trial's evening sessions attracted young socialites out for a night's entertainment. Two debutantes in full flapper garb posed for souvenir photographs perched on the chancellor's bench.

The jury was composed of the customary twelve white men. All prominent citizens, they included a president and vice president of local companies, a factory manager, a department store sales manager, an architect, a cotton broker, and other assorted businessmen. These were a jury of Millsaps's peers, but not Mary Louise's.

As the trial opened, Millsaps's lawyer, Colonel John Walter Canada, a veteran of the Spanish-American War in Cuba like Captain Fitzhugh, introduced his client as a well-known attorney and the son of a prominent family. The mother-in-law, meanwhile, Mrs. Walter Baird Perkins, he said, was an "arrogant, nagging and domineering type of woman" who began "a course of conduct that destroyed all his young wife's love and affection." Millsaps Fitzhugh charged that he had been constantly insulted and looked upon merely as a commercial asset. When Mary Louise was not visiting Clarksdale, her mother, Josie, was in Memphis bossing around the servants and dominating his household. Called to the stand, Millsaps described in detail why he had resented his mother-in-law from their earliest encounters. "She called me a shrimp on a number of occasions," he complained.

Under oath, Millsaps recounted his many grievances—specifically, Mary Louise's insufferable conduct toward him. Mainly, he disclosed, she did not love him and probably never had. During their married life she had written him only four letters and had sent him just one wire. She had only once called him over long-distance telephone (and then only to say she had missed the train from Clarksdale). She never called, he said, "just to talk."

On June 29, Mary Louise's lawyer tried to persuade the judge to dismiss the case, saying the accusations hadn't risen to the charges of cruel and inhuman treatment. The motion was denied, and so the trial-going crowd could look forward to hearing Josie Perkins's testimony.

In Josie Perkins, the Memphis newspaper had found its surefire paper-selling villainess. They continued to portray Josie as unattractive, truculent, and nosy, the mother-in-law from Punch and Judy hell. Her frequent visits to the Memphis establishment of her better-heeled daughter, her unpolished manners and rural accent, her supposed control over Mary Louise's behavior—all were dissected in clamorous tabloid style.

When Josie took the stand at last, those expecting something of a virago must have been disappointed. She was a short, plump, soft-spoken woman who often broke into tears. Sometimes the judge had to ask her to speak up. He also had to occasionally ask her interrogators to pause so she might compose herself. During his cross-examination, Colonel Canada produced a letter Josie Perkins had written to Captain Fitzhugh criticizing his son's treatment of her daughter. It declared that if he attempted to demean her daughter's character, she would "inform the Elks, the Masons and the Knights of Pythias"—all organizations to which her late husband had belonged. Addressing Josie Perkins, but playing to the rafters, Canada asked, "You wouldn't appeal to the Ku Klux too?" He was implying that the late Mr. Perkins was a member: Wouldn't she want to defame his client's father with all the men's clubs in the area? Josie said she wouldn't, since she only felt she had clout in those clubs to which her husband, Walter, had belonged. "My husband wasn't a Ku Klux," Josie said. It was a rare moment of triumph. Josie showed that the fancy lawyer certainly hadn't known her husband, who despite the local pressure to join had had the strength of character to resist recruitment.

On the following day, Mary Louise took the stand to forthrightly deny Millsaps's allegations of extravagance and mendacity.

She said that early on in their marriage he had lied to her, that he gambled—notably, on Al Smith's chances to win the presidential election of 1928—and that he drank to excess. She said everyone in his family was high-strung and quarrelsome, and that Millsaps liked to trumpet his social rank and prestige. Even though he had a perfectly good car, he preferred to be driven to work by his father's chauffeur. In her most dramatic testimony, Mary Louise added details about Millsaps's recurring abuse. For over eighteen months she had endured his profanity, mockery, accusations, and threats. He had called her a whore, he had threatened her with violence, and he had slapped little Louise when the baby was just one month old for putting her finger in her mouth.

Mary Louise's lawyer, Gerald FitzGerald, put her thrifty household account records into evidence. He described Millsaps's nefarious attempts to punish her, including, at one point, forbidding her access to their shared home, then permitting its foreclosure by nonpayment of their mortgage. As to the wedding gift of $5,000, from Millsaps's parents, Mary Louise told the court, "I don't remember having seen that check." Under cross-examination, Colonel Canada produced what may have been the most damning piece of evidence against her, trying to show that Mary Louise must have been either calculating or mentally unstable. He started by brandishing a pen and paper.

"Mrs. Fitzhugh," he said, "Will you please write your name several times?"

Reclaiming the page and flapping it to dry, he played the moment, pausing to build suspense. "I now hand you a five-thousand-dollar check, given as a marriage gift by Mr. and Mrs. Fitzhugh and made payable to you and Mr. Millsaps Fitzhugh. Please look closely, is that is your signature on the back of the check?"

She hesitated, and then replied, "It looks like my signature but I don't remember having signed the check or having seen it."

It is possible that Mary Louise did sign the check during the honeymoon phase of their marriage. It seems unlikely that Millsaps would have deliberately tricked her at that point, but it's also unlikely that the practical Mary Louise would have forgotten signing a check for such a large sum. There is no certain conclusion to this mystery. Under oath, Mary Louise would not say that Millsaps was a forger, although she did call him a liar.

Canada pressed his advantage to show that Mary Louise was the bigger liar and the worse parent, positing that she was exaggerating matters out of self-interest. Baby Louise, he contended, had never been *permanently hurt*. "How many times did Millsaps slap the baby?" Canada asked.

"Once," she said.

"Beat it up pretty badly?" he asked.

"He slapped its hand," she said.

"Did the hand swell considerably?"

"No."

"Break any fingers?"

"No," she said.

"Bleed any?" he asked.

"No."

From there on, a terrifying duel of recrimination and rebuttal proceeded for hours. Everything Millsaps said, Mary Louise denied, and everything she said, he denied. Finally, it was time for closing arguments.

Colonel Canada began with his entreaty that the jury rule out any hope of reconciliation. Millsaps wanted out *and* he wanted complete custody of his child. Mary Louise "did not deserve a dime in alimony." Gerald FitzGerald summed up the defense's case with a sentimental ode to Mary Louise as a young and virtuous wife of sweetness and character who had been cruelly mistreated and ruthlessly abused.

Despite this poignant defense, popular sentiment was not with Mary Louise. The Fitzhughs' media strategy had influenced public opinion, and in the courtroom they successfully built a case against the monstrous mother-in-law, Josie Perkins. Some gossips whispered that the person who deserved the most sympathy was dear old Mrs. Fitzhugh, Millsaps's mother, who had so graciously extended her hand in friendship to that marauder, keeping her dignity and biding her time. Others said it was wily Mrs. Fitzhugh who was the real force behind the marriage breaking up. She could not abide her eldest son's entanglement with a common Mississippi dancing girl. Old Mrs. Fitzhugh was the culprit who set the canker in the rose. It was she who held the purse strings to the family fortune, and it was she who wanted to raise that baby girl—in her own way.

Mary Louise had continued to hope for the jury's sympathy, and their unanimous verdict in favor of Millsaps Fitzhugh was a crushing blow. Neither Mary Louise Fitzhugh nor Josie Perkins were in court when the verdict was announced. After the trial, they immediately returned to Clarksdale, where for two weeks Mary Louise's mental state continued to deteriorate. Josie rushed her back to the hospital in Memphis while her lawyers appealed the case on the grounds that Mary Louise was suffering "temporary insanity" brought on by the strain of the divorce. The chancellor allowed her counsel to introduce the testimony of her neurologist, who cited a diagnosis of acute mental psychosis. "She has evinced a desire to kill herself on two occasions," he wrote. "She has twice tried to walk through a window, clad only in negligees." Beyond that, Mary Louise was unresponsive—indeed, catatonic.

Millsaps's lawyers rebutted with the argument that she had been, in fact, a credible witness throughout the trial, when she had expected to be taken at her word. The chancellor, siding with

Colonel Canada, denied Mary Louise's motion for retrial, and the divorce decree was ruled in Millsaps's favor.[1] Mary Louise was denied alimony. She failed in all her appeals, and as he promised, Millsaps did not give her "one dime."

Through many appeals, Mary Louise fought fiercely for her child. She used all the weapons at her disposal. She was permitted to take baby Louise back to Clarksdale, where expensive lawyers soon drained the family's savings. As a last resort, Josie Perkins sold the family business, the Sunshine Lumber Company. This was 1929, and the Perkins family's financial crisis coincided with a worldwide catastrophe. When the stock market crashed on October 29, baby Louise had just turned one year old. She and her mother were living in the Perkinses' Yazoo Avenue home along with Josie's other children: Mary Louise's older sister, Inez, and her daughter, one-year-old Regina Inez; her brother, Billy; and her younger sister, Josephine (called Dodie). Their home was crowded, but Mary Louise's mental health improved dramatically once she was surrounded again by friendlier faces.

When she was well enough, Mary Louise began to teach dance again and to produce musical shows, casting family members in the roles. In one vaudeville-like spectacle at the Paramount Theater in Clarksdale, Dodie and Billy performed a tap duet. As the acts gathered on stage for a final bow, Billy rolled baby Regina Inez onto the stage in a highchair for her theatrical debut.[2] Mary Louise had nixed bringing out baby Louise too, fearful that the Fitzhughs would find out and hold it against her. She felt that Millsaps was somehow always watching, and she was running out of time. As the appeals process ground on, Mary Louise formed a last-ditch plan to keep her child and salvage her self-respect. Such circumstances demanded drastic measures. She announced her plan to go to Hollywood and find a job as a dancer in the movies, or maybe as a teacher of dance, in order to show she could support a child.

Mary Louise phoned Millsaps on May 16, 1930, to say she was leaving for Hollywood and would be gone for six months. Once she found work she would have baby Louise sent to her in California. In the meanwhile, she was designating Josie Perkins as their child's custodian.[3] Millsaps strenuously objected, but neither he nor anyone else could dissuade her. Mary Louise understood she didn't have much time to make her fortune, but it was a gamble she was willing to take. And while Millsaps informed the court of his ex-wife's extraordinary conduct, optimism, confidence, and the irresistible allure of a Hollywood fortune drove Mary Louise onward.

Josie Perkins, encouraging her daughter, promised to keep baby Louise safe and away from the clutches of the Fitzhughs. This was no easy task. When Millsaps unexpectedly came to Clarksdale to visit his daughter, Josie, caught off guard, rushed out the back door with the child in her arms. Millsaps chased Josie and baby Louise around Clarksdale, from store to soda fountain to the home of a family friend. It may have had the choreography of a slapstick comedy, but his Javert-like pursuit was tragic. Millsaps considered Mary Louise's quest delusional. He and his mother now demanded nothing less than complete custody of baby Louise.

Of course, six months was not enough time for Mary Louise to meet the talent agents and other gatekeepers who booked appointments with casting directors and choreographers. She was ambitious and bright and pretty and talented, but so were a thousand other would-be starlets and entertainers. Mary Louise had no clout or contacts, just a burning desire to find a job that would allow her to support her baby. If her life had been a movie, she might have rocketed from chorus girl to star, but this was reality and she had no such luck. She cut her visit short and returned to Mississippi that summer, without success.[4]

Mary Louise and her mother fought every step of the way to the custody endgame, but they were outmatched. The Fitzhughs' argument focused on Mary Louise's unreliability. When they learned of her excursion to California, their lawyers added abandonment to their complaint. They said Mary Louise consistently failed to show up for custodial visits, and when she did produce baby Louise, the infant seemed fretful and in clothes that had not been washed. Under oath, Mary Louise affirmed that she had sometimes resisted their demands, but only because she thought them a cruel and untrustworthy bunch. At one custody hearing, she beseeched the court, "She's very dear to me and I pray that the little thing will not suffer. . . . I will send her to you regardless of the damage to her health; I do not want you to put me in jail. But please don't make fun of the dear little thing."

Finally, when Louise was two and a half years old, after every appeal had been exhausted, Millsaps was granted sole custody. He brought his daughter to live with him and his parents on Central Avenue in Memphis. Mary Louise's supporters agreed that their once vivacious and charming friend had been tricked and treated unfairly by a system rigged for the wealthy and powerful. Mary Louise continued to feel the profound loss of her reputation and the unforgivable theft of her daughter. Millsaps was given the discretion to decide future visitation rights, and he refused to permit his ex-wife to see their child.[5]

If Mary Louise was devastated by losing her daughter, the Fitzhughs were embarrassed by the spectacle of the court case. To reestablish their place in society after the scandal, they needed a grand show of confidence. Josephine Fitzhugh, in particular, sought a platform from which to reassert her position. She and the Captain purchased a splendid mansion on Rose Road in Memphis.[6] They named it Samarkand—after the great Silk Road city with ties to both Alexander the Great and Genghis Khan—and moved there in 1931 with Little Gus, Millsaps, and baby Louise. Although she was a difficult mother-in-law, Josephine proved a gentle grandmother; she would sometimes sing lullabies in her beautiful voice as she rocked the baby to sleep.

As the Great Depression deepened, baby Louise's millionaire grandparents suffered small declines, but they were in no danger of losing their fortune. Baby Louise had the best of everything, including a handmade walnut cradle, lace baby clothes from Paris, and several servants just for the nursery. There were gardeners and a handyman, a furnace boy, a chauffeur—who always made a fuss over baby Louise—and a stern butler.

The household cook, Allie McSwain, had been twenty years old when Louise was born. She'd worked for Mary Louise in the Central Avenue house, then moved to the Fitzhugh mansion after the divorce. For Allie, who was African American, life at Samarkand would have offered more space and marginally more privacy. The African American staff employed there were typically ill paid, and often underestimated, but Josephine Fitzhugh's position was generally one of noblesse oblige, and she knew the value of her kitchen employees, at least, even if she didn't compensate them fairly. She relied on (and acknowledged in print) the cooks who advised and test-cooked the recipes she would later include in her two cookbooks. These books instruct on matters of hygiene and hospitality and include recipes for many of the desserts the little sweet-seeking Louise came to love, like peach pies and silver pies and Queen Tarts.[7] They also offer a guide to Josephine Fitzhugh's principles of "dainty service." For instance, "A dainty housekeeper is not always the one who has unlimited means, for her meal may be simple but her table is set with immaculate linen, her China is neat, her silver whether plated or solid, is shining, her glassware is glistening. Her meal is well lined up. If one plate service, the plate is not sticky, but delicate to the touch."[8]

Josephine Fitzhugh would have thought nothing about race and everything about it. In her world, white supremacy was a condition, like the weather. Her children were expected to be polite and obedient to the Black help, and when they were older, to be tolerant and condescend with courtesy. Millsaps's future brother-in-law, the author Peter Taylor, would later publish stories examining many such convoluted acts of etiquette. His worldly fiction, much of it set in the Fitzhughs' milieu, dissects the lopsided power dynamics between men and women, white and Black, boss and employee, parent and child.[9] In one of his stories, "A Long Fourth," an affluent white woman, similar in status to Louise's paternal grandparents, confidently expresses her view that African Americans are a sort of "medieval peasantry": "Their whole race is in its childhood . . . with all the wonders and charm of childhood. And it needs the protection, supervision, discipline, and affection that can only be given by Southern white people who have a vital relationship and traditional ties with them."[10]

This is the sort of nonsense that Louise and her more enlightened friends would have rejected as disgusting and, well, "medieval." The Middle Ages—which had given the world sophisticated torture techniques and religious fanaticism—could only be a favorite reference for those who lived, as Louise later remarked, like fish gasping in the "cesspool" that was the Jim Crow South.[11]

Between the ages of two and a half and five, Louise's most intimate relationship would have been with her nursemaid, Aunt Jane, whom Millsaps had rehired once he'd been awarded custody. She loved Aunt Jane and the rest of the household staff, who cuddled and cared for her. The nursery world was closed to the remote white elders—who loved her, but only visited her when it fit into their adult schedules, which made them considerably less influential. It fell primarily to Aunt Jane to field Louise's questions about her mother. When Louise was no longer satisfied with vague replies, Aunt Jane urged her to ask her father, but

Millsaps didn't care to discuss his former wife. It wasn't until he was on the verge of remarrying that he finally told his five-year old daughter the lie: *"Your mother is dead."*

By then, Louise hardly remembered her mother. She knew nothing of Mary Louise's efforts to get custody, and later, to see her. But Aunt Jane knew, and she felt sorry for the lonely little girl. One day Mary Louise had even marched up the path to Samarkand's ivory painted door, but that was as far as she got. The servants had been told never to let her inside.[12] Later, Louise would tell friends that as a child she had watched this pantomime from her window, but had no idea who the woman was.

four

INTELLIGENCE

In 1932, when Louise entered Miss Hutchison's School for Girls, Miss Mary Grimes Hutchison, who had founded the school thirty years earlier, was still its director. Known as a pious businesswoman and a dedicated educator, she wore long, old-fashioned dresses with brooches—and shoes so soft she could silently sneak up on her charges. Miss Hutchison was incongruously a great fan of Richard Burton, the adventurous explorer, writer, and spy, who was also known for his translations of erotic literature. On every Monday morning, when she would gather her students into the school's assembly room to wish them a productive week, she might leave them with a valedictory line from the Bible or from Burton. Her students would bow in turn and chirp, "Good morning, Miss Hutchison," then disperse to their classes.

Respect for ritual, routine, and legacy were all part of the experience at Miss Hutchison's school. The school catalog, which stated its founder's educational philosophy, said that "attempts to equalize abilities and performance among all people are contrary to the laws of God and nature." Miss Hutchison cites Christian scripture (Matthew 25:29) to support her view that "of the richly endowed much should be demanded in performance of herself and others, and should be rewarded accordingly. Of the meagerly endowed less should be required and in turn they should be content with less."

Among the compensations provided to even the most meagerly endowed student was the useful knowledge of etiquette. A Hutchison's girl was taught the manners "of a perfect gentlewoman, intellectually firm and having poise, simplicity and graciousness."[1] French instruction was provided throughout the curriculum, and ballroom dancing classes offered from the fifth grade. Indoctrination (and rebellion) began at once. In photos of Louise's kindergarten class, the five-year-olds posed during a May Fete are dressed in Revolutionary War–era costumes. These are not homespun types, but instantly recognizable as the slaveholding planter class. Some girls are in white mob caps and ruffled dresses. Others, including Louise, sport breeches and tricornered hats. Louise is brandishing a cardboard sword.

A year after Louise began attending Miss Hutchison's school, Millsaps married Sally Taylor in a modest ceremony at her parents' home in Memphis. Some humility may have been imposed by the economy—1933 was three years into a Depression that was a long way from improving. Sally also wished to put her imprimatur on their fresh start, and such simplicity was in contrast to the extravagance of Millsaps's previous marriage. The bride wore a white satin gown with a lace overdress that her sister, Mettie Taylor, had worn several months earlier. Louise is not listed as a member of the wedding party, but in her brief appearance, she impressed one guest "with her wide brown eyes, high coloring and a head of blonde ringlets."[2]

Sally was a smart, funny, unsentimental young woman who had been educated at the Finch School in Manhattan and Ward Belmont College in Nashville for a life as a social doyenne. Her parents had not immediately favored the match with Millsaps, who was older than their daughter by seven years, and the divorced father of a young daughter. Sally's father, Hillsman "Red" Taylor, knew Millsaps as a fellow member of the Tennessee Bar—wealthy, educated, and a rising politician in the Democratic Party—but Millsaps was also known for his temper, and the end of his first marriage had been a public scandal. In any case, Sally made up her own mind. She wanted Millsaps, and with little Louise, the newlyweds set up their household on Lombardy Street in Memphis. Aunt Jane left to nurse other, younger children, while Louise was cared for by a series of young women who were hired help and also "did" for Sally as maids and cooks. In later years, Louise would say that the household staff were the grown-ups for whom she cared most and to whom she turned for love and affection. She'd memorialize some of them in her books. Ole Golly, the nurse in *Harriet the Spy*, is in large part an amalgamation of her beloved nannies; depictions in this and other books of an irascible cook, a wealthy recluse's independent maid, and a sensitive housekeeper are all likenesses drawn from memory.[3]

Louise's new stepmother's family were a prominent clan. Their political connections included colorful senators, a governor, congressmen, and an array of Revolutionary War veterans and Confederate officers. Politicians on a family tree may be all well and good for some, but geniuses outrank them. For little Louise, who was five years old when her father remarried, the most prominent and influential member of Sally's family was her new uncle, Peter Taylor, older than her by twelve years. Peter's wide-ranging mind, impatience with old-fashioned things, and pleasure in new ways of seeing would have an indelible influence on Louise. She adored him. He was an Ariel to Uncle Gus's Caliban. Millsaps would also come to serve as a father figure for Peter. Millsaps was unpredictable and sometimes cruelly misogynist, but where Peter was concerned, he was unfailingly generous and sentimental. He took particular pleasure in introducing the teenager to his beloved Russian writers: Tolstoy, Dostoyevsky, and Chekhov.

And Millsaps clearly enjoyed playing the parental role. Over the course of his life, he had enjoyed a reputation as the best of sons, best of students, and, for a time, even best of beaus, so appearing to be an excellent father was important to him. For a set of family portraits taken before his marriage to Sally, Millsaps posed with Louise on his lap. Louise was dressed like a little Edwardian boy, in a velvet suit, with her blonde curls to her chin. In one photo, Millsaps, with brilliantined hair, holds Louise encircled in his arms, amused by his daughter's giggling and wiggling. There is a Shirley Temple, goody-goody tone to these photographs, but, looking back, Louise would later recall a nasty aftertaste associated with the games she and Millsaps had played when she was small.[4] In one of these games, later described in her novel *Nobody's Family Is Going to Change*, an affectionate father playfully encircles his four-year-old daughter in his arms, then encourages her to try to escape. She pushes but fails to break free until at last she cries with frustration. The same character gloats after beating his young daughter at a game of checkers. Insistence on such insignificant victories shows the lengths to which an insecure father will go to control even the smallest exchange with his child.

Louise and her best friend, Ann DeWar, weren't outrageously naughty, but it took very little to fall out of step at Miss Hutchison's School for Girls. Ann called Louise *Fit*, short for Fitzhugh; Louise called Ann *Der*. First grade was all about conforming to the rules of conduct. Even a little friendly patter while turning to the right page or passing an innocent note could land a girl in first-grade hoosegow. Once, to punish her chattering charges, their teacher sent Louise to one corner and Ann to another. She expected them to stand quietly for twenty minutes while the rest of the class silently practiced penmanship. Ann didn't wear a watch and was too short to see the class clock from her cloakroom prison. She tried to count minutes by sixty seconds, but lost track. Time slowed, and such a strange muffled silence prevailed that Ann sang softly to herself for courage. A very long time seemed to pass, until Ann was quite certain she'd been forgotten and the class dismissed. At last, Ann sauntered out from her prison among the cloaks, like a miniature Maurice Chevalier, jauntily singing his celebrated love song "Louise," about a girl beloved by birds, bees, trees, and the breeze.

Her classmates, still practicing their elegant rolling script, fell over themselves laughing. Their teacher's voice rang with irritation: "Ann DeWar! You've not yet been released! Is this your doing, Louise Fitzhugh?"

Louise was on the other side of the room, her face to the wall. She turned around to stare down her interrogator. While Ann had counted the seconds spent in confinement, Louise had likely been stewing on a revenge scenario, some big plan to get back at her teacher, once she was older and bigger. She was mad as a hornet and she wouldn't forget the injustice of being punished just for talking. She and Ann would run away together, to a place where they'd be understood, never corrected, and never banished to a corner.

"She didn't have brothers and sisters," Ann later said about her friend. "She had me." The two girls played together every day after school. They roller-skated and shot marbles and shared their favorite books about adventures on the high seas and animals that talked to children. On Saturdays, they would go to matinees at one of the lavish nearby theaters, where the ceiling was painted to look like a night sky, spread with sparkling stars. They would listen to an organist play popular songs before the show and gorge on popcorn. Once they saw the silent film actress Anita Louise play her harp in the stage show after the movie. Another time they went together to see an exhibition of the former silent film star Colleen Moore's dollhouses at the Memphis Auditorium.[5]

As best friends, they spent time with one another's families. Ann knew Louise was fondest of her Uncle Peter, her grandmother, and strange Uncle Gus, whom Ann considered "a pleasant enough person, but he just wasn't all there." The girls typically avoided discussing Louise's mother, whom Louise still believed to have died. Ann thought Louise's stepmother had "a perfectly wonderful sense of humor." She was game when the two little girls tried their luck digging a hole to China and came running when they thought they'd hit a rooftop with their spades. On weekends, Sally would sometimes make them fudge in the kitchen, and she never minded when they hollered out their favorite expressions: *Doggone it!* or *Phooey!* or *Oh Golly!*

The mothers of Hutchison girls generally spent their afternoons independent of their children, who were raised in segregated Memphis by Black nurses and maids. Memphis during Louise's childhood was brutal in its punitive application of Jim Crow laws. As an affluent white child, Louise would have played in segregated parks, paddled in segregated pools, and visited zoos, libraries, and museums on "whites-only" days. She may not have witnessed the daily threats, humiliations, and abusive treatment of the Black population firsthand—and she certainly wouldn't have been exposed to the horrors of the system the way she would have if she had been an African American child—but she was a thoughtful and perceptive little girl. She would have overheard grown-ups use pejorative words, and she would have seen African

Americans routinely disparaged and denigrated. But there was a lot that would have been kept from her, too. At Miss Hutchison's School, where a white teacher's duty was to uphold the moral tone and promote the social graces, as an elementary student Louise would have been taught nothing about the Reconstruction era, nothing about resistance and opposition to Jim Crow, and nothing about Ida B. Wells, the African American leader of an international campaign against lynching, and perhaps the greatest journalist to come out of Memphis. It's unlikely she knew much about the relationship between her own grandfather, Captain Fitzhugh, and his mentor Senator Edward Carmack, whose public attacks contributed to Wells's persecution and exile from the city.[6]

If five-year-old Louise was persistent, at six years old she was indefatigable. She was a precocious only child, the darling of the household, and used to getting her way. She had been pampered by her grandmother and was naturally suspicious of Sally's intentions. Louise was an expert cajoler, and she soon had the staff of the new house under her spell. One of her favorite habits was sitting at the top of the stairs to listen in on the grown-ups at cocktail hour. This could be especially rewarding when her grandparents were visiting. She'd hear glasses clinking and liquids pouring. It was on one of these nights that she'd have heard Sally say, "Mary Louise has been seen outside Miss Hutchison's again." Mary Louise had been seen outside Louise's school more than once, and outside their church as well. She couldn't be stopped from stalking the places where she might get a glimpse of her daughter. Louise must have been excited and troubled by the information—or perhaps just confused. Her mother, *Mary Louise*, had been seen *again*.

Louise, who had been told repeatedly that her mother was in heaven, and had no reason to doubt that version of reality, must have wondered at this fascinating turn of events. Perhaps she thought the grown-ups were discussing her mother's ghost haunting Miss Hutchison's. Louise had no reason to believe the adults in her life were lying to her. But Sally had come to believe that the longer they waited, the worse it would be when Louise finally learned the truth.

For her part, Mary Louise had exhausted all remedies. Custody had been awarded to Millsaps alone, and he was under no legal obligation to allow her to see their daughter. His mother was also opposed to permitting Mary Louise visitation; she didn't want her to have any influence whatsoever over her granddaughter. But surprisingly, Sally's will prevailed. Sometime after Louise entered first grade, the Fitzhughs permitted infrequent, supervised visits.

Years later, Louise would tell her friends that reintroduction to her living mother was agony. The first time Mary Louise visited their house on Lombardy, all the grown-ups were polite. Her grandmother was there, and her father, who left the room after a moment. Sally stayed, and Louise's mother just smiled, stared, and burst into tears. Louise was baffled and began to cry too. After that experience, her mother never came to the Fitzhughs' home again. She would meet Louise in a restaurant or hotel for the length of a meal. Millsaps would drive Louise there and wait in the car. Nobody ever relaxed, although, over time, Louise was better able to understand what custody meant and how her mother didn't have it. Sometimes Louise brought Ann DeWar with her, and once they met at the DeWar house. Ann thought Louise's mother was a nice lady who looked like Louise; she noticed they had the same short curly hair.

Louise and her mother only met a few times a year. Once, her mother brought along Louise's cousin, Regina Inez, who was just Louise's age and informed Louise she had a grandmother in Clarksdale. Another time, Mary Louise came with her second husband, William Baker "Jake" Trevilion, who was an officer at a Clarksdale bank.[7] At least once, Mary Louise and Jake attended a Hutchison school dance performance. Ann remembered that little Louise's stepmother and grandmother had sat close to the stage, while her mother and her mother's husband had sat in the back of the hall. According to Ann, Mary Louise didn't come backstage for lemonade after the show, but when they met again, she said she was proud and complimented Louise's pirouettes. Millsaps always grumbled about the parade of Clarksdale visitors. Sometimes, Louise wasn't sure who she liked anymore, but she knew her father had lied to her, and that wasn't something she would forget.

Louise's Grandmother Fitzhugh and her friends liked to think of themselves as progressive and enlightened citizens. Most were not fans of the Memphis mayor, Edward Hull "Boss" Crump, whom they saw as a vulgar upstart from Mississippi without an authentic interest in the arts, in philanthropy, or in social benevolence. Crump and his Democratic cronies were on record as manipulating elections, offering patronage in exchange for support, quashing the opposition press, and repressing dissident political rivals. Captain Fitzhugh and his cohort of middle-aged attorneys, all Democrats, made it their business not to run afoul of Crump, who customarily dressed in an ice-cream white suit, but Millsaps decried Crump's political control. In 1936, willing to test the conventional wisdom that "no young man can succeed in Memphis unless he's friendly to the Crump organization," Millsaps took the extraordinary step for a man of his social standing and milieu of joining the Republican Party.[8] It wasn't just Crump who had pushed him over the edge. He claimed to be fed up with the national Democratic Party, and, in particular, with President Franklin D. Roosevelt.

Millsaps was also an opportunist who believed that as a white man he could rise quickly through the ranks in Tennessee's weak and mostly Black GOP.[9] His new Republican politics and subsequent strategic associations with African Americans would make him odious to many Memphis Democrats who had been steeped in the politics of white supremacy.[10] Her father's conversion also meant that Louise, an eight-year-old schoolgirl, became something of a double outsider. She was a child of divorce, and her father was a Republican in a Democratic stronghold. Some classmates teased her by parroting their parents' remarks about *damned Republicans*, but their words weren't crushing. Louise was small, but she was tough; if her smart replies didn't stop their insults, she was known to inflict worse punishments. "We could be naughty," Ann DeWar admitted.

One girl whose Democratic father did not approve of Millsaps's Republican apostasy was Elizabeth Prichard, known as Betty. One day, when Betty proudly arrived for class in a new hat and matching circle skirt that her mother had made, Louise grabbed the homemade hat and tossed it to Ann DeWar. The two girls played keep-away until Betty's hat was lost behind the radiator and Betty indignant. Louise could be "devilish," said Betty Prichard Dunn. "Not one of my favorite friends."

When Louise was about nine years old, she began to draw in an artist's sketchbook. She was small for her age, and the sight of her lugging the big, heavy black book seemed comic to Sally, who teased, "Here comes crazy Louise with her sketchbook." Louise stood on her dignity. She did not appreciate Sally's light mockery and logged this incident as one in a growing list of unforgettable offenses. Louise's intensity amused the adults, who rewarded her at Christmas with an adult-sized easel. When her Uncle Peter began taking classes at the newly opened Memphis School of Art, they would sometimes set up their easels side by side.

Louise in those days kept her hair short and wore bib overalls. A schoolmate described her as always tiny, rather fairy-like in figure, but with a fiery temperament. Peter, who was usually quiet and studious, was notably chatty and at ease with Louise. He would recommend his favorite blues and jazz records, along with new books she might enjoy, and answered her questions—to the best of his ability—about the baffling lives of grown-ups.

It was Peter Taylor more than anyone else who influenced Louise's growing awareness of class distinctions and bigotry. His stories and novels, many set in Memphis neighborhoods like those in which the Fitzhughs lived, would speak of pride of place, but at the same time they exposed inequities and deep-seated prejudices. His characters are often in thrall to people or events in the past. His writing is not sentimental, but his characters can be deeply nostalgic: for lost youth, lost time, lost opportunities, and lost power. His sister Sally and her husband, Millsaps, must have sometimes remarked at the way Peter's stories captured people like themselves, feeling both pride and chagrin.

Guston Fitzhugh Sr., the Captain, died on January 16, 1940, and afterward, Louise, her father, and her stepmother often visited the grieving Josephine Fitzhugh. Eleven-year-old Louise was fond of her grandmother, and she particularly admired her musicianship. Josephine could still perform a serviceable aria, and she was a strict piano teacher who would slam the lid on Louise's hands when she played the wrong notes.[11] She also carefully patrolled Louise's manners, complimenting her when she obliged by walking slowing and gracefully. (It was well known that haste was a middle-class predilection.) And she could be cutting when Louise used vulgar slang or slouched (uncouth conduct attributed by all the Fitzhughs to the *Perkins's influence*).

When Louise was in seventh grade, the Japanese attacked Pearl Harbor. After war was declared, Peter Taylor was drafted;

he served on a base near Sewanee before going overseas. Millsaps received a deferment, but many of Louise's friends' fathers enlisted and were gone for the duration. Ann's older brother joined the Army Signal Corps and served on an aircraft carrier. When he came home on leave, he'd tease his sister and Louise, barking, "Hit the deck . . . Flat as a pancake," just as he had been commanded by his senior officers. The girls giggled and obeyed. Sometimes they'd stand at attention and give him a smart salute.

Soldiers on leave came from the bases that surrounded Memphis for a good time in the joints of Beale Street. They bought records by Memphis Minnie and Bessie Smith and carried Memphis blues songs and sheet music back to their bases as well as overseas. When Louise and Ann went downtown, they saw streets crowded with loud young servicemen in olive drab uniforms, some not a whole lot older than they were. In classrooms and clubs, the girls also did their bit for the war effort. They wrote letters to soldiers abroad, and they tried to learn to knit hats and scarves, with uneven results. What Louise and Ann liked best was collecting the tin cans that would be sent somewhere to make bullets. With the neighborhood boys, they loved to jump on these cans and smash them to a pulp.

Louise didn't write about the war years in the Deep South from the viewpoint of a twelve-year-old child, but her contemporary, Carson McCullers, did.[12] In McCullers's novel *The Member of the Wedding*—which as an adult Louise would read and admire—Frankie Addams, the novel's protagonist, comes of age in the American South during World War II. There's much that is Louise-like about Frankie.[13] They were both tomboys, and Frankie's ideal world, where "people could instantly change back and forth from boys to girls, whichever they felt like and wanted," would certainly have appealed to Louise. She was also, like Frankie, an only child who turned to the household staff for company and advice.

Louise's family kitchen would have been a frequent destination for an inquisitive little girl who loved cake, and it's likely she got under the cook's feet from time to time. Perhaps this was the cook who introduced little Louise to the simple delights of a delicious tomato sandwich with lettuce on white bread with mayonnaise. As an adult author, Louise would repay the debt by writing scenes into *Harriet the Spy* between an ornery cook and a stubborn little girl who would only ever eat this one meal for lunch.

During the war years, Josephine Fitzhugh remained a staunch matriarch within Memphis society, and she tried to interest her granddaughter in the welfare organization she had formed years earlier called The Josephine Circle. This organization bestowed charity—such as educational scholarships—on young women of suitable religious uprightness and careful, receptive character. Louise, who was rapidly losing her religion, was distinctly uninterested in her grandmother's style of social work: her early domestic rebellions were characterized by sulky nonparticipation in the grand old traditions of her family's philanthropy. She didn't care to attend banquets, and she was embarrassed by the idea of meeting the recipients—girls her own age—of the Josephine Circle's largesse. Eventually, her elders stopped asking her to be involved.

Louise wasn't any more petulant than other thirteen-year-olds in her social set. At ease with her friends and some chosen adults, including her Uncle Peter, she could be charming and ebullient.[14] Uncle Peter wasn't often in Memphis now, but when he was on leave from military service he made time to visit with Louise. He noted how she was growing from a "courageous little girl" into a tough-minded young woman, a person "already fighting for her existence."[15]

five

BEST ASSETS

Louise's fourteen-year-old beau, Charles McNutt, thought Louise liked him because he wasn't a southerner. He was an army brat with some experience of the world; he was just as smart as she was; he was not a bossy or show-offy type of boy; and he was very good looking. His father was a career military officer posted abroad. In the summer, the rest of his family lived with Charles's grandfather in Memphis's Morningside Park. In the heat of the summer of 1941, just about every day, Charles would walk the three or four miles to Louise's house on Lombardy in the Chickasaw Gardens neighborhood. Sally would answer the door and invite him in.

"Louise will be right up," she would say, and Charles would climb the stairs to the outside deck above the family's large living room. Louise would come up to meet him carrying her sketchbook, and sometimes some magazines with articles marked that she wanted to discuss with him. They would lay on the couch talking about new movies, the novels they were reading, and the records they liked. Charles was more interested in Memphis blues than Louise; she liked jazz and torch songs. They also talked about school, and which teachers they liked or did not like—to varying degrees, they were "respectful, terrified, or disdainful" of them, Charles later said.

They never discussed their parents, so Charles was surprised to discover from a mutual friend that Sally was Louise's stepmother. He thought Louise was "a serious young lady, pensive at times. Sometimes petulant. She was something of a rebel . . . not a wild one." He judged her to be "a little different from the other girls, a little bit more serious and very smart." She was also impatient, often quarrelsome, mischievous, and intolerant of stupidity at home and in the world. He thought her beautiful and was head over heels in love. They'd do a little necking, always aware that the deck wasn't terribly private and at any moment Sally might appear with lemonade.

Louise and Charles went steady for two years during eighth and ninth grade. When Louise graduated into Hutchison's upper school in tenth grade, Charles went to the Sewanee Military Academy, a boarding school about three hundred miles from Memphis. They kept up a correspondence and met when he came home on breaks. He escorted her to dances and social events. But the intensity of their 1941 meetings would not come again. Louise confided in her best friend, Ann DeWar, that although Charles had grown more devoted over time, she had come to see him as more of a friend than a sweetheart.

In Miss Hutchison's upper school, Louise and Ann's class expanded to include several new friends, including Peggy Land and Joan Williams. Louise and Joan already knew each other from church; in high school, they became close friends, sharing an ambition to become writers. For much of high school, Joan and Louise would be a team of rivals, confidantes, and competitors for writing prizes; outside of school, they dared each other to be more reckless and rebellious. Joan thought they were drawn together because they were both only children, both idiosyncratic and sensitive types, and both looking ahead to escaping Memphis.

As a sophomore, Louise followed the fashions. Girls applied blood-colored lipstick and wore their cardigans backward. Louise let her hair grow, curling it around her shoulders in a long page-boy style. Tenth grade also meant pledging sororities and clubs, whose acceptance might establish a girl's social standing for the remainder of high school. Candidates would be evaluated and assessed for personality and appeal, talent, and amiability, with added stress on the value of family connections.

Louise was the child of a scandalous divorce, and of Republican parents. Her conversations with her Uncle Peter had given her a worldly perspective. She was an arty girl, rarely seen without her sketchbook. These distinctions, which might have stigmatized her, seemed instead to play in her favor. Louise, like her friends, wanted to be invited and accepted, and those desires overcame any misgivings she might have had about being judged by sorority sisters like a prize sheep. Peggy Land thought any sorority would want Louise. In Peggy's estimation, Louise Fitzhugh "got everything": "She was well-liked and attractive. . . . She got to do pretty much what she wanted. . . . She could have whatever clothes she wanted. Never had to worry about money or things that lots of people had to worry about. . . . She was one of those fortunate people who never even had a skin problem."[1] Louise was invited to join Sigma Kappa Sigma, as were Peggy and Joan. "We were both still conformists," Joan Williams conceded, and they would remain so for a little longer.

Pledge week signaled the start of the season's cascade of parties. Charles commuted on weekends from Sewanee to be Louise's date at city events and country events. At balls held at the high-end Peabody Hotel, the girls dressed in tulle and satin and wore gardenias in their hair. At farm dances, some of Louise's school friends raced their horses. Another Hutchison student, Audrey Taylor Gonzalez, described how sometimes they'd dance on the grass to a bluegrass band that played on washboards and banjos and fiddles. They'd dine on "green and white coleslaw, yellow and white potato salad, black barrels of baked beans, and pink half-moon slices of watermelon with black teardrop seeds . . . chicken parts and pulled pork pieces," served on a red-checked paper plate.[2] The Memphis Country Club, whose membership was restricted to white, male Protestants only, hosted tennis tournaments and pool parties, where the menu was typically chocolate malts and club sandwiches prepared by African American women, who were paid a pittance in wages.[3]

Before long, Louise had grown tired of the parties and insipid small talk. All the high school boys just wanted to brag about which branch of the forces they would join. Meanwhile, Beale Street swarmed with good-looking soldiers and sailors with real war experience. Louise and Joan sometimes dared each other to talk to one or another young serviceman they'd see at the counter of a soda fountain. Sometimes they'd flirt and ask for a light to a cigarette, but these encounters were never serious. They still cared deeply about their reputations, and there were gossips everywhere.

Unlike the fathers of their friends, Joan and Louise's fathers stayed home during the war years. Joan's father was too old to enlist, and Millsaps received a deferment. An attorney on the home front, Millsaps was involved in city politics and active in the Republican Party. Louise's stepmother, Sally, also did her bit. Her Junior League chapter collected scrap, rubber, and rags and held benefits to build morale and raise funds for the war effort. She and Millsaps were a charismatic couple. They were noted for their sophisticated repartee and invited everywhere.

Louise didn't care for her father's sarcasm or cutting wit. She confessed to Joan that, frankly, she didn't like her father much at all. Joan couldn't understand, since Millsaps seemed smart and "very nice . . . very attentive." She found it fascinating that "Millsaps would play tennis with [Louise]." Her own father was older and would never play. Millsaps seemed modern. Louise conceded that her father was well educated and good looking, but he was also unpleasantly competitive. He *had* to win every argument and every tennis game. He was also old-fashioned regarding women in the workplace. He hated the very idea, for instance, of women lawyers. Louise wanted to be a writer, not a lawyer, but she would boil with anger at his implication that women were inferior. Her father had plenty to say on the subject of women writers, too. Where were their Dostoevskys? She could not wait to get out from under his thumb.[4]

Joan saw Louise as a deeply sensitive girl, later reflecting that she was someone who had been "essentially hurt by the enforced absence of her mother." On the subject of mothers, Peggy Land said any discussion whatsoever of Mary Louise Perkins Fitzhugh Trevilion was strictly *verboten*. Louise did still occasionally see her mother, although Millsaps discouraged their meetings and stopped shuttling her to lunches. When Mary Louise visited Memphis, there was almost always something off. Mother and daughter didn't really know one another, and as a teenager Louise could be silent and moody around adults. By 1940, Mary Louise had given up her dancing school to work as a librarian for the Carnegie Library in Clarksdale, so they mainly talked about books. On the rare occasions when Louise visited her mother's home in Clarksdale, they would listen to music together on the radio or record player, and Mary Louise might demonstrate a few fancy dance steps. Despite her mother's efforts to bridge the gulf, Louise still resented having been spirited away as an infant; as a teenager, she blamed everyone concerned.

One Sunday, Louise invited Joan to lunch at her grandmother's grand old house. Joan found the place a little spooky, silent, and empty. The servants who cared for Josephine Fitzhugh, who was then in her late sixties, kept it in impeccable order, its floors and furniture polished and gleaming. Joan's family was well enough off, but what she saw that day struck her as true wealth; she concluded that her friend, who had grown up surrounded by such riches, had been "pampered." Before lunch, Joan and Louise visited with Josephine upstairs in her bedroom suite. To Joan, the elderly woman looked remarkably tiny, taking up very little space in a very big bed. After a spell of polite small talk with their hostess, the two girls went downstairs to eat in a formal dining room at a table laid according to the principle of dainty service, with pristine linen, sparkling silver, neat china, and glistening crystal. A butler in a white coat arrived to serve them lamb chops, and Louise joked with the man, who had been with the family for years.

When Joan ventured to remark on how "lonesome" Grandmother Fitzhugh seemed, Louise laughed. "Oh no, Joan," she said, "nobody but you would have the courage to say that." In other words, it took an innocent to state such an obvious truth. Josephine Fitzhugh may indeed have been a lonely lady, but according to family mythology she was a paragon—unassailable, self-sufficient, and the final arbiter on subjects of etiquette and morality. Pity was on par with disrespect.

Louise was just starting to see a pattern: the indomitable lady and all the relics of the past were stultifying. In the roadhouses out of town and on Beale Street, where Louise and her friends would sometimes drive just to say they had been there, new dances and music were luring teenagers to show a little more of the rebellion they'd been holding inside: to curse a little louder, stay out a little longer, show some disrespect to the dead hand of history, and act a little more uncouth, just to see what might happen.

By the time Louise was sixteen, the Scopes trial was almost twenty years in the past. The controversy over evolution seemed to Louise and Charles like a sepia postcard, old-timey and holy-rollerish. (Nevertheless, it would remain illegal to teach evolution in Tennessee public schools until 1967.) Louise didn't much like math and science, but it irked her that her state was so ill informed. Private schools often took a more enlightened view, but at Miss Hutchison's, math and science studies were distinctly underdeveloped. In the school library, a student with an inclination toward science might have found books from the Great War era and before on the theories of eugenics, relating race to disease, intelligence, human development, and delinquency. The school's whitewashed history textbooks taught the accepted notions—not unique to the South—that Reconstruction had been a disaster, and that the annexation of Native American lands and the destruction of tribal people were essential to American progress. Even if she wasn't fully aware of the alternatives, Louise would have questioned these status quo interpretations of history. Peter Taylor's influence and her own wide-ranging reading would have given her the ammunition to do so.

In their senior year English class, Louise and Joan were the two top girls who competed for the attention of their teacher. Mrs. Polk favored brown clothes, wore her glasses low on her nose, and had a passion for poetry. When Joan read aloud an emotional story she'd written in the voice of a mother whose son had died in battle, Mrs. Polk spontaneously burst into tears.[5] Louise, determined to surpass Joan, performed a dramatic monologue she'd written in which she personified war. "I'm so tired, give me rest!" she declaimed at a school assembly. An audience member remembers there wasn't a dry eye in the house, with the possible exception of Joan's.

Moving at last beyond her conformist phase, by her senior year Louise was dating women. Joan knew this, but they didn't talk about it. Virginia L. Wolf, the author of the 1991 book *Louise Fitzhugh*, briefly mentions Louise's high school romance with an unnamed classmate.[6] After the affair was discovered, Wolf says, the Fitzhugh family succeeded in sending the other girl away and "having the whole incident hushed up."[7] Wolf's sole informant was Peggy Land, who would not say how she had gained this information. Peggy referred further questions to Joan Williams, who replied, categorically, "I don't know anything about that girl getting expelled."[8]

Louise's romance rings true, but her girlfriend's expulsion remains something of a mystery. There were only thirty-one students in Louise's graduating class. One girl getting sent away, or expelled—no matter how powerful and efficient the combination of administrative and parental authority may have been—could hardly have remained a secret. Ann DeWar said that if it were true, "I can't imagine that I wouldn't have known about it. . . . None of us knew where [Peggy] got that story, and she won't tell." Would Louise have permitted her elders to send her girlfriend away without a struggle? Even if they had already broken up, even if they no longer loved each other? Would she have continued to attend school as usual despite the injustice? "That's not likely, not Louise," said Ann DeWar.[9] On the other hand, perhaps her closest friends did know who the other girl was and what happened to her. They might have sworn secrecy to preserve Louise's reputation—a vow Peggy perhaps outgrew.

In the Hutchison upper school, there would have been other lesbian or bisexual students and teachers, and every one of them would have been endangered if their secret had been discovered. Still, even under the constraints, they found each other. Louise would soon enough come to understand the risks attending exposure: condemnation by family, denunciation by the church, punishment by state and federal laws. As a child of wealth, she'd always been able to obtain whatever she wanted, all her mistakes forgiven. In the future, she'd have to be less impulsive and more guarded. She'd have to bide her time and keep her nerve until escape to a freer place became possible. Meanwhile, she'd manage her family and friends carefully. What mattered in Memphis was how you presented yourself, and sometimes you had to lie.

The day the war in Europe ended, Miss Hutchison gathered her pupils and made the joyous announcement in the school's assembly room. The girls could hear people singing and shouting, church bells ringing, and the unusual noise of car horns blaring, a sound normally forbidden by regulation in quiet Memphis.[10] Ann DeWar's brother, who had served on an aircraft carrier, came home safe; so did Peter Taylor. Uncle Peter and his new wife, Eleanor Ross Taylor, visited Memphis after demobilization, coming to Christmas dinner at Sally and Millsaps's Lombardy Street house. That year, as was customary, Millsaps performed his holiday tradition of pitching bottles of whiskey to members of his staff and their family and friends, who gathered in front of the house. As an attorney and politician, Millsaps received many bottles as gifts from his clients. He never liked to keep any whiskey but Scotch, so he'd toss twenty or thirty bottles of all shapes and sizes, some more expensive than others, to willing recipients, some of whom had waited for hours for this largesse.[11]

Peter regaled the guests with a story about meeting Gertrude Stein by accident in Paris: he had been invited to visit and talk with her for two whole blissful hours. Stein, whom every enlightened reader of books and magazines knew about at that time, was openly a lesbian, and she lived with her partner Alice B. Toklas in Paris. Whether or not Louise had read Stein's books at that point, she would have read articles that celebrated Stein's confidence and famous lack of concern for convention. She would have known of Stein's domestic relationship with Alice B. Toklas, whom Stein called her wife. Her uncle's encounter with Gertrude Stein sparked a new ambition in Louise. Getting the hell out of Memphis would only be a baby step. Now that the war was over, Louise longed to see Paris for herself.

six

MASTER OF DISGUISE

In the spring of 1946, Louise met a like-minded young rebel who shared her strong sense of social justice. Handsome and serious, Ed Thompson was a senior at East High, bound for Vanderbilt. A photograph from the time has him dressed in a bomber jacket with Buddy Holly hair, sitting on a stoop and dangling a pair of horn-rimmed glasses. He wrote poetry, and he shared Louise's interest in W. H. Auden and W. B. Yeats. He also liked the fiction of Peter Taylor, which was starting to be published more and read widely. Ed's family had considerably less money than those of most of his crowd. His father had died when he was young, and he and his sister were being raised by a single mother in a modest bungalow that was tucked amid the more lavish homes of the Central Gardens district. His mother, Sammie Agee Thompson, worked for Helen of Memphis, an upscale dress shop where women like Sally and Josephine Fitzhugh bought high-priced frocks. She had cultivated the hauteur her patrons expected in their fashion consultant. As a teenager, Ed was guarded and sensitive like his mother.

Ed had grown up feeling like an outsider. Louise had plenty of material things, but they hadn't made her any less lonely. She told Ed about her parents' long and pulverizing custody battle and explained that, as a child of divorce, she'd felt wrenched between both families. She'd had the sense since childhood that in loving one parent, she'd betray the other. Ed thought this had made Louise hesitant to put her trust in people. She spoke to him of her impatience to get away. He said, "Like everybody else you want to get rid of your parents and be your own boss."[1] Ed knew of Millsaps as an attorney and a "big Republican" when that was still a rare thing for a white man to be, and not "real popular." Sammie did not belong to clubs, but she knew that Sally Fitzhugh was especially influential in the Junior League.

Ed and Louise agreed they were both sick of the South. They talked about "what a lousy place the world is, and how we were going to make it better," Ed later said. They also talked "about running away—somewhere up north—together." Louise said that north was the right direction, but she wanted to keep going, all the way to Paris. It wasn't a far-fetched dream; the young people of their parents' class had all gone before the war. She wanted to visit the Louvre, where the artwork that had been evacuated and hidden in chateaus and caves for the duration of the war was finally being returned. If Miss Hutchison's hadn't been good for anything else, at least Louise spoke excellent French, which would come in handy when she was painting pictures on the Left Bank. Maybe, like her Uncle Peter, she'd run into Gertrude Stein, or maybe she would meet Picasso. Ed wanted to do everything he could to make Louise's dreams come true, whether in Memphis or Paris. He was smitten.

Despite their dissatisfaction with the status quo, Ed and Louise still attended some of the parties and dances sponsored by their social clubs and Louise's sorority. Louise played tennis and Ed played baseball. The Louise Ed knew also seemed to have read everything, and she wanted to write serious novels. She impressed Ed because of just how many artistic talents she had. She was an accomplished painter and she had a lovely singing voice; she could play the piano and was learning flute. He said that by contrast, he sometimes felt "clumsy and socially backward."[2] But Louise was an intrepid companion, and they encouraged each other's sense of adventure, exploring alternatives to their insular high school society.

On one of their dates, Louise and Ed went to the home of an older man named Vernon Watkins, who held a literary salon in Memphis. Watkins was a polyglot with a library of volumes in many languages. As an icebreaker, he'd hide books between the cushions of the sofas and chairs and bid his guests to search for them, a game that gave their colloquy the ambience of a treasure hunt. Once Ed came upon a small volume written in Greek, from which his learned host later read aloud. Ed suspected Watkins of putting on a show to impress young women. Louise, for one, seemed dazzled by their host's erudition.

Ed enjoyed his evenings at Watkins's but as a high school student sometimes felt he was in over his head. He was jealous of the older man's knowledge and charisma and the attention Louise paid to him. Watkins was also a more experienced poet. Ed had shown Louise some of his "crude attempts to write adolescent poetry," which she had critiqued—but "in a nice way," he said. "She just let me know that I wasn't so good and I stood corrected there." Her own work, Ed believed, was "deep and esoteric." He thought she would certainly become a writer of "dead serious" books. By that point, she could have been writing in invisible ink: he had fallen in love and thought everything about her brilliant.

On their excursions around town, the couple read *The New Yorker* at the public library, and the *New Republic* and the *Partisan*

Review at Watkins's salon. Louise jumped in when the Watkins crowd discussed articles and books about the nightmare of Hiroshima and the horrors of segregation. There was a side of Louise that always felt in the right. She had a short fuse, and when contradicted she was quick to defend her side. Her school friends never thought of Louise as tempestuous, however. She seemed more amused than anything by the social ups and downs of their crowd, and her quips made people laugh. She was fond of saying, "Bury me north of the Mason-Dixon line," provocatively mocking their elders (there had been reports of nonagenarian veterans of the Confederacy in far-flung places who'd insisted on their burial down South). She wasn't interested in showing much respect, and she didn't care when she was called uncouth. The Louise Ed knew scorned status and prestige. She was more of a "proletariat," he said, with a special loathing for the debutante types who allowed themselves to be inspected and paraded for the marriage market.

Ed rarely disagreed with Louise. "I never did debate with her that much," he said, instead deferring to her passionate opinions. Sometimes he would get a scolding for accidentally coming up against her politics. During one of their conversations regarding prejudice—a common topic—Louise had reprimanded Ed when he'd referred to a Jewish storekeeper in a way Louise thought smacked of casual anti-Semitism. "What difference does it make that he's Jewish?" Louise demanded to know.

"I stood corrected," Ed said. He regretted having leaned on a noxious stereotype. "In the South the Jewish storekeeper was sort of a label you put on people and an unfair one. . . . She set me straight real quick, and I never will forget the rebuke that I got."

Louise graduated from Miss Hutchison's School for Girls at its thirty-third annual commencement exercise on May 30, 1946. She and her sister graduates wore white formal dresses and carried arm bouquets of yellow roses tied by yellow satin streamers. Louise planned to attend Southwestern at Memphis College in the Fall (formerly Rhodes College). She wanted to study writing, and the Southwestern English Department had a good reputation, according to her Uncle Peter. He had studied there before transferring to Kenyon College. But she wasn't thrilled by the prospect of staying in provincial Memphis. She abhorred Jim Crow and rejected the expectations her milieu had for women. She especially wanted to escape her father's dominion.

The summer ahead was heavily scheduled with parties and dances. The long-suffering Charles McNutt had agreed to escort Louise to them, although her interest in such affairs was dropping precipitously. Charles wanted to be near her and was prepared to play any part she would allow. By then, Charles was aware of Ed Thompson, and he was jealous of Ed's height and good looks. Louise assured Charles that Ed wasn't a serious rival, but that wasn't entirely true. One night, when Louise and Charles had arranged to attend a formal dance at the Memphis Country Club, Charles had dressed in his formal military uniform for the occasion, but Louise showed up at his house wearing Bermuda shorts. She said she didn't want to have anything to do with the debutante-types anymore. No more parties or dances or soirees: she was making a clean break. "You might as well get out of those ridiculous clothes," she told him. "I'm not going to join those menstruating minstrels."[3]

Charles diagnosed Louise with fashionable "ennui." But Louise wasn't suffering boredom; instead, she was feeling increasingly hostile toward social obligations. With a few exceptions, she also felt alienated from her former friends. She reproached herself for being wishy-washy as she pondered her escape from Memphis. She understood her advantages, among these the privilege to choose between many possibilities. She had seen how, among

Sally's friends, this gift had frozen into indecision, where society luncheons and bridge games filled the void. In Louise's view, Sally's role as president of the Junior League made her a minipanjandrum, a large fish in a small, polluted pond. Louise wanted a different kind of life.

Louise had other plans for the night, she told Charles. She was on her way to meet someone. "Is it Ed?" Charles asked.

"No," she said. "A girl named Amelia," a college student studying art at Southwestern, whose family had a farm in Arkansas. Louise told Charles they were sleeping together. At the time, he persuaded himself that Louise was only "experimenting with sex": "I thought it was silly, frankly," he said. "I wasn't going to let a little thing like [her bisexuality] stand in my way. I didn't think that was an ongoing thing. . . . I thought she was trying everything."

In the fall, Charles returned to Sewanee to begin his studies at the University of the South. Louise attended Southwestern, and over the next year she dated both Amelia Brent and Ed Thompson. Ed considered her his girlfriend and praised her as a prodigy, saying her poetry was profound. He was Louise's first dedicated literary fan—the first of a string of admirers throughout her life who appointed themselves protectors of her genius. Amelia was just fun.

On Friday, August 8, 1947, Ed impulsively proposed to Louise. She surprised him by accepting, perhaps because he praised in her the talents she most admired in herself. What followed was an afternoon of strategizing. Ed had always assumed there would be opposition from the Fitzhughs, who would have wanted their only daughter to marry somebody from Memphis's upper strata, perhaps even Charles McNutt. But Louise said none of that mattered. She had no intention of telling her parents. She would only marry him if they eloped at once.

Beyond Ed's admiration for her writing, there are many reasons Louise might have made this impulsive decision. She may have had an argument earlier with Amelia and wanted to make a dramatic, defiant statement. Perhaps she thought this shock would be the best way to declare her independence from her father. In any event, elopement was a subject much discussed among Louise's circle of friends. Joan Williams had eloped while still in high school with her own longtime boyfriend, though her underaged marriage had been quickly annulled. Perhaps this was even a factor in Louise's decision: Joan would later speculate that Louise was being competitive again.

In any case, Louise and Ed hopped into his car. Before they were across the border to Mississippi, they stopped to collect Peggy Land, whom Louise insisted on taking along as a witness. Peggy, part of Louise's crowd at Hutchison, also attended Southwestern. Most importantly, Peggy knew about Amelia Brent. Peggy also had her own wild streak, which had driven her to run away to Los Angeles the previous winter, when she was seventeen. Peggy had waited until both her parents had been out of town, then taken a cross-country train alone and under a false name. Along the way, she'd mailed separate letters to her mother, to her father, and to her best friend, Joan Williams. In her mother's letter, Peggy had written that she was "unhappy" and "going away for a trip." She didn't state her destination, but asked that her mother communicate with her through the personals section of the *Memphis Commercial Appeal*. Her mother placed the following ad: "Peggy darling, everything is all right. Anxiously waiting to hear from you. Call me at home. Mother."

The "Co-Ed Heiress," as Peggy was dubbed by the tabloid press, became the subject of a nationwide search. Her photograph was distributed to police, and her "mysterious disappearance" became an item on the radio broadcast of the influential gossip columnist Walter Winchell. Just five days after she'd left Memphis, Peggy Land was run to earth in Los Angeles's Mayflower Hotel, registered as Mrs. William King. The Mayflower was a sturdy downtown building with a rooftop terrace bar, not far from Union Station. Built in 1927, it was one of many such stops on the avenue of broken dreams where would-be starlets and ingenues, who arrived from Memphis and Topeka and Walla Walla, abandoned their Hollywood fantasies. (Mary Louise might even have stayed there on her failed job search in 1930, when she still hoped to find enough work as a tap dancer to support baby Louise.) Peggy told reporters eager for an explanation that she was "amazed by the commotion"; she wondered if in her letters she hadn't been "explicit enough." After her return to Memphis, Peggy's mother announced that her daughter had been studying too hard and damaged by reading books on psychology.

So when Louise needed a witness for her own out-of-state adventure, she knew who would be game. The three of them set off for Hernando, Mississippi, just twenty-five miles from Memphis and a world away. Mississippi was like Tennessee—still a dry state—but for the adventurous, black market alcohol was available. And Hernando had a reputation as a rowdy border town, a destination for drinking to excess, hearing musicians play the blues, and dancing.

Ed, as their driver, wasn't drinking, but it's likely Louise and Peggy sipped from a celebratory bottle. They arrived in Hernando in an ebullient mood and searched for a marrying judge. Fast weddings for out-of-staters were something of an underground industry, and there was not much oversight of the business. At least in the case of the newlywed Thompsons, neither the minister who performed the marriage, nor any witnesses, were required to ratify their official-looking Mississippi state board of health document, titled a "Statistical Record of Marriage." In 1947, Mississippi law permitted men to marry at seventeen and women at fifteen with parental permission. Without permission, both bride and groom were required to be twenty-one. In the circumstances, Ed and Louise, both nineteen years old, lied about their age.

When the marriage was concluded and the license documented, the couple found that their mood had lost its fizz. Within an hour of her wedding, Louise told Ed that she had changed her mind. She didn't wish to be married anymore.

Ed was disappointed, but always a perfect gentleman. If his bride didn't want him, he wouldn't make it hard for her. The three of them got back in the car and returned to Memphis. In the short time it had taken to drive home from Hernando, Louise and Ed hardly spoke. They already knew it wouldn't have worked.

It was the middle of the night when Ed turned down Lombardy Street. All the lights in the house were on, and Millsaps and Sally were waiting. Peggy's parents or Ed's mother may have informed the Fitzhughs, whose response was as confused as the newlyweds' escapade had been. Ed and Louise had eloped? But they didn't necessarily want to stay married? Louise shook her marriage license at Millsaps and Sally to signal her independence, then she stormed up to her room, leaving the rest of them to assess the damage.

Millsaps quizzed Ed. "What were you thinking? You don't have a job. Aren't you just about to start college? Find yourself a lawyer," Millsaps advised. "Your marriage is on its way to being annulled."

Within days, Millsaps filed papers in court. Their marriage license was declared illegal, since they had been under the legal age to marry without parental consent. Ed also testified under oath that their marriage had not been consummated. All of that was sufficient grounds for a speedy annulment.

By September, the decree was final. The events and outcome seemed harder for Ed—particularly once Louise said she didn't want to see him for a while. Ed had a close friend named Bill Brown who had watched Ed's relationship with Louise evolve over time, and he consoled Ed in its aftermath. Memphis was a small town, and Bill had seen Louise and Amelia around together; he may have guessed that they were more than friends.

Even with the annulment and Ed largely out of the romantic picture, Louise was still in a love triangle. When Charles next returned to Memphis, he ran into a mutual friend who said, "Did you hear? Louise went off and got married and Millsaps had it annulled!"

Charles thought she would explain about Ed, but Louise only wanted to talk about Amelia. She announced she was truly in love with her. Later, at Charles's insistence, she would explain that she "had tried sex with a man," but hadn't gone all the way, because she'd found it unsatisfactory and disappointing. Then she had been with Amelia, "and sex that way was more satisfying."

Charles told himself she was just being Louise, testing to see how outrageous she could be. If he argued that she was just being rebellious for the hell of it, she'd just dig in deeper, and he didn't want to hear any more intimate details. If there was one thing he knew about Louise, it was that she was recalcitrant to a fare-thee-well. She delighted in being stubborn and arguing her point until everybody else had closed up shop for the night and gone home. "You ought to be a lawyer, Louise," Charles said once. Which was of course the worst thing a person could say to her. She would *never* be like her father. She was going to be an artist in Paris, and she would have lots of satisfying sex, with lots of different women.

seven

PRIVATE INVESTIGATOR

In the formal photograph taken when she was a twenty-year-old student attending Southwestern College at Memphis, Amelia Brent's intelligent dark eyes are all business, her long brown hair is brushed back over a high forehead, and her brows and lips darkened and sharply defined. Amelia was the only daughter of a successful cotton broker and socialite whose family owned farms and an old plantation in Arkansas. She and Louise had much in common. Their families had been acquainted at least back to their grandparents, when Amelia's grandfather, an attorney, had given evidence of Millsaps's upright character during his divorce trial from Mary Louise Perkins.

Through girlhood, Amelia had belonged to all the requisite clubs and sororities. She had dressed in styles bought on city shopping trips to upscale emporiums like Helen of Memphis, and she practiced French, ballroom dancing, and all the arts expected of young southern ladies. She didn't care to learn how to embroider her beau's initials on a handkerchief, however, and at some point, between the cotillions and elocution lessons, she had balked, unsatisfied with the life she was on track to inherit. Perhaps, because she was a great reader, she felt called to explore the great world. (Amelia's custom-printed book plates feature text in black and white around an inset of a vessel with sails aloft: *"With ships and books I sail all seas" Ex Libris Amelia Riddick Brent.*)[1] Memphis society must have felt as small and small-minded to her as it did to Louise.

After high school, Amelia had spent a year at Ward Belmont College, one of a crew of fashion setters who wore their brother's white shirts untucked over blue jeans, landing them a mention in the *Nashville Tennessean*'s "College Capers" column.[2] The following year, at Southwestern, Amelia joined the sorority for ambitious, smart girls, Delta Delta Delta. She had a lot of drive and the alternative career plans to go with it. If she couldn't make it as a photojournalist like Margaret Bourke-White or Dorothea Lange, she would get a job in magazines or in advertising in New York City; she would be the kind of brainy, independent, no-nonsense career woman that Eve Arden and Rosalind Russell played in the movies.

Louise's career at Southwestern, by contrast, was a damp squib. She intended to be an original and didn't model herself on anybody. There was nothing she wanted in Memphis anymore, except Amelia. It was the real first love for them both, a passion that demanded attention and a considered strategy to manage. There could be no careless sighs and kisses for two girls. If Louise was more of a shout-it-from-the-rooftops-type, the practical Amelia convinced her to have patience. Through the winter and spring of 1947, they plotted their getaway.

Louise and Ed's annulment was granted in September 1947, and Louise returned to Southwestern the same month. Together, she and Amelia accelerated a plan that would get them away together by increments. They'd begin by going deeper south, to Florida Southern University, where Amelia would finish her education. At first, everything went beautifully to plan. Louise took the semester off to enjoy the sunshine in Lakeland, Florida. Their first weeks together were a blissful vacation, spent sunbathing and watching the Detroit Tigers play baseball in their winter home. Ed Thompson visited them on his spring break from Vanderbilt. He thought there might be a chance that he and Louise would get back together and remembers being "full of optimism back then." Louise was not persuaded, but she wanted to remain friends. After he returned to Tennessee, he and Louise often spoke on the phone. Ed didn't understand her relationship with Amelia at the time. He still loved Louise.

Once their vacation ended and the fall semester began, reality set in. Amelia became absorbed in her schoolwork, but Louise grew bored, tired of waiting for her own life to catch hold. She wanted to study writing and literature with published poets, and art with masters of painting and drawing. Recognizing that they'd have to separate for a time to achieve what they wanted together, Louise and Amelia parted, vowing to meet again in New York City.

Louise reluctantly moved back into the Fitzhugh home on Lombardy. It was the worst possible retreat for her. By then, she knew well enough what she wanted: to get out of the South and not look back. Joan Williams was also home that summer after a disappointing sophomore year at Chevy Chase Junior College in Maryland. Both of them wanted to be writers and to escape the narrow world of white gloves and garden parties.

When Louise turned to her Uncle Peter for advice, she was disgusted to hear that Kenyon College, where he taught creative writing, did not accept women students. Peter recommended

Bard College, which, like Kenyon, Bennington, and Oberlin, was known for progressive thought and a fine arts curriculum—and admitted women. It seemed a brilliant solution. In one fell swoop, Joan and Louise would get out of the South and drop into the middle of one of America's great intellectual milieus.

Surprisingly, and perhaps out of respect for Peter Taylor's opinion, Millsaps didn't object. He agreed to pay for his daughter's education, but he urged her to get some work experience first on a summer job at the *Memphis Commercial Appeal*. Millsaps was its legal counselor, and its editor, Frank Algren, was one of his best friends. Millsaps enjoyed the idea that his daughter would earn her first paycheck on what was almost a family paper.

Louise didn't have much feel for local journalism. Her summer job was most valuable for the way it gave her access to the newspaper morgue, where among the old photos and yellowed clippings, she found a treasure trove of Fitzhugh family history. She read how her Grandmother Fitzhugh had founded the Josephine Circle and published two popular cookbooks. Her Uncle Gus's literary accomplishments had also received much flattering coverage. It may have been surprising to see the photo of the author—a handsome, trim Gus in profile—because since then he had grown obese and increasingly mentally ill. Gus's physical transformation haunted Louise; for much of her youth, she'd conflated the horror of gaining weight with the horror of going mad. There were other articles, too: stories she half-remembered, overheard in fragments spoken by gossips and distant relatives. One of these was that her grandfather had been a protégé of Senator Edward Carmack, the scoundrel who'd viciously persecuted Ida B. Wells and incited a mob to burn down the Memphis offices of her newspaper, *Free Speech*. After Carmack was shot in the middle of the street on a Nashville afternoon, the Captain had prosecuted Carmack's alleged killer, but lost the case.

And there was more. Within a massive collection of stories about her mismatched parents' sensational divorce, Louise couldn't help but notice the newspaper's Fitzhugh bias. Her father, Millsaps, came off as some kind of hero, and his mother, Josephine, Louise's grandmother, as a saint and a martyr. Meanwhile, Louise's mother, Mary Louise, was reported to be a half-mad gold digger, and Josie Perkins, Louise's maternal grandmother, manipulative and trashy. According to this newspaper's record, Josie was clearly the villain of the affair; her meddling, the paper implied, had destroyed her daughter's marriage.

Reading the coverage of her parents' divorce was a wrenching experience. After work that day, she went straight to tell Joan Williams what she'd discovered. Louise was deeply disturbed by all the sordid details, Joan said, but there was one story that made her especially distraught: the incident with the divan. As Joan listened, Louise just kept repeating, "I was a baby and they threw me on the couch." Louise was angry, and from Joan's perspective, her attitude was "a plague on both their houses." She didn't need any encouragement to distrust her father, but her mother didn't come out of the story that well either. Louise just wanted to get far away and be herself.

In August, with passengers Joan Williams and Sally Taylor Fitzhugh, Louise drove to Bard College in her beautiful new 1948 sky-blue Plymouth, a curvy, shiny creature with bulbous fenders, a short snout, and a long, sloping trunk. She dearly loved that car, despite it having been a parting gift from her father. Thrown together on their road trip, Joan grew to like Sally, who always seemed slightly amused by everything. Joan thought Sally liked her particularly, because she was straight and might exert a good influence on Louise. Louise and Sally seemed to get along, so Joan was surprised later when Louise announced she had never liked Sally, ever since she had felt that her stepmother was mocking her when she called her "crazy Louise," the child with the too-big sketchbook. Joan had learned long ago not to take her friend's likes or dislikes too seriously. She regarded Louise as capricious, someone whose opinion could change based on her mood at the moment.

Located forty miles from New York City, Bard was a postwar sanctuary for war-weary émigré professors and left-leaning scholars as the Red Scare gained steam, as well as for artists seeking refuge from an indifferent world. For many idealistic students, Bard was part of a meaningful experiment in progressive thought and arts education. One student journalist at the college wrote, "As students of a small experimental college, in a country terrifyingly large, and in love with bigness, in a world which we feel to be increasingly apathetic to innovation, we realize that we have the responsibility to imagine and create."[3]

The college began enrolling women in 1944, when many of its co-eds were already used to doing the work of their male counterparts in wartime factories, in construction, and as political organizers. Some were transfer students like Louise and Joan, who knew what they wanted and seized the chance to study in male bastions. According to *The Bardian*, the college newspaper, its students did not adhere to "meaningless tradition" and rejected "assembly line" education. The women of Bard wore "pants and jackets, lounging and smoking as men." For even the most cynical teachers, students, and veterans, Bard, located in the remarkably pretty Hudson River Valley, was a peaceful refuge. For Louise and Joan, it would also provide a radically different perspective on race, sex, and class.

When Louise left Memphis to live with Amelia, she'd led an insular life. In Florida, she hadn't taken an outside job, and she hadn't made new and lasting friends. She'd stayed near home while Amelia attended school, and apart from Amelia, she'd been miserable. But at Bard, Louise plunged into the social world of parties and poker and excursions to roadhouses, where students would drink and swing to a jukebox that played Billie Holiday, Hank Williams, and Edith Piaf. Louise had a lovely singing voice, and thanks to Miss Hutchison's impeccable French, she could sing a perfectly accented rendition of "La Vie en Rose."

Bard, as it turned out, was a haven. Louise loved both the students and the faculty. She wanted to know *everything* and, in exchange, told all—in her fashion. Her fellow students couldn't get enough of Louise imitating the southern socialite's plight, a comic performance that let her new friends know just how dull and odious the life she'd escaped had been. And if, in telling stories, she liberally borrowed details, elided facts, compressed timelines, and elaborated the shenanigans of her high school years in Memphis, she was just exercising her storyteller's license. At Bard she began to tell the tale of her grandmother's eccentricities, with added Gothic flourishes. Josephine Fitzhugh was a musical millionaire who threw money out the window for the birds, while servants stood below to catch the cash in baskets. Her Uncle Gus was obese and insane and lived in an attic, where he cut up dolls for entertainment. Her stepmother, Sally, was mean. Her father, Millsaps, who had stolen her from her mother when she was a baby, was hateful. Her mother had *thrown her on a couch.* She would tell these stories in slightly different ways through her college years, and later to her friends in New York. With each retelling, she honed these family portraits for later use in her autobiographical books and plays.

Joan and Louise's academic advisers, both relatively recent hires, were a contrast in writerly personalities and style. It was rumored that literary fiction writer William Humphrey, Joan's adviser, had butchered a goat to commemorate his new job at Bard. He was a Texan who set his stories in the southern plains, and he roamed the hills with his students. Louise's adviser was the urbane, formalist poet James Merrill.

Raised among the upper crust of New York, Palm Beach, and Southampton, Merrill had arrived at Bard determined to avoid the distractions of New York society and to focus on his writing. "I want to make myself be alone, and this is the only way I can see it can be done," he wrote.[4] Merrill's first book of poetry, called *The Black Swan*, had been privately published in 1946. Five years later, Alfred A. Knopf would bring out his collection *First Poems*, which established Merrill as one of the leading poets of his generation. His "ornate, dense, obscure and very literary poetry," which often employed elaborate, fixed rhyme schemes, was part of the conversation surrounding metered and free verse much debated in academia and literary circles throughout the 1950s.[5] Louise enrolled in Merrill's poetry course on metrics, and at their first tutorial she brought him a villanelle (a highly structured nineteen-line poem with repeating lines and refrains).[6] Louise made a profound first impression on her professor, as he would write in his memoir, as "a bright, funny, tiny tomboy from Memphis."[7]

Before long, they began going out together to a nearby roadhouse. On one such outing, Louise had a few drinks and then asked Professor Merrill (or Jimmy, as she'd come to call him) to dance. Practiced in the music of her native Memphis, she knew how to do the "mess around" and to grind and stomp. Merrill entered into the spirit of it, and they returned to his apartment, where they danced toward the bed. Merrill, who was gay, had not been with a woman before. He would write in his memoir, "She began undressing me," and "what we found ourselves doing proved to be a thrilling discovery."[8] Louise put the brakes on. Despite what she had told Charles McNutt, Louise hadn't yet had sex with a man, and although she wasn't entirely opposed, she wasn't sure that was the night she wanted to sleep with her faculty adviser.

In fact, Louise would come to love Jimmy Merrill, but she wasn't any more prepared to *make love* with him than she'd been with Ed or Charles. For a time, Jimmy pursued her. He said he "slipped pleading messages into her campus mailbox, bought prophylactics, sought to waylay her on the paths between dormitory and classroom." Their college romance ended once Louise made it clear that she was more interested in women. Instead, Merrill said, they "made do with a lifelong friendship."[9]

Jimmy wasn't Louise's only devoted beau. Charles McNutt showed up at Bard one winter day to propose marriage. Saying he wanted to rescue her from her doomed life as a lesbian, he asked her to come away with him. She gently refused. "I don't want rescuing," she said. "I'm happy here." She didn't wish to hurt her old friend, but what she really wanted, she told Charles, was to get back together with Amelia and be an artist. She'd begun hanging around with a group of hard-driving student journalists as well as with a crowd of artists who studied with Stefan Hirsch, a painter in the precisionist, Mexican muralist, and surrealist styles.[10] In a photograph taken in a painting class in 1949, Louise is posed as *girl slumping with ennui* as Fred Segal (brother to Hollywood actor George Segal) paints her portrait.[11] Upon the half-finished canvas in view, Louise's face resembles the frog's-mouth helmet of a jousting knight precariously perched on a bundle of rags and flesh. (But to be fair to Fred, the reproduction is not good.)

Charles didn't hang around. After a night of drinking with Louise, he left Bard without her. In 2017, at the age of eighty-nine, he would still say he was "a little in love with her."[12]

On January 24, 1949, Louise's grandmother, Josephine Millsaps Fitzhugh, died in Memphis. Their complicated relationship was one that Louise would write about in several unpublished biographical plays. In some of these, the grandmother character is eccentric but kind; in others, she is conniving or malevolent. Louise had loved her grandmother, but she had also blamed her to a large extent for engineering the custody battle in which she had been taken from her mother. In Louise's second novel and the sequel to *Harriet the Spy*, called *The Long Secret*, she portrays an elderly Fitzhughian grandmother, soft and powdery and impeccably correct. Called Mrs. Hanson, she mostly keeps to her bed in a mansion in the New York Hamptons while still managing to manipulate the lives of those around her. She exerts a powerful influence on her granddaughter, which the younger girl only realizes after the fact (the universal and posthumous fate of grandmothers). She has a lovely smile.

Josephine Millsaps Fitzhugh left her granddaughter an inheritance, which gave Louise her independence. After receiving the first check, Louise declared that now that she could afford to do as she wished, she'd never wear women's clothes again. Six months shy of graduating, she dropped out of college to move to Manhattan. She and Amelia had found an apartment on the third floor of a building at 315 Seventeenth Street across from Stuyvesant Park.

Their upstairs neighbors were Betty Grayson, Louise's friend and former psychology professor, and seven-year-old Mitch Grayson, who, fascinated by all things vehicular, shared Louise's love of her sky-blue Plymouth. Mitch was mesmerized in particular by its exotic Tennessee license plate—a skewed parallelogram.

Mitch considered Louise to be something like his sensible big sister. She spoke in a soft, relaxed accent and looked very young, almost like a child herself. Some afternoons, Mitch, home from the Downtown Community School, a progressive elementary school, would do his homework on their kitchen table while Louise sketched.[13] Almost as soon as she and Amelia unpacked, they'd signed up for classes at the Art Students League, which offered students the opportunity to experiment in various styles in small studio groups. Louise was studying portrait painting, and Amelia was studying photography. Louise worked on her assignments while Mitch worked on his.

Young Mitch had never met anyone from the South before and he found their rounded accents and references to that world quite fascinating. Once, after learning that Mitch knew nothing about Christianity, Amelia tried to explain the resurrection. Louise, who no longer believed in God, had only laughed through the perplexing lesson.

In 1951, Greenwich Village was several generations past Djuna Barnes's and Kenneth Burke's heyday. The Cedar Tavern had a new crowd of antiauthoritarians, sexual acrobats, and drunks. There was no uniform constituency among the lives of the subterraneans who made their home in the Village to which Louise arrived, except perhaps in their resistance to conformity. The Beatniks were taking up residence at places like the San Remo, where a dedicated eavesdropper might experience an audio banquet of blooming egotism, insecurity, drunken sophistry, wild wit, and the noisy devouring of so many cannoli. The talk was of phonies and alienation, free verse and abstract expressionism. Robert Motherwell, both practitioner and theorist, would write that an abstract painter's work "reflected alienation from bourgeois society"; it formed "a kind of spiritual underground . . . isolated from the consumer driven property loving world."[14]

Louise admired abstract expressionism for what she called the "beauty of its line," but she wasn't impressed by the monumental dominance of abstract art. As an artist influenced by Works Progress Administration muralists and the masters of the Renaissance fresco, she opposed the dominance and commercialism of abstract expressionism, and later, pop art. Her response to any kind of assertion of supremacy: white, male, heterosexual, abstractionist, or garden-variety pomposity, was typically to oppose it. It was no secret that women with ambition and guts weren't particularly welcome in the abstract painter's "spiritual underground." Those bohemians gaining notice for their art, from bebop musicians to beat poets, were mostly men, with a few affiliated women, girlfriends, and wives. In making a considered decision to pursue the figure, and in particular, to paint portraits, Louise was being iconoclastic and true to her artistic confidence. Her teachers at the Art Students League had worked with great Mexican muralists like Diego Rivera, Frida Kahlo, and José Clemente Orozco.

For Christmas 1951, Louise gave James Thurber's new book, *The 13 Clocks*, to little Mitch Grayson.[15] Mitch found its incongruous cast and eccentric rhymes wonderfully funny. Its characters undergo impossible trials against implacable villains, and there are spies named Hark, Whisper, and Listen. Thurber described his book as an escape for people whose reason was under threat from the irrationality of modern life.[16] Louise admired its originality, and especially its illustrations, by Marc Simont. She was casting around for various ways an artist might make a living without compromising, and illustrating children's books seemed an honorable profession. The money she received from her inheritance was sufficient, but the euphoria she'd originally felt at the prospect of being independent from her father was soon tempered when she learned that it was Millsaps who would manage her trust fund—and thus dole out her monthly allowance.

Still, she could afford art supplies and a larger apartment. She'd just moved with Amelia to Waverly Place when Louise's former husband, Ed Thompson, turned up. Betty Grayson, who had met Charles McNutt at Bard, must have wondered how many more southern beaus would come courting.

Unlike the stalwart Charles, Ed Thompson had a poet's cast of mind and was philosophically contemplating *what ifs*. The way Ed saw it, his marriage to Louise had been annulled, but they hadn't argued or declared themselves broken up forever. He thought it possible they might have gotten back together if Louise hadn't left for Bard. At first, he'd wanted to follow her; he had planned to attend Columbia University, just so he could be near her. But circumstances conspired to keep him in Memphis. He was an only son, with a working mother who did not want him to go far away. He'd begun dating a lovely Memphis State student named Jolee Taylor. But he hadn't been able to get Louise out of his mind. He wanted to learn for himself what she thought of him.

The scene made the kind of searing impression that, after forty years, Ed could still see vividly in his mind's eye. They were at 110 Waverly Place, the studio apartment where Louise lived with Amelia Brent. He and Louise sat at a table surrounded by paints and other art supplies amid the acrid tang of turpentine. Some paintings hung unframed on the wall. On the table was a bottle of brandy and two shot glasses, into which she poured their drinks. The window was partially open, and car horns blared in the street. The rest of the studio was all bed and clothes. Louise hardly had to explain. It was clear to Ed, scanning the room, that Louise and Amelia were lovers, and any illusion he still held that she'd get back with him was foolish. Louise raised her glass to toast him goodbye. She was sympathetic, but not sentimental. It was the last time they would meet.

Ed Thompson married Jolee Taylor in 1952. Louise would sometimes send the couple woodcut Christmas cards, and later signed editions of her books for their children, a daughter, Becky, and a son, also called Ed. Jolee met Louise once at a party that Bill Brown gave in Memphis. Ed did not attend; Jolee said Louise was lovely. Much later, in a conversation with her grown granddaughter, Robin Jacks, who was fascinated by their family connection to *Harriet the Spy*, Jolee was succinct: "Louise became a lesbian in that Green-Witch Village."[17]

PART TWO

I couldn't possibly be interested in books for dead dull finished adults, and thank you very much but I [have] to get back to my desk to publish some more good books for bad children.[1]

—*Ursula Nordstrom, publisher and editor in chief of juvenile books at Harper and Row from 1940 to 1973*

eight

CLUES

Louise felt her solitude and something verging on liberation on March 15, 1952, as the SS *Île de France* pulled away from a New York pier to begin its journey to France. She hadn't intended to travel alone, but at almost the last minute Amelia had been hired as an editorial assistant at *Time* magazine and canceled her ticket. Louise was disappointed, but *Time* would not wait. It was no small thing for a young woman to find work on a top newsmagazine, and Amelia's ambition to become a photojournalist was every bit as great as Louise's long-held desire to paint in Paris. They'd argued at first, then acknowledged that they'd both been sentimental over the remnants of their first love. They obviously weren't the same kids they'd been when they'd separated three years before. Greenwich Village had launched them in different directions. They parted with the agreement that their friendship would remain indestructible no matter who else they'd come to love.

The *Île de France* was a gorgeous art-deco-designed ocean liner that had advertised that season—most appealingly—as "Your gayest entrée to Paris." Louise, who was traveling in cabin class, carried, like other tourists, the latest *Fielding's Travel Guide to Europe*. This indispensable book provided insider scoops about hole-in-the wall boîtes and bistros and out-of-the-way markets. In France, where 350,000 lives were lost under Nazi occupation, survivors were swinging back from "listfulness, weariness, and disintegration of moral fiber," the guide said—and the bargains would never be better.[1] *Fielding's* and other guides to vacations in recovering Europe advised travelers to take everything they needed, as some things may not be available. Visitors brought care packages and filled steamer trunks. Gifts like cigarettes and LPs from the United States, in particular, were golden.

It was already seven years after the war's end, but despite the euphoria of the movies and the cautious optimism of the guidebooks, many passengers sensed that there was no telling what they'd find. For many of the European-born travelers returning home, the uncertainty was even worse. Their homes might have been demolished, or might be occupied by strangers. Some of the Jewish travelers were still seeking their lost relations. This uncertainty lent an odd cast onboard the *Île de France* that spring: the kind of anxiety that comes with feeling somehow overdressed for the occasion.

Some of the younger passengers—like Louise—felt, by contrast, during mile after sea mile heading eastward, an unencumbering giddiness, a feeling of shedding layers upon layers of responsibilities and expectations. In France, there would be less Cold War mongering, less of Joseph McCarthy, less of House Un-American Activities Committee (HUAC)—and goodbye, FBI, hello art! Louise had packed her art supplies, her jazz records by artists like Billie Holiday and Charlie Parker, and some books, including *The Catcher in the Rye* by J. D. Salinger; *Spring Fire*, the new lesbian pulp novel by Vin Packer; and *The Origins of Totalitarianism*, by Hannah Arendt.[2]

It so happened that Hannah Arendt and her husband, the philosopher and poet Heinrich Blücher, were on the same ship, returning to Europe for the first time since the war ended. The *Île de France* could transport 1,500 souls, but its cabin class accommodated only about 500. If Arendt and Blücher had met Louise by chance on the promenade deck, or in one of the ship's bars, they would have discovered the coincidence that Louise had studied at Bard, and Professor Blücher had been hired to teach philosophy there starting the following fall.

After the seven-day ocean journey, Louise disembarked at Le Havre, then went on to Paris by train. Through the grapevine and trial and error, she found the most hospitable cafés to write or sketch in. She ate the best, cheapest meals available, like those at the Café des Beaux-Arts on the Rue Bonaparte, where just a couple of dollars bought a filling and delicious dinner.[3] And she collected the addresses of gay bars, which came in all shapes and sizes—like the women who frequented them. There were places of refuge, places to drink in company, places to meet students, secret clubs in which one could hear jazz ballads sung and poetry read aloud, and even grander venues where litterateurs, philosophers, and fashion models, wearing the latest urchin haircuts and toreador pants, danced to all-women orchestras.[4]

Louise hated the slow work of writing letters; instead, she memorialized the trip in her sketchbook. She was particularly fascinated by the spectrum of quick-sketch caricaturists she observed on the sidewalks of Montmartre. Among the charlatans bewitching tourists with their chalk profiles and hasty silhouettes were some artists who could instantly capture a subject's backstory. Painting portraits wasn't for the faint of heart—truly looking into someone's face and rendering their emotions and history through their expression took tough-mindedness and stamina. More than anything, it would take technique, which she would have to study.

Before Bard, Louise had thought she'd like to write poetry. After encountering some truly gifted poets, starting with Jimmy Merrill, she recognized that her writing talent lay elsewhere. It was never easy for her to dislodge her father's acid observation that any literary work that wasn't Tolstoy was hardly worth the trouble. She was also stymied by her own unyielding belief that painting and poetry were at the top of the art pyramid, and that other forms of design and literature somehow counted for less.

By the time she arrived in Paris, though she could hardly eke out a letter home, Louise was thinking again about novels and plays she wanted to write. She hadn't forgotten Thurber's *13 Clocks*. But writing for children, à la Thurber, seemed like something writers did *after* they were successful, more a digression than serious work. As it happened, Marc Simont's illustrations of Thurber's book may have had a more immediate influence than the text. Louise's early portraits had a storytelling, comic quality—satiric, and often grotesque. Captivating in their honesty, portraits would be Louise's métier for the next decade.

When September came, Louise returned to New York on the RMS *Queen Elizabeth*. Amelia was still living at Waverly Place and still working at *Time*. Louise parked with her for a while before finding her own apartment. Although they felt affection toward each other and would remain the best of friends, the separation had caused a lasting break, and there was no going back to being high school sweethearts. After Louise moved out, they still saw each other often.

Meanwhile, Louise's old schoolmate Joan Williams was also making her way in New York, and she and Louise rekindled their friendship. She was writing for *Look* magazine while completing a novel. From the time she and Louise had arrived at Bard, Joan had been preparing for a future as a self-supporting writer, polishing work for submission and entering contests that offered cash prizes and prestige. Three years earlier, then nineteen-year-old Joan had won an award from *Mademoiselle* magazine, a prize won in other years by Sylvia Plath and Joan Didion. Before that, during the summer of 1948, while Louise had worked for the *Memphis Commercial Appeal*, Joan had launched a charm attack on William Faulkner in Oxford, Mississippi. She'd arrived at Faulkner's house uninvited and introduced herself to him as a writer and dedicated student of his work. The Nobel Laureate, not known for returning fans' attention, had been impressed by Joan's tenacity and beauty. Their subsequent correspondence turned into a relationship of several years between the married novelist and his young devotee.[5]

After Joan had left Bard, her clandestine meetings with Faulkner moved from Memphis and Mississippi into her one-room Greenwich Village apartment, which Faulkner, as a former house painter, helped her redecorate.[6] He became, in a manner of speaking, Joan's guru, while she saw herself as the caretaker of his genius. Later, she would write, "We were soul mates, and if that was sentimentality, we were not against it."[7] Faulkner had encouraged her writing and made a diagnosis: that her bourgeois mentality—which he warned might hold her back from becoming a great writer—was also preventing her from acting on her passion with him in bed. He was fifty, she was twenty. She loved him, but felt no sexual attraction toward him. Nothing Faulkner said would diminish Joan's ambition to become a writer on her own terms. And on that front, Joan was happy to tell Louise the great news that her first short story, "The Morning and the Evening," had been accepted for publication by Seymour Lawrence at *The Atlantic Monthly*.[8]

To celebrate, Louise took Joan out for a drink in a gay bar. They dressed up and made a smashing entrance. Louise, who at twenty-three could easily look like a sixteen-year-old boy, wore trousers, a vest, and a tie. Joan wore a chic dress with a nipped-in waist and wide skirt, her red hair in a wavy, shoulder-length page-boy. The juke box in the bar was a good one, with Ray Charles singing "Hey Now" and new records by B. B. King, whose performances on Beale Street were a Memphis sensation. The most popular song of the night, hands down, was Kitty Wells strumming "It Wasn't God Who Made Honky Tonk Angels." Wells was from Nashville, and the burgeoning country music industry in their home state was a subject of fascination for both women. Louise, intrigued by the fashion for cowboy costumes and yodeling, could do a fair imitation of Hank Williams.

Louise had a new swagger that Joan hadn't seen in her before. She was more assertive and suffered fools even less. When a pretty young woman stopped by their table to compliment Joan's hair and flirtatiously ask, "Why don't you cut it short?" Louise sent her on her way with a proprietary growl, saying, "Leave her alone. She's not gay."

Over beers, then bourbon, Louise brought Joan up to date on her breakup with Amelia, whom Joan also knew from Memphis. Louise insisted they were still best friends, but she had a new French girlfriend in New York. Her name was Lilyan Chauvin, and she was very stylish indeed. She'd just given Lilyan the present that Millsaps and Sally had sent Louise for her twenty-fourth birthday. "A mink stole," she said to Joan. "You would have loved it."

"I'm sure you're right," Joan said. A fur stole was an immensely desirable possession, like a diamond bracelet or a Cadillac, something a well-heeled husband or older lover might give a girl. *Wrap yourself in luxury*, the magazine ads urged, *over a blindingly sequined evening ensemble, accessorized with just the right mother of pearl cigarette holder.* Such high style was way beyond Joan's clothing budget, and she was faintly annoyed by how lightly Louise took the whole business. She didn't like taking an admonitory tone, but sometimes with Louise, Joan felt like the only adult in the room.

When Joan warned Louise not to squander her inheritance on hangers-on, Louise scoffed. Lilyan was a self-supporting actress and photographer, she said. She also tutored French, which they spoke when they were together. Louise's only complaint was that Lilyan wouldn't stop calling her "Lou Lou," a name Parisians very often gave their darling dogs.

On Thanksgiving Day in 1952, Louise met France Burke. Over a turkey dinner the two women discovered they'd been in Paris at the same time. They'd lived in the same *quartier*, eaten at the same cheap restaurants, gone to the same lesbian bars, and returned just weeks apart. It was funny that they hadn't met previously—and a little humbling to realize that there were other young American lesbian artists, perhaps hundreds, following the same well-worn track.

In short order, the women began sharing an attic garret at the top of a lovely two-story brownstone in Greenwich Village. A pen-and-ink drawing by their friend Jean Sherman, in whose studio they took art classes every Thursday, catches their block's street life on a summer afternoon with a slight surreal inflection. On the sidewalk, a rotund mother pushes a baby carriage as two other women, with equally expansive bodies, and dressed in sack-like dresses to their ankles, gossip and share cigarettes. One little boy sits exhausted on the sidewalk; another is peeing on the pavement. Across the street, in a two-story convent, nuns in wimples stare out of second-story windows holding crosses. All the nuns are nude from the waist up. At the corner is France and Louise's house, and curled asleep on the roof is France's black and white cat, MacDuff.

The garret was small, cluttered, and cozy. A radiator along one wall served in summer as a surface for extra books. In cold weather, the radiator dried (and stiffened) the clothes they laid upon it. Together they had a choice library, a typewriter, and a growing stockpile of artist's paraphernalia. At first, the Leroy Street garret was also their primary artist's studio, where Louise and France sketched and sculpted and painted. It was there that Louise rendered many versions of France's handsome, square face—in graphite, ocher, chalk, pastels, acrylics, oils, and ink. In one of her earliest oil paintings, she painted her lover in bed with pneumonia. France's dark hair is in contrast to a bluish-gray face upon a white pillow; her supine body is in a pink and violet cloud of covers. MacDuff the cat sleeps nearby, curled on the carpet.

Theirs was a love affair of equals. At home in Greenwich Village, the center of art and radical thought in 1950s New York, each seriously began to commit themselves to making art. Louise took classes at Cooper Union in addition to the Art Students League, and both women painted at the atelier of their friend and teacher Jean Sherman. Sherman, as she was called, was a remarkably tall woman. When some fellow students saw Sherman and Louise walking together, they jokingly called them "big and little" until Louise got wind of it. She made it clear that some people are one way and some people are another way, and everybody ought to get used to it. (This was Louise's practical philosophy, which later she'd include in *Harriet the Spy*.)

France admired Sherman as a friend, artist, and teacher whose critiques were astute and unfailingly honest. Louise didn't typically take well to being told what to do, but she willingly suffered through Sherman's critiques. She wanted to be a great painter, and there were still so many things she knew she had to learn.

Louise primarily painted and drew, while France began modeling in clay. In her sculpture journal, begun in 1953, France wrote, "Have started a head of Louise." Later she would report, "Head of Louise drying slowly from rich terra cotta to pale, going over the whole thing [with] steel wool. The profiles are somewhat alive but the front is flat and meaningless." In another entry, France noted that after class Louise had said the pose of their model gave her an idea for a piece of sculpture. And in a third, she wrote, "L's doing sculpture has given me a wonderful opportunity to learn how to cast. I produce my own work so slowly and when I am finally finished an error in casting would flatten me. Louise is wonderfully indulgent."[9]

Frances Burke, born on July 14—Bastille Day—in 1926, and thereafter known as France, was a sensitive and rigorously self-interrogating young woman. Her family was Greenwich Village intelligentsia: artists, radicals, and philosophers. In 1952, France was twenty-six years old. She had attended Manhattan's Dalton School (surely a model for the Gregory School in Louise's novels *Harriet the Spy* and *Nobody's Family Is Going to Change*), then college-hopped, first to Cornell, then New York University, then Bennington in Vermont, where her father taught philosophy. There, she had discussed the subject of life with difficult fathers with her classmate Miriam Marx, Groucho's daughter (called Little Marx). Louise met France's father, Kenneth Burke, when he was around fifty-six years old and a lion of American letters; he was credited with retooling midcentury literary criticism and advocating for new writers, including Richard Wright and Susan Sontag.

Through the Burkes, Louise met other mandarins of modernism. Among these were Djuna Barnes, the author of *Nightwood*, and photographer Berenice Abbott, who used France as a model for some of her work.[10] The poet Marianne Moore was France's godmother, and Dorothy Day, the journalist, social radical, and founder of the Catholic Worker Movement, was France's aunt. Louise also became friends with France's sister Eleanor "Happy" Leacock, an anthropologist, and her husband, filmmaker Ricky Leacock. Their circle included the documentarians Al and David Maysles and D. A. Pennebaker as well as the influential pacifist and civil rights leader Bayard Rustin.

Robert Penn Warren and his wife, Eleanor Clark, were also summertime visitors to the Burkes' family compound in rural New Jersey, where France also had a cottage. While Burke had been celebrated since the 1920s as a philosopher, critic, and teacher, Warren had gained popular fame after his best-selling novel *All the King's Men* was adapted to an award-winning movie in 1949. Warren had won a Pulitzer for his novel and would win a second Pulitzer for his poetry. He had written the introduction to Louise's Uncle Peter's first collection of short stories.

France and Louise were sufficiently relaxed in the Burke family atmosphere to demonstrate their affection. The extended Burke family had to greater and lesser extent a bohemian acceptance for the varieties of human love, starting with France's father, who had divorced her mother, Lily Batterham, to marry Lily's younger sister, Elizabeth Batterham, called Libby. Sam Shea, who would later become France's life-partner of forty-eight years, observed, "There were too many complex, contorted, convoluted relationships of all kinds—both within the Burke family and among their friends—for two young gay women in the family to be remarkable."[11]

There was, however, one notably intolerant figure in their circle: France's brother-in-law, Henry Hart, who was married to France's sister Elspeth.[12] He condemned France's relationship with Louise and refused to allow his wife or their sons to have any contact with them. France had to sneak around small-minded Henry to visit her sister and nephews.[13] The other Burkes derided Hart's bigotry, but his homophobia was still a shocking reminder to be on guard. Louise was outraged that a perfectly normal love affair could still give the Henry Harts of the world palpitations. As for her own family, by her early twenties Louise may have sometimes felt insecure and doubtful of being in the right place with the right person, but she no longer changed her clothes to oblige the company she kept. She'd let the Fitzhughs believe what they wished about her, then left them and their prejudices behind in Memphis. In Greenwich Village, she had felt a safety in numbers against the judgment of the world.

In Greenwich Village in 1955, Kafka was all the rage, European film ruled cinema, and to many artists and intellectuals, Freud and his couch still held a fashionable appeal. Louise liked the idea that a psychiatrist might help her understand her shifting moods, sort through what mattered in her love and work, and perhaps offer guidance to living in the fucked-up mid-twentieth century. She wasn't particularly set on seeing a Freudian; she just wanted somebody *good.* At a writers' group that she attended, Louise was lucky to meet Dr. Bertram Slaff, a psychiatrist with whom she'd begin a long-lasting relationship, one of the most important of her life.

In the 1950s, homosexuality was a diagnosis in treating mental health patients, a disorder to be overcome. Luckily for Louise, Dr. Slaff, whose primary field was as a practitioner in adolescent clinical psychiatry, was himself gay and supported Louise's sexual identity. Under his counsel, Louise tracked her self-doubt back to a father whose phantom grasp she hadn't yet escaped. She pursued this theme in the poetry she sent to Jimmy Merrill to review.[14] As Slaff's patient, Louise didn't become much less moody or drink any less, but his support may have counted for at least some of her increased focus. The next decade was the most productive period of her life.

Louise encouraged her girlfriend to also enter analysis and paid for France's sessions out of the allowance she received from

Memphis. France went to a Dr. Nancy Peters, and as part of her therapy she kept a notebook in which she grappled with her own various family dynamics. She also wrote about Louise, whom she described as "the firebrand, the disturber, the quicksilver, ranting or magnificent, at my side." In the same entry, she wrote, "I have to learn to fight, because I want to keep Louise."

France's therapy notebooks also poignantly track the slow unraveling of their relationship. Louise was on occasion drawn to others. She told France about her "one-night stand" with the young writer Anatole Broyard, whose rakish memoirs tell of his many sexual conquests among the young women of Greenwich Village.[15] Louise told France that Broyard characterized their encounter in a most ungentlemanly way, saying, "I wanted a meal and all I got was a ham sandwich."[16] In fact, she was still technically a virgin in her sexual relations with men, and the chase tantalized Broyard. Louise found him amusing, and their on-again, off-again semi-affair continued for some months. Louise had other male companions, both gay and straight, including Ed Thompson's good friend Bill Brown, who was then living in New York and working in advertising. Bill was a voluble storyteller, and like a gossip columnist he knew how to unearth the juiciest details. He loved to dish and gossip and carouse with Louise and their mutual friend Joan Williams.

In 1956, with two gallery shows on the horizon, Louise impressed a reporter from the *Memphis Commercial Appeal* with her poise and native genius. "Miss Fitzhugh is almost entirely self-taught," the reporter wrote.[17] In fact, Louise had attended two different colleges and had taken plenty of art classes at various institutions. Her art education wasn't slapdash; she just never took instruction well. Despite her stated intentions to study hard and learn from masters, her habit was to scan what she needed, then wander her own way.

As a young painter, Louise had a series of successes, which encouragingly included the sale of a few pieces. In October 1955, she showed a painting of France's cat, MacDuff, at the Village Art Center. An art critic's review in the *Village Voice* praised its charm: "An especially handsome composition in matte surface is Louise Fitzhugh's sleeping cat, with his tabbyship sprawling in ancient ease, and lending his slumbering dignity to the painter's wide-awake perception."[18] Louise also showed a picture called *Masquerade* in Memphis as part of the Brooks Museum's Fifth Biennial Exhibition. The exhibition's grand prize of $200, supplied by the Memphis Publishing Company, was awarded to Agnes Bradley, whose *Merry-Go-Round* featured a blond child with Keane-esque eyes and plump thighs riding a carousel horse, circled by the shadows of other riders. Louise's response to the winning entry might have come right out of her favorite *Mad* magazine: "Blecch."

In October, Louise showed several new paintings at the Panoras Gallery on Fifty-Sixth Street. During this period, she painted nudes, interiors, several versions of MacDuff, many portraits, at least two paintings set in public buses, and other New York street-life subjects. Her stylized figures were often inspired by random encounters and eavesdropping. Observing underdogs and outsiders in action, she was drawn to faces and to cityscapes and to a style that incorporated storytelling and allegory. Louise's new work was influenced by the scene painting of the Works Progress Administration and Mexican muralists; by Käthe Kollwitz and German expressionists like Max Beckmann, Oskar Kokoschka, and Egon Schiele; by Alice Neel, Francis Bacon, and other portraitists—and, to an increasing extent, by medieval tapestries and frescoes by Bolognese Renaissance artists such as Pellegrino Tibaldi.

Louise kept working to reveal the lives behind the faces she portrayed—their *backstory*—and began to introduce some southern imagery from her own memories. She was fascinated by the story beneath the surface and whatever metaphysical qualities she could draw from the depths of her subject. Between September and November 1955, she painted a mural on a wall in a building on West Fourth Street.[19] She primed the plaster walls and painted a story in oils about daily life in Washington Square Park. According to a reporter for the *Commercial Appeal*, "while painting the mural, Miss Fitzhugh became so absorbed in that medium that she enrolled at the Academia Bella Arte in Bologna, Italy, to study mural techniques, with emphasis on fresco, for the spring term."[20] This is one of the very few feature articles written about Louise. It is accompanied by a photograph of the young artist as a very serious woman. Her hair is mid-length and fashionably styled. It is the kind of article guaranteed to convince a doubtful parent that the struggling artist they were supporting wasn't wasting her time.

In the summer of 1955, Louise and France began taking Italian lessons in preparation for their trip to Italy. No one had answered Louise's letters to the Fine Arts Academy, but she didn't sweat the details. She had another reason for visiting Bologna: she believed it to be a communist city, one of the few outside Eastern Europe or China, and she was curious to learn what life there might be like. Her language teacher, Fabio Rieti, was an Italian American artist who was born in Rome; after becoming a naturalized citizen, he had served in the US Army during the war. He was a year older than Louise—and a charming, intelligent, and very good-looking young cosmopolite.

Fabio and Louise discovered they had been in Paris at the same time. They had seen the same museum exhibitions, and they knew the same cheap artists' cafés and the regulars who drank there. Fabio, like Louise, was a dedicated and self-taught artist. He had won first prize in a design contest for Condé Nast several years earlier. Louise interrogated him about becoming a working muralist in Italy. Her studies in mural production had made her, in Fabio's words, "yearn after walls to that effect." She asked for his advice. Might there be crews she could join in Italy? Were artists hired to restore or paint new frescoes? In Bologna, under communist leadership, were male and female artists treated equally?

When Fabio suggested that she might more easily find a fresco master in America, Louise thanked him and proceeded to buy her ticket to Italy. She completely disregarded his advice, and it could have been the end of their accord, a why-did-you-even-bother-asking, see-you-around-sometime moment between two strong-minded personalities, but Fabio admired her courage and pertinacity. He thought her charming and strong willed, unpredictable and irresistible. They encouraged one another's mocking tones and dry humor. Like Louise, Fabio was in a monogamous relationship, and by mutual consent they agreed, at first, to keep their affection platonic. Louise wasn't sure she wanted their flirtation to progress beyond tipsy smiles across the room and the Italian endearments he taught her at private lessons. Fabio was charismatic, so frankly un-American. Perhaps it mattered that he was a wonderful dancer, too. At rooftop parties on scorching nights, they cha-chaed and sambaed and had a reckless, drunken slow dance or two. In one another's company, they enjoyed a passionate multilingual logomania; in French, Italian, and English, no subject was off limits. They stayed up many nights drinking, smoking, and schmoozing, and in the morning found it hard to separate. At summer's end, as Fabio made plans to return to Paris, Louise agreed to meet him in Bologna the following year.

By the spring of 1956, after about four years together, France and Louise's romance was winding down. There may have been a rupture caused by Louise's continued interest in Fabio. By early spring, they were no longer lovers, but still planned to travel together as friends.

They had tickets to embark for Europe in March, where Louise intended to study fresco painting and France would work on her sculpture. Before then, they had to complete their work for the Downtown Community School Show, Exhibition, and Sale. Louise had an earlier show, opening March 5 at the New York Public Library's Hudson Park branch, which she shared with the painters Julie Arden and Robert LaHotan.[21] Her paintings for the library show included a portrait of Frederick O'Neal, founder of the American Negro Theater and later the first Black president of the Actors' Equity Association. (In the 1960s, an era when there were few visible Black actors on national television networks, his day job was as a policeman on *Car 54, Where Are You?*) Louise's other paintings in that show were mainly of New York street life, specializing in outdoor festivals and markets. These titles included *Feast of St. Anthony 1955*, *Garden Party*, *Monmouth Park*, *Butcher Store*, and *Luncheonette*.

Like other artists anticipating the reception of their new work, Louise and France shared the sense that these shows might be life changing, even career making. Add to this whatever emotional tumult each suffered internally at the end of their romance. They were still living together at Leroy Street. Zooming on coffee and adrenaline, aided by alcohol, they worked many nights all the way through to prepare. Euphoria built from excitement and exhaustion has a way of crashing down into doubt and anxiety, but they kept at it, pushing each another to the deadline. At the last minute, they still needed to find a professional photographer to document their finished work, typically an expensive undertaking. Amelia Brent, still at *Time* and still Louise's best friend, did the job for free.

In the days before the exhibition opened, Louise fervently hoped for positive attention from the critics, whom she alternately courted and despised as phonies and finks. France invited her father, Kenneth Burke, to the Downtown Community School show and asked him to please pass along the details to his acquaintance Robert Coates, who was at that time *The New Yorker*'s art critic.[22] In fact, Coates may have already had that exhibit on his schedule, since it was a perennial benefit for the school's scholarship fund and featured new and emerging artists alongside established painters and sculptors. In 1956, the exhibition featured work by Jacob Lawrence, Ad Reinhardt, Moses Sawyer, and Louise Nevelson. At any rate, he was there to see the expansive, many-roomed gallery that the school had created for the occasion.

The *Memphis Commercial Appeal* article and interview with Louise published partial reproductions of two of the paintings she would show at the Downtown Community School. Two were among her recent paintings set on or around buses. Rosa Parks's refusal in December 1955 to be bound by Jim Crow laws had ushered in the Montgomery, Alabama, bus boycott, and Louise registered her admiration by painting a Parks-like portrait in which a woman wears a hat and coat very much like those in an iconic photo of Parks. This painting was one of three she exhibited, alongside *Three Figures Aboard*, in which Louise painted herself as a little boy being comforted by an adult woman in a red dress. The bus driver, Louise said, was Millsaps. She painted his face in profile, with a notably deep brown complexion. Louise's third painting was a nude of France posed more or less as a classic *femme couchée* but, in this instance, straightforwardly inspecting her viewers.

On March 21, with ten days left to run for Louise's exhibit at the Hudson Branch library, Louise and France left New York on board the Compagnie Générale Transatlantique's ship *Liberté* bound for Plymouth, England. Both were veterans of transatlantic journeys and careful to avoid the rookie mistakes of either the "Eager-Beaver-Culture-Vulture with the list ten yards long" or the cool, suave, sophisticated "Take-your-own-toilet-paper set."[23] Amelia promised to meet them at the pier to wish them bon voyage, as she had when Louise went to France four years earlier. She was still working for *Time*, but she was now on the verge of taking a vacation of her own. She and Louise spoke of meeting in Rome after the worst of the summer heat, to drink espressos at a café like those they'd seen in the film *Roman Holiday*.

Over the course of several weeks, Louise began an illustrated journal that captured her breakup with France, their shipboard journey, and their arrival in Bologna. The first of four drawings, each on a single sheet of medium-weight, lightly lined notebook paper, is of their bedroom in Leroy Street. Everything in their bedroom has been packed away. Only MacDuff, curled up under an open window, is serene. The second drawing is of France and Louise storing the contents of their apartment in France's cottage on the Burke compound. France's arms are full of packages and she stands to one side, observing as Louise ascends the three porch steps. The door is open to a lit scene within, unfurnished except for a table and a curtain at the window. Louise has drawn herself as heavy and hunched, wearing the costume of an older Italian woman: dark skirt and sweater, dark stockings, and slippers. She carries a suitcase in each hand. Her posture is that of a refugee, suspicious of the sanctuary she's found.

The third drawing is of their cabin on the ship. Although they shared a cabin, they did not share a bed—as a couple, they were definitely kaput. Louise emphasizes its compressed space, the bunk beds, and all things shipshape. The fourth drawing is at their table in the ship's dining room. France is seated, looking confident and speaking calmly to an intelligent- and sympathetic-looking waiter. In contrast, Louise looks like a hunched, bad-tempered elf, older than her years, gripping the tall dining-room chair. Her feet barely touch the floor, her lips are pursed and eyes narrowed, nose wrinkled, and she is wearing large hoops in pointy, oversized ear lobes. Is she seasick? One dinner companion, a very tall man with an enormous blond mustached and bearded head, looks like a Viennese psychiatrist in resort wear. Behind their table is a man sitting alone. He has a soft, sad face with a brush mustache, a bald dome, and a fringe of hair around his ears. There was something about this man's face that particularly appealed to Louise, and she would draw and paint him several times in various media. He looks sentimental, and he looks a little anxious. She'd paint him into the crowd scene of murals, and a decade later, cast him in a leading role, as Mr. Waldenstein, Ole Golly's husband, in *Harriet the Spy*.

Louise in 1956 was a sophisticated, attractive person. Fabio said that when he met Louise that year, she was "very pretty," with "lively features." In those self-portraits, Louise drew herself as a lost little boy, or as a comic sort of goblin, or a dumpty middle-aged woman, resigned to her fate. It isn't fair to say that's how she always saw herself, but gives a hint. When she arrived in Bologna, she was ready to start something completely new, apart from France and the life they'd made together. Her studio on Via Castiglione had a wood-burning stove, and outside its walls were lilies, nasturtiums, and a Judas tree. At dinnertime, the street smelled of rosemary and garlic. She was more than ready to abandon herself to the possibilities of this life-changing landscape.

nine

ROUT

Louise's summer began happily. In a letter she told Jimmy Merrill of her delight to have found a refuge without telephones, television, or even doorbells. The pace and tranquility of Bologna was conducive to making art, and she was painting every day. Her original plan to attend the Accademia di Belle Arti di Bologna hadn't panned out, either because the school was not in session, or because classes in fresco weren't offered (perhaps Fabio had been right, and fresco would have been easier to learn in New York). From the new friends she made in her language classes—tutoring English and studying Italian—Louise learned that many local churches were under renovation, and some might hire artists to paint new frescoes. She was enthusiastic about the prospect, but in no hurry. Through June and July, she was unencumbered, without distractions or responsibilities, living *la dolce vita* at Via Castiglione Uno.

Then, in early August, she received the shocking news that Amelia Brent had been killed in Arkansas in a horrendous accident. The news was unfathomable and haunting, the circumstances almost incomprehensible. An Associated Press brief was headed "Propeller Kills Vacationer," but Louise could not take it in:

> HUGHES, Ark., August 5 [1956] (AP)—A few hours after arriving on a vacation, Miss Amelia Brent walked into the whirling propeller of her brother's airplane. She died ninety minutes later. The tragedy happened at the Stump City plantation owned by Miss Brent's parents, Mr. and Mrs. Gordon Brent. Miss Brent was an editorial employee of Time, Inc., in New York.[1]

Louise was shattered, as France described in a letter to her sister:

> [Louise's] dear friend from childhood, Amelia, was killed last week by an airplane propeller. Amelia was her age, also a southerner in New York and very close. Louise has to some extent collapsed under the shock. I have been taking care of her. Had a fever of 104 and frantic crying, but it is better now, and she has begun to mend. It was the first close death for her. And so unexpected. Amelia was 29 and in the best of health. Especially horrible as there are strong implications of some unconscious suicide wish. She walked into the propeller. No possible explanations for such a thing really.[2]

Louise lay in bed for weeks. France brought in food and books and read aloud from the *International Herald Tribune*, which is how they discovered that Jimmy Merrill's father had also died. Louise wrote at once to commiserate.[3] She said she didn't know what kind of relationship he might have had with his father, but losing a parent was catastrophic and debilitating; she added that she'd suffered a terrible loss too, and she couldn't seem to overcome her endless sense of dread, shock, and emptiness.

Fabio arrived in October. Louise welcomed his company but was grieving and subdued, with little appetite for making art or love. Their attraction the year before had been as intellectual as it was sensual. Two intense personalities, they'd slipped into a cool Beatrice-and-Benedick manner of flirting by disavowal. At times, Fabio was irritated by Louise's stubbornness, and his self-confidence annoyed her. But they always rebounded. She found him sensitive, resolute, magnetic. He found her witty and pretty, a terribly charming and terribly moody person, whose mood might change instantly. He thought curiosity was Louise's distinguishing characteristic. She wanted to know everything.

Fabio was no nurse, but he had resources. It fell to him to try to reignite Louise's interest in the walls she'd once longed for. He went to work, persuading his cousin Dina, who had a cement basement in Bologna at Via Corsica 20, to permit Louise and him to paint a mural there. Although they would not be making "frescoes," in the technical sense of working on wet plaster so the pigments would sink in, they would each have two walls about ten meters wide and a little over two meters in height to paint a mural of Bolognese markets. It was just the sort of project to get Louise back into her artist's routine of spying and eavesdropping. Louise even told Jimmy Merrill that she and Fabio had plans to expand their partnership, decorating houses and possibly churches with modern frescoes.

Through that fall Louise and Fabio worked on their walls. At first Fabio had his own place, but after a while they moved into the same apartment and the same bed, to which Fabio added a longer mattress. Louise told Fabio that he was the first man with whom she had ever fallen in love.

France often joined them for dinner, and over pasta—gnocchi a frequent choice—and bottles of wine, they played music, read poetry aloud, and in various languages discussed and debated art and politics: the Algerian War and the Suez Canal, the antinuclear marches in England, Elvis Presley's rise to fame, and the astonishing endurance of the Montgomery bus boycott. They were all three dedicated antifascists, and they debated the sustainability of any totalitarian regime. Louise was attracted to socialism, especially in contrast to American capitalism, but she despised ideologies and ideologues. It was Fabio's position that "ideals were fine, but there was no way to materialize them: either the whole world was communist, or, if such weren't the case, a communist state had to be perforce a police state in order to defend itself against inner and outer aggressions."[4]

On November 4, when the Russians moved into Hungary to crush the Hungarian uprising, Louise was outraged that the Soviet tanks had invaded the country. To Fabio, the invasion was further support for his *realpolitik*. He thought "collapse in Hungary could mean collapse of the whole Eastern Europe and finally in the USSR [Union of Soviet Socialist Republics] too. . . . Which only proves my point of view: communism had to walk hand-in-hand with police." Louise didn't like the implication that her perspective was naïve. Even at night, mellowed by wine, when they would play music together, Louise found their harmony increasingly unsatisfactory. France played her violin, Louise her flute, and Fabio the piano. "No!" Louise declared one night, insisting the piano was an instrument for solitary playing. "Fabio should buy an oboe," and he did. He adored her.

During the daylight hours, Louise and Fabio worked on opposite sides of Cousin Dina's garage. France's letters to her sister track their progress. "This weekend the owners of the garage are giving a party to show [the completed mural]. . . . Louise hopes the party (about 35 people) will produce a paying customer."[5] A photo of the party shows Louise and Fabio standing in front of a table piled with plates and pastries; Fabio looks ebullient, Louise a little skeptical. Her mural on the walls behind them is composed of eight lush tableaus teeming with street life.

She regularly included her friends in her work, and the faces of France and Fabio pop up among a hundred characters in the crowded market scene, which also includes the Mr. Waldenstein prototype. There is a tailor's shop where a disappointed seamstress sits at her work, and a butcher's where shoppers line up for meat. A religious procession threads through, led by a priest with a long, narrow skull. At another tableau of a winter street scene, workers outside an arched arcade are warming themselves at a brazier as a lone diner inside (with Fabio's face), ignored by waiters, gestures for attention. There are several other lively café scenes. In one, an acrobatic waiter juggles plates above two men who only have eyes for each other. Five women crowded together at a table speak animatedly. At a city intersection, an impatient boulevardier in sunglasses, befuddled tourists, a snobby dog walker, and anxious lovers forced to wait too long at a stoplight cross paths, all bringing their history forward into that frozen second.

After the party ended, for a time the mural remained, in Fabio's words, "the liveliest garage one could imagine." Its life, though vivid, was short, however. The artists didn't deliberately plan its obsolescence. But because of the watercolor base they employed, said Fabio, once the garage returned to its original function, the crowds on the wall were doomed to disappear "the first time they washed a car."

Louise and Fabio would live together for two months. In December, she broke up with him. It wasn't just that they argued endlessly. She had to tell him the truth (best to imagine this in a Tennessee accent): "I can't abide a male human being in my bed." Fabio considered his inability to "bring about the conversion" (to bisexuality) that she had earlier seemed to wish for as "a major failure in his life." Their friendship continued. It was no longer a love affair, but it was always intense. Fabio returned to New York, and Louise returned to the habit of confiding in France Burke.

In the New Year, both women started looking homeward again. France wondered if the sculpture she'd placed in Henriette Stoner's Talents Unlimited gallery on Grove Street had attracted any interest. Before their departure, they'd had to crate all their work. The sheer physicality of shipping artwork made every voyage slow and complicated, and Louise told Jimmy she envied his easier style of travel, carrying a notebook and a couple of pens.

Louise and France sailed from Naples on May 3, 1957, on the SS *Cristoforo Colombo*, arriving back in New York on May 11. They said their goodbyes at the dock, and in New York and on her own, Louise continued to grieve for Amelia's inexplicable loss. She looked up her scattered Village friends. Betty Grayson, her professor and friend from Bard, had left on a multiyear voyage with her son, Mitch, first to Israel, then Casablanca. Jimmy Merrill and his partner, David Jackson, had moved to Connecticut, into something of a bohemian enclave in Stonington. Louise wrote to tell him that being back in New York was maddening, but she still wouldn't want to live anywhere else. She wondered whether it helped to be a little mad oneself when living there. She and her friends agreed that a touch of personal craziness might be beneficial, like an inoculation.

Of all the old gang, Louise found Joan Williams's circumstances most transformed. Joan wasn't the single Manhattan career woman she had been the year before, or Faulkner's muse. She had married Ezra Drinker Bowen, a writer and editor for *Sports Illustrated*, and moved to suburbia, and they'd had a baby boy.

Despite those changes, Joan was the same dedicated and ambitious author as before. She was working on a novel and had short stories in the works. They made plans to meet, and Louise arrived at Joan's Connecticut home in a vulnerable and philosophical state. Her four-year relationship with France had ended, her romance with Fabio had fizzled, and she was staggered by Amelia Brent's strange and tragic death.

They naturally discussed Faulkner, as Louise was one of Joan's few confidantes on that subject. The Nobel Laureate had recently been in Paris to speak at a writers' festival there. He had asked Joan to join him, conveniently ignoring her husband and child. In letters, Faulkner conceded, rather ungallantly, that she had become the bourgeois he'd prophesied.[6]

Louise confided how daunted she felt by the prospect of ever finding a soul mate, as Joan seemed to have done. The gay microcosm of bars and house parties and introductions of friends to friends, which in better days had seemed exciting, now looked lonely and chaotic. Louise said she wanted to have children. She asked whether Joan and her husband had any single male friends she might meet. Joan didn't know any eligible men and, when she asked Ezra, he made it clear he wasn't going to introduce a lesbian to any of his friends.[7]

Louise and Joan had both read Jimmy Merrill's first novel, *The Seraglio*, published the previous November.[8] Jimmy had been their teacher at Bard, but he was also their friend and an indisputably brilliant poet. Louise had wanted to love his book, but she found it a disturbing read. She hadn't yet told him so, though. Joan and Louise had been brought up with the same conventional view that small fibs lubricated social relationships and that in many circumstances it was kinder to lie. A girl, especially, needed to calculate the odds in an unforgiving social code that could turn a misunderstanding into a lifetime grievance. In *Harriet the Spy*, when Ole Golly gives Harriet frank advice meant to help her negotiate a world in which she has little power and few allies, Harriet realizes that "sometimes you have to lie."[9] Louise as an adult was less inclined to compromise. She believed utterly in an artist's responsibility to be honest, and lies had no place when it came to discussing art.

In Merrill's case, she just had to find the words. When she finally sent a letter, she told him how much she admired his book overall. The first part was beautifully written, she wrote, and she delighted in its humor and sensibility. The second half of the book, in which a character castrates himself, was, in short, a punishing experience, and it was hard for her to stay engaged. She confessed it troubled her that he might regard her remarks as carping; she hoped he'd understand that she was truly impressed by his book but that it really had upset her. Louise wasn't alone in her confusion. Jimmy's most devoted readers found much in the second part of his novel baffling.

Jimmy didn't directly reply to Louise's criticism. Over the years ahead, he rarely pulled punches when it came to critiquing Louise's work. Such truth-telling on both sides seemed to add meaning and perhaps longevity to their friendship.

Sometime in the summer of 1957, Louise fell in love with Alixe Gordin. They'd met briefly before Louise had left for Italy, when they'd been introduced by Lilyan Chauvin, a mutual acquaintance, whom Louise had dated. Lilyan, an actress, spoke Spanish, German, Italian, and Russian, and among her several jobs she was employed by the popular French actor Charles Boyer to help him refresh his French accent. She would later make her own Hollywood debut in the film *Silk Stockings*. Alixe, who was working at the time as the casting director for the live television series *Studio One*, was attracted to Lilyan's androgynous and swashbuckling style. She hired Lilyan, whose golden hair and luminous complexion had earned her the sobriquet the "Parisian Garbo," to play a spy in the episode "Letter from Cairo."[10] It was around that time that Lilyan asked Alixe on a date to a place the actress touted as a wonderful out-of-the-way club, where all the chefs of Manhattan went to cook for each other.

Their night together was a disaster. The club turned out to be in a nondescript motel in New Jersey. The food was underwhelming, and Lilyan was not at all an attentive admirer; by the end of dinner, they were hardly speaking. Instead of the romantic encounter she had anticipated, the typically confident Alixe plunged into the kind of self-doubt that occurs when somebody you like, and thought liked you, rejects you once they get to know you better. Among the millions of reasons why, perhaps the power dynamic between casting director and actress played a part. The casting couch is a notorious abuse of power, and a trap which many performers have had to cautiously elude. Male casting agents, directors, and producers sometimes assumed their *lèse majesté*, and although such conduct was much less prevalent when the casting agents and performers were women, it's certain that Alixe was used to being in the driver's seat when it came to interaction with actresses.

Late into the night, Alixe cursed her fate. She was lonely and stuck in a cell-like room in New Jersey. Lilyan had rented a room of her own and, as Alixe lamented, "hadn't even wanted to sit up late and talk." Then, in the morning at breakfast, Lilyan brusquely informed Alixe that a friend would be coming to drive them back to New York.

Years later, Alixe, recalling the event, said, "I guess I was feeling sorry for myself and feeling totally alone."[11] When an old convertible pulled up, Lilyan jumped into the front and Alixe got into the back. "I started to cry. I couldn't stop myself," Alixe said.

"The driver, who Lilyan hadn't bothered to introduce, turned around and looked at me with *such compassion*. That driver was Louise. Right there, I knew we were meant to meet. She really was the person I loved most in my whole life." Louise must have been thinking about Alixe, too, because she phoned soon after she returned from Italy.

On their first date, Alixe invited Louise to see a show. Free tickets were the perks of a New York casting director, and she attended as many first nights as she could. At intermission, they stepped outside so Louise could have a cigarette. Although they were wildly attracted to each other, law and custom forbade any outward display of affection. Alixe, always hyper-aware, felt then and always that her job was precarious. If anyone who couldn't be trusted learned that she dated women, she'd be disgraced and unemployed.

Louise understood—of course, that was the way of the world. In the dark of the theater, they touched hands and knees. In the light of the marquee they joked and, as young lovers will, stared and waited impatiently for a later time, when they could act as themselves. When a handsome, perceptive woman in her fifties approached to ask Louise for a light for her cigarette, Alixe recognized her immediately as Janet Gaynor, the Oscar-winning actress of *A Star Is Born*.[12] Gaynor sized up the situation and gave them her benediction: "You two kids look so happy together," she said. They were charmed and thanked her. Later they would joke that Gaynor had to have been a messenger from the Hollywood firmament—a true star had blessed their union.

Alice Gordin Glas was born in Dayton, Ohio, in 1922. Her parents, a Midwestern Jewish couple, had a rocky marriage and divorced when she was young. She was separated from her brother and educated in boarding schools. When her peripatetic mother moved from Texas to Tucson, Alixe attended the University of

Arizona for two years. In those days, she often argued with her mother, who, fearing her daughter's exposure, derided Alixe's wardrobe of jeans and cowboy boots as too masculine. In one memorable episode, her mother followed Alixe out the door yelling, "I'm going to cut those jeans off you!"

By the time Alixe was twenty-one, the arguments and provincialism had become too much. She fled Tucson, dropped her last name, and, with fifty dollars in her pocket, set out for New York. Her nickname in those early days, the consequence of (or tribute to) her western-style footwear, was "Boots." As an artist-at-large, Alixe was a singer in a band, an overnight deejay on a jazz station, and an actress. In those days, she would forgo many comforts because of her limited income, but not psychotherapy. Like many other artists in midcentury America, she felt that getting therapy was the baseline for self-improvement—and self-improvement was the baseline for an ambitious young woman in New York City. Alixe favored the life-coach variety of shrink; she credits one such therapist with the suggestion that she investigate all the employment opportunities in the new television industry. She'd proposed herself to the big cheeses at Columbia Broadcasting System, who at the time didn't have many other casting directors.

There are special talents needed for this profession, and Alixe possessed them. First, a casting director has to have a dramatist's imagination. Every script, of whatever quality, deserves to be viewed as its writer sees it, then enhanced by adding the most simpatico performing artists. Next is a psychologist's awareness of the personalities that might fulfill the director's vision, which means understanding what each different director requires. Finally, a casting director has to have an eye for beauty: not only must the performance be truthful to the script, but, in most cases, the actor has to look good. In the early days of television, that disqualified a lot of wonderful lesser-known actors who might have been brilliant on stage, but whose bags and pores and morning-after eyes were not going to read all that well onscreen. Alixe's line of work—promoting some performers and rejecting others—required a kind of tough emotional resilience. Women in her profession had to be seen as above reproach. Alixe was a quick study and just a bit of a snob, combining the warmth of advocacy with professional froideur. In the era of the two-martini business lunch, she would only ever have one.

In the mid-1950s, the world of television and established stage society were also being rocked by informants and threatened by the Hollywood blacklist. Under deadline, after hours, as Alixe and her colleagues sorted through head shots, an actor's background was impossible to ignore. In that paranoid age, gossip had outsized power. A talented person might be rejected because of a rumored tendency to drink too much, a taint of unreliability—or a leftist affiliation in their youth. When conversation turned to politics, Alixe was liberal and outspoken. At CBS, she objected to the way performers could suddenly be blacklisted and rendered unemployable. The McCarthy-era Red Scare, apart from its political ramifications and its destruction of so many reputations, made it that much harder to properly cast a show. Alixe saw it as her responsibility to try to help get performers off the blacklist. She would call an actor's agency, one of the industry gatekeepers for political purity, and vouch that the actor in question was a Democrat, not a communist sympathizer. More than once, she had been warned to act with caution. "People would say to me, 'You're going to lose your job, somebody's going to find out you're doing this.'"[13]

In the years before meeting Louise, Alixe's social life had relied on work relationships and a few select and discreet friendships. Her career took her out late to a show most nights, then early into the office. It was exciting to be part of the industry, but it was lonely at 84 James Street, where she lived with her two cats, Barnaby and Jerusalem. She rarely went to bars on her own, and she approached friendships with other women cautiously—which is how she came to be in New Jersey with Lilyan Chauvin and how she met Louise.

According to Alixe, who could be regarded as something of a raging romantic, it was a *coup de foudre*. She fell in love at first sight with Louise's wonderful laugh and her beautiful legs. Alixe had an inch on Louise. Each wore her brown hair short, but Alixe's was curlier. Louise's complexion was a little paler, her frame less sturdy. Neither had finished college. Alixe had eradicated all evidence of a western twang through careful practice, so her enunciation was precise and bordering on East Coast elite. Louise had long since dropped her Tennessee accent (deploying it for play or emphasis). There were even some words Louise pronounced in a deliberately Brooklyn way. Alixe praised Louise's musical ear, her ability to speak several languages and play various instruments, among them piano, flute, and trumpet. They sang folk songs in harmony—including "Hang Down Your Head Tom Dooley" and "Long Black Veil"—and went to classical music and jazz concerts. (Alixe's favorite was Coleman Hawkins.) They both loved musical theater. It was still a golden age for the genre, when *My Fair Lady*, *The Music Man*, and *West Side Story* were all on Broadway. In the early days of their love affair, they saw Federico Fellini's film *Nights of Cabiria* and talked about adapting it for the stage.

They moved together into the entire first floor of an old brownstone near Fourteenth Street. Alixe, who had a talent for interior design and a passion for home renovation, threw her considerable energy into establishing their conjugal home. They shopped for furnishings at antique stores and flea markets, bought a lot of flowering plants, and set a dozen avocado pits to germinate around the house. While she searched for an outside studio, Louise used watercolors at home, a medium that represented the dreamy quality of their honeymoon and was free of the oil-paint smells that Alixe found oppressive. On one of their Saturday flea-market excursions, they found a beautiful old brass bed and purchased it. Louise would feature it in two horizontal life-sized paintings. In the first, Alixe's and Louise's naked bodies are entwined—Louise's face looks like a mature and ardent Harriet M. Welsch. In the second, they are asleep amid billowing covers. Both paintings represent a serene domesticity, before the noise and disruption of home renovations began.

It took a few months for Louise to also find the right painting studio, one with enough space for all the many projects she had in mind. At last, she rented a storefront on the Lower East Side, at 533 East Twelfth Street. It was noisy in the day, with markets nearby and kids playing dodgeball in the street after school; a wild cross-section of neighbors made for endlessly fascinating people-watching if she wanted to fritter away her time. At night, the street was strangely peaceful, although it wasn't known as the safest area; sometimes stores were robbed and there were occasional muggings. There were some street people and junkies who panhandled, but Louise took it all in stride. She described it to Jimmy as a fantastic refuge that she was happy to have found.

One of the first paintings Louise completed in her new studio was a life-sized watercolor portrait of Alixe. Alixe, wearing a rose-colored men's Oxford-style shirt and yellow trousers, is posed on a step stool. The wall immediately behind her is streaked with blues and greens and grays and pinks, intersecting clouds that perhaps stand for the many paint chips Alixe considered before settling on a color to finish the room. Once, as she'd stood modeling, Alixe had asked the artist to describe her painting process. Louise said it was difficult to describe inspiration, but it was something like painting dreams or a picture of her brain.

Louise was still seeing Dr. Slaff, and Alixe was also in therapy. Telling the truth to themselves and others, and not being a phony, was the goal. Alixe hadn't had many other people in her life with whom she felt capable of revealing her true self, but she tried to do so in therapy. She wanted to be completely open and honest, and was gratified when Louise opened up about her artistic process. From their earliest days together, Alixe said, Louise was a compulsive sketcher. "Louise drew as she breathed," she said. "She never sat still without drawing." It was Louise's habit to start sketching as soon as she awoke in the morning. "She drew on the telephone, or when she was talking to you. You'd be sitting, talking, she'd be drawing." This might have unnerved lesser mortals, but Alixe was dazzled by Louise's artistry and devoted herself to smoothing her way.

To Alixe, their relationship went beyond a love affair; she said they were "sisters who bonded especially over family horror stories." Alixe told Louise of being separated from her brother and father and boarding with strangers in a sequence of different schools and cities as her mother moved around the Southwest. Louise related how she hated her father. She was haunted by an image of being thrown across a room when she was an infant, a story for which she blamed Millsaps. Alixe thought Louise's father held a terrible power over his daughter. He was so very rich; and somehow, the fact that he would never disown Louise, no matter what she did, seemed to Alixe not evidence of a generous nature, but the game of some malign puppet master.

By 1958, Louise and Alixe viewed their relationship as a companionable marriage. They both had fulfilling work. Alixe had a successful career, and Louise's life as an artist was satisfying when her painting was going well. She could be gregarious, and after a day spent painting or writing, she liked having her circle of friends around. These young women were intense, flirtatious, and jokey. There was a lot of drinking (a very lot of drinking), and there were a lot of hangovers. It was a hectic, frenetic lifestyle. On many nights, Alixe might have preferred a quiet house, a light dinner, a late-night movie on TV, and not Louise's version of the Algonquin Round Table.

Then there were the doldrums. When Louise's work was not going well, she could be beset by doubt. Alixe, who believed in solutions, tried her best to lend support. She would want to do anything she could think of to help. Sometimes, Alixe's micro-ministrations just made Louise feel more restless, more doubtful, sometimes even trapped. Alixe may have sensed this, but her own character led her to move inexorably forward. She either could not or would not stop trying to cultivate her friend's genius.

ten

SNOOP

Early in 1958, Louise met the young writer Sandra Scoppettone at a downtown drinks party on West Thirty-Third Street. Sandra, a gamine with a pixie cut, had arrived in Greenwich Village in 1954, soon after graduation from high school in Morristown, New Jersey, where she had been voted the senior class wit. She was fortunate in having sympathetic, sophisticated parents who had been supportive when she had come out of the closet at the age of seventeen. "As long as you're happy," they said. Also, Greenwich Village, just forty-seven miles away, was where a would-be writer *went* to try her luck. For generations, the Village was a destination in sharp contrast to Uptown, not least for its role as an incubator of underground arts and its bohemian hospitality toward love affairs between women, between men, and between people of vastly different incomes, different marital statuses, and different races.

Louise kept a painter's hours, and after long periods of discipline and focus, she would flee her studio, sometimes to carouse with Sandra, her drinking buddy, who was eight years younger. Sandra was ironic and ingenious, a spirited and funny woman with a penchant for martinis and the music of Frank Sinatra. She knew a lot of people and introduced Louise to a bustling community of downtown women writers and playwrights. As refugees from square, straight white America, they'd visit each other's studios, listen to the music they made, tolerate each other's poetry, drink rough wine and cheap beer in someone's pad, and troop together to some dark den of a gay bar.

Each bar had its own character. Some had restaurants—some had good food, mostly the food was crummy, but at least girls could show affection for each other, hold hands, and dance to the jukebox in a public space. Some bars appealed to butch-femme cliques, others to gay bohemia, and some made an effort to appeal to slumming uptowners.[1] One bar could be merry, another a dive. What they all had in common was the booze. Everybody drank too much.

Sandra was a sharp contrast to Alixe, who rarely went to bars. Few of her professional friends did, and there wasn't much about the bars to attract Alixe.[2] She didn't drink much and she had everything to lose by exposure. Even in the most private gay bar, you would still be seen, with all the meanings of that word: scrutinized by the manager, the bouncer, and the bartender as you entered (*On your own? Troublemaker or cop?*); recognized by a potential friend or lover; observed by a stranger, who could—in the worst-case scenario, at another place and time—expose you. Even at her loneliest, the risk for Alixe of being publicly outed was just too great. Whispers were a stealth weapon threatening her job, status, and income. Sometimes, during the vice raids that were still intermittently staged, women were questioned and detained. Alixe found most bars disagreeable, their exclusivity a constant reminder that society condemned her for loving women.[3]

For Louise, Alixe provided comfort and refuge, while Sandra offered a different kind of sympathy. Louise and Sandra had begun to write plays, and they both understood the struggle to get something right on paper, to fail and feel desperate, to succeed and feel euphoric—all on account of a word or phrase or punctuation mark. This might not have mattered quite so much if they were older, but they were young together—and art and literature were everything.

Alixe considered her new rival a bad influence and hoped that Louise's friendship with Sandra would flame out. Instead, they grew closer, brainstorming potential fortune-making books or movies they could write together. Louise longed to be free from her father's allowance. Sandra's underpaid day job as a telephone reservation clerk for an airline took too much time away from novel writing. They just needed one brilliant idea.

As Christmas of 1958 approached, Louise and Alixe began to quarrel intermittently. After one particularly fierce argument about the amount of time Louise was spending with Sandra and her friends, they broke up. That was the season Louise took her only job in retail—doing temporary work at the department store S. Klein on the Square, wrapping gifts. She may have imagined gift-wrapping as aesthetically exciting. Perhaps she heard through friends of the Christmas temp who was asked to wrap a sofa not just with a big bow, but full-on gift wrap. Or maybe she was inspired by the character of Therese, a seasonal gift wrapper in Patricia Highsmith's novel *The Price of Salt*, who keeps a copy of *Portrait of an Artist as a Young Man* on a shelf under the wrapping paper. (*The Price of Salt* was especially prized throughout the gay women's community as a singular novel; its lesbian couple does not end up in a loony bin or commit suicide.) Or maybe Louise just wanted a bit of extra pocket money.[4]

Whatever the reason, Louise didn't fare well during her brief employment. She wasn't used to working on anybody else's schedule and she wasn't practiced (or any good) at taking direction from bosses. Her allowance had always given her an out, although it was one she resented. She quit wrapping and beribboning gifts after just a few weeks to throw herself into the production of seasonal greeting cards. She illustrated Christmas carols with linoleum-cut images of reveling monks and nuns like those she'd created for her mural in Bologna. She sent a card with the drawing of a blissfully singing nun (more Ethel Merman than Julie Andrews) to Ed and Jolee Thompson with the caption "Peace on Earth and Mercy Mild."

Christmas Day found Louise enjoying a traditional meal with Sandra and the Scoppettones, an Italian American feast in which pasta and meatballs in a spectacular sauce preceded the turkey. Christmas also marked a turn in Louise's relationship with Sandra to something more serious. They spent New Year's Eve 1959 together and, afterward, Louise gave Sandra a portrait she had drawn of her as she'd been on New Year's Day—hungover. "We were friends, then lovers, then friends again," Sandra said. Louise's affair with Sandra hadn't lasted very long. After she and Alixe reconciled, they agreed to work harder on making their relationship work for the long term. Among friends, they said they wanted to save their "marriage." At the same time, Louise and Sandra kept up a creative friendship that would soon change both their lives.

Louise felt encouraged to try her luck as a professional writer after meeting another of Sandra's friends, Marijane Meaker. M.J., as she was known, was making a decent living writing paperback suspense and mystery novels. She had arrived in Manhattan in 1949 with a prestigious degree in journalism from the University of Missouri, talented, ambitious, and impatient to become a self-supporting writer. M.J. published her first lesbian pulp novel, *Spring Fire*, under the pen name Vin Packer, then produced scores of stories in multiple genres: suspense, horror, crime, romance, true confessions, intrigue, mystery, hard-boiled, and soft-core, under various pen names. She sold fiction to women's magazines under the name Laura Winston, her *True Confessions*–type stories as Mimi Stone, and a series of subjective social histories about lesbian life in New York under the name Ann Aldrich—but her pseudonyms for crime, mystery, and suspense were invariably male.[5] Early on, an editor of paperbacks had counseled, "You tell a fast tough story, but you lose your credibility with a name like Marijane."

Those were the glory days of the mass-market paperback, when the spin racks at drugstores, train stations, and airports spilled over with easy reads feeding the public's hunger for spies, murderers, sinners, dastardly villains, swamp monsters, lords and ladies, and butlers who might have done it. Readers could carry a paperback in their jeans, handbag, or between the heavier pages of a school loose-leaf notebook. The stories were meant to be page turners, and M.J. had the knack. Compression, fast dialogue, and plot twists and turns were most desirable. Good typically triumphed. Characters could be outrageous and suggestive, but eventually, even the antiheroes had to satisfy the reader's expectations—and every book needed a big finish.

There was a distinctly nonconformist, gender-fluid hum to the workforce of the paperback industry in its early gold-rush moment. The price of paper, printing, and marketing were all relatively cheap when produced in great quantity. A stable of fast-working writers, for whom the word "hack" was an affectionate recognition of professionalism, churned out content of a vivid intensity. The freelance artists who designed the books made covers that popped with primary colors.

Although many of the pulps ended with hypocritical and banal morals, along the way many buxom women, first seen lounging around scantily clad in furs, might—in the advancing genre fiction of fantasy, mystery, and romance—lead revolts against tyrants and liberate worlds. Many of these pulp fictions were essentially utopian, and their purple prose could be a subversive education.

It wasn't all marvelous, though, and it had some of the same dangers as those associated with other unregulated economic booms. Freelancers were at the mercy of fly-by-night enterprises, and some snobs called mass-market paperbacks the lowest of lowbrow. But, it was work in publishing, and you didn't need a college degree to get under way. Many young women, in particular, found it a liberating apprenticeship in all sorts of styles and forms and subjects. It was also a decent job, at a penny for every book sold. And then there was the strange phenomenon of high- and lowbrow publishers occupying the same real estate. The upper floors of one building would house the elite offices where hardback books and refined literary standards ruled, while the pulp offices occupied the lower floors. A young pulp writer with aspirations could imagine her future as just one elevator ride away.

M.J.'s novel *Spring Fire* was the first successful mass-market lesbian novel in English. Written in the tradition of and for the same audience as *The Well of Loneliness*, by Radclyffe Hall, it sold over 1.5 million copies. The original cover of *Spring Fire* from 1952 shows two sorority girls dressed in lingerie. The blonde, in a black slip, looks off into the distance, while the brunette, with her modest, downturned eyes, wears red. An orangy-red background matches the lipstick on their pillowy lips. Under the title, crawling in black Courier font across one nude shoulder, are the words, "A story once told in whispers," and "Now frankly, honestly written."

M.J.'s novel of thwarted love, set among sorority sisters at a Midwestern college, brought its author fans from all over the country. Hundreds of women wrote her letters about their fear of coming out of the closet, or, having come out, they asked for advice about where to live, how to find kindred spirits, and how to get published. One such young writer was Ann Weldy, who wrote *The Beebo Brinker Chronicles* under the name Ann Bannon.[6] After their encounter, Weldy wrote a character like M.J. into her novel *Journey to a Woman*. The character Nina is a worldly, canny, and successful writer who takes everyone's measure. Weldy's pulp novel sales may have rivaled M.J.'s, but she didn't have the same fearless, literary flair. M.J. didn't bother to create her own Weldy-like character, but she wasn't immune to literary revenge plots. In 1962, after her intense love affair with Patricia Highsmith ended badly, M.J., again writing under the name Vin Packer, included the murder by claw-hammer of a Highsmith-like character in her novel *Intimate Victims*. The same year, Highsmith published *The Cry of the Owl*, which featured the stabbing death of a character based on M.J.

M.J.'s first impression of Louise was of a "Judy Garland–like moppet." There was something childlike in the timbre of Louise's voice and in the sulkiness to which she would sometimes revert. She was younger by five years, shorter by six or seven inches. She was also pretty, lively, very funny, whip-smart, and excitable. From the first, one thing was clear: Louise was unshakably out, "always herself, never in the closet." Many of their friends led double lives. Some people had jobs, different friends in different lifestyles, but to M.J., "Louise was very much in the lesbian world."

M.J. and Louise also became regular drinking buddies. M.J. had a special affection for the gay bar scene. Unlike Alixe, M.J.

didn't feel particularly vulnerable. She liked the sense of being recognized in some bars (indeed, she was a celebrity) and anonymous in others. She liked their exclusive, clandestine quality, their secret locations, and their typically hard-boiled managers, like the one who came running out to chastise M.J. when her taxi stopped too close to the bar ("Didn't she know every cabbie was a potential informer?"). Bartenders confided in her about paying protection money to the Mafia, which provided background material for her crime novels. M.J. could drink with just about anyone. She liked a jolly party, admired a pretty person, and had a special sympathy for the lonely and lost.

It was still common practice for women to wear hats and hose in restaurants above Fourteenth Street, so when Louise and M.J. met for lunch, they'd stick to comfortable places downtown, where Louise could wear jeans and paint-splattered Oxford shirts. Clothes were a constant topic of conversation. When the spirit moved her, Louise would dress up in vest and tie. She had a treasure trove of her grandfather's jeweled stickpins. When "Alixe used to beg her not to wear anything masculine to the theater," M.J. said, Louise would be blasé. "These clothes are worth a fortune," Louise would say.

At lunch, over cocktails and clams casino, they would gossip about who was in town or out of town, who was sleeping with whom, who had sold a book or a painting, who was depressed or drinking too much or not drinking at all. M.J. had recently begun writing a book about suicide, and Louise helped her make lists of famous people who had done themselves in.

By the end of their meal, Louise would have likely recounted a sensational story or two from her childhood, which M.J. perceived as rich, proper, and eerie: she saw Louise's unhappy childhood as paradoxically lucky, in that it contained a wealth of material for an artist. There was the eccentric opera-singing grandmother who would fling money out the window while somebody stood below with a basket. A crazy uncle confined to the attic, sawing up dolls. The father who kidnapped her, then told her, falsely, that her mother was dead. Not to mention the servants who would turn her grieving mother away from the door of her father's house.[7]

Meanwhile, the heroine of the tragedy, Louise's mother, Mary Louise Perkins Trevilion, was still employed as a librarian in Clarksdale, Mississippi. She adored her daughter and worked very hard to cultivate their relationship. They had stayed in touch, but Louise hated writing letters. On the rare occasions that Louise visited the South, they got along reasonably well, but Louise didn't have much family feeling. Many of her friends felt the same, especially those who had suffered parental disapproval, and worse, for their sexual orientation. In the mid-1950s, there was a gentle social trend among some artists toward claiming deracination. It was personhood that mattered, not regional identity or association with a class or religion. Those things were only chains that could hold a nonconformist back. Louise wasn't a declared proponent of the theory, but when she was in her twenties it was an easy way to justify having few ties to the past.

It wasn't until after Louise moved in with Alixe that Mary Louise began making regular visits to see her daughter in New York. Mary Louise's neighbors and other family members respected her as an experienced and knowledgeable authority on books, art, and music, but Louise—now a New Yorker, down to her casual use of Yiddish curses—saw her mother as a conventional, middle-brow provincial, someone whose accent and reactionary opinions regarding race relations were "antebellum," forged among backward white Mississippians.[8]

Mary Louise's acceptance of the status quo was a position that infuriated Louise and drove Alixe bonkers. "How could she continue to tolerate the evil of segregation?" Alixe asked. After one exhausting and unresolved argument between Alixe and Mary Louise, Alixe slammed out of their apartment. She stayed away for days to avoid running into their house guest.

Alixe would later say that Louise longed for a mother who would love her unconditionally—just not the mother she had. Jimmy Merrill observed dryly that Louise "really didn't like mothers much," a characterization Louise protested as too general, since *some mothers* she found enchanting. Louise may have once imagined an ideal champion, rescuer, and advocate, someone whose maternal love she could rely on to bind old wounds. Instead, she found a real woman with her own quirky character. Mary Louise prided herself on being courteous and fair to everyone. The library where she worked was segregated because that was the law of the land, not because she herself was a bigot. Perhaps Louise had been away from the South too long to understand. Eventually, Louise made the conscious decision not to discuss injustice or inequality with her mother—and considering how rarely Louise kept opinions to herself, perhaps this is the greatest testament to her desire to have a relationship with Mary Louise.

Like other divided families, Louise and her mother found ways to get along. Mary Louise was a warm, religious person who counted her blessings. Louise thought she understood what her mother had suffered, and she came to recognize, with the help of Dr. Slaff, that the residual resentment she felt toward her mother was something that might come and go. She understood that it was up to her to master her anger toward the entire family. She couldn't make herself love her mother in the unconditional way her mother loved her, but she tried at least not to argue with Mary Louise about the things she cared about.

One subject that appealed to both Louise and her mother was the Perkins matriarchy and how close-knit the family was. As adults, the Perkins women and their husbands and children had all lived in one house together. For years after they had their own households, they still vacationed together. Mother Josie and her three daughters, Mary Louise, Dodie, and Inez, and Inez's daughter, Regina Inez, would crowd into one car and drive south to Florida or west to California. "We'd talk about you," Mary Louise told her daughter, "and wish you were with us."

Inez, who was a movie buff, liked to drive by the homes of the stars in the Hollywood Hills. She and Mary Louise were in a movie theater in California when they heard the news that Pearl Harbor had been bombed. In more peaceful years, they had traveled to Yellowstone National Park, taking Glenda McCoy, Regina Inez's daughter, born in 1953, in a baby carrier. Another subject on which mother and daughter could agree was food. Louise maintained a lifelong fondness for the cakes and pastries of southern cuisine. Mary Louise, who never cooked, loved seafood, especially boiled lobster.[9] After a night at the theater, mother and daughter might eat out at a New York institution like Sardi's, or after a concert, at the Carnegie Deli. On their outings to fancier locales, like the Twenty-One Club, they'd linger after a delicious meal of flambéed Steak Diane and New York cheesecake to people-watch and joke about the season's more outrageous styles in clothes and jewels. For instance, they liked the look of chandelier earrings dripping with emeralds, but agreed it wasn't a style for everyone. Both Louise and her mother were petite, and both had been athletic in their youth. In middle age, Mary Louise still hiked and swam, and she encouraged her daughter to keep up her exercise, or the cakes would start to show. Louise in her early thirties was still lithe and could eat anything she desired without adding a pound, but she had a secret horror of suddenly becoming fat and mad like her Uncle Gus.

After her New Year's fling with Sandra, Louise reconciled with Alixe, and they continued to live together. Sandra and Louise stayed friends and worked as writing partners. They discussed writing a play together, then a movie—but nothing gelled until they started to ponder take-offs and spoofs. In 1959, the writer Kay Thompson and the illustrator Hilary Knight published *Eloise in Moscow*, the fourth in a series of children's books.[10] It hadn't escaped Louise's notice that all that upper-class folderol about a funny little girl named Eloise who lived in the Plaza Hotel had proved to be a gold mine. It seemed ripe for parody and for commercial success. Instead of residing at the highfalutin' Plaza, Louise and Sandra dreamed up a beatnik child who would live on Bleecker Street. They decided to call her Suzuki Beane.[11] The name paired the brand name of the Japanese motorcycle manufacturer with an upper-class Anglo surname, which they borrowed from one of the Wall Street partners of Jim Merrill's father.

Louise began by sketching several preliminary portraits in pen and ink: mama, papa, and baby beatnik. She drew Suzuki to look like a young Sandra: fierce and spiky, with hair that sprung irrepressibly over eyes and ears. These drawings were waiting in Louise's studio one winter morning as Sandra tore over from her cold-water flat. Over the course of that night Sandra quickly wrote the whole book, first pasting down the finished drawings, then adding text fresh from her typewriter while leaving space for the many illustrations to come.

The following day, Louise designed the book and hurried to complete her illustrations. Sandra wanted to keep the text in typewriter typeface, lowercase, nothing fancy. Louise wanted there to be dancing children, and sketched cartoons of a funny, intelligent little girl twirling in midair. They agreed that the book should work as a kids' book as well as a novelty gift for adults. It opens with Suzuki introducing her family. Her father, Hugh, writes "cool poetry," and Marcia, her mother, "makes sculptures out of tin cans."

Sandra's collaboration with Louise was often tense and quarrelsome. They were both strong, opinionated artists, and their arguments could break up their partnership for days, weeks, and sometimes longer. Sandra said, "Louise could be totally uncooperative but she was never dull company." They agreed that their friendship was worth working on, and for years they kept trying. Collaborating on *Suzuki Beane*, they were equally focused and disciplined, albeit with customary though manageable bickering, until they came to discuss the book's dedication page. This triggered an explosive conflict. Louise wanted them to dedicate the book to their mothers, leaving out their fathers. Sandra wasn't alienated from her father like Louise was, and she wanted to dedicate her first book to both her parents. After a cooling-off period, they agreed at last to each write their own individual dedications. Louise's is *To My Mother*; Sandra's is *To my Mother and Father*.

When the manuscript was finished, they gave it to Gloria Safire, a literary agent and friend, who promptly sold it to Doubleday. Sandra said the speed of *Suzuki Beane*'s acceptance blinded her to the reality of publishing. She would go on to publish many books, become a popular success in various genres for adults and young readers, and receive awards and good reviews—but no book ever came together or sold as swiftly and easily for Sandra or Louise as *Suzuki Beane*.

eleven

DETECT

In February 1960, four students protesting segregation in Greensboro, North Carolina, staged a sit-in at a Woolworth's lunch counter. In Memphis, there would be sit-ins, marches, and other student protests over the next year. Supported by a community boycott of downtown stores, these actions—and the pressure of lawsuits—led the Memphis City Commission to grudgingly make some changes. By the fall of 1960, the public libraries, the zoo, and the Memphis parks would begin to desegregate. The following year, Memphis schools unwillingly began to desegregate, and the University of Tennessee started to admit Black students.[1]

Louise Fitzhugh was keenly aware of the politics of the area. Her father had retired the year before as US Attorney for Western Tennessee, and he had long since moved beyond the reach of white Democratic powerbrokers. Louise considered her father a pillar of the ruling class, and she believed his support of incremental racial advances was essentially self-serving. But he was marginally better than the pack of white supremacists who ran the place; she gave him that. As a member of Tennessee's integrated Republican Party, he had worked alongside Black politicians and helped promote their local and national causes, including voter registration.

During his six years as US Attorney, Millsaps had mostly prosecuted income-tax fraud cases, but as a prosecutor of federal laws during the Red Scare, he had also been a bona fide spy-catcher. When FBI agents in his jurisdiction had famously arrested Junius Irving Scales, a twenty-six-year-old antiracist organizer for the Communist Party of the United States of America, on November 18, 1954, they brought him directly to Millsaps Fitzhugh's office. The *Press Scimitar*'s headline the next day read, "State's Top Communist Seized Here by G-Men." In his record of the events, Scales wrote of making a telephone call for assistance while "seated at the great man [Millsaps's] desk, facing a half-dozen FBI men at extension telephones."[2] Scales, born in 1920, was from North Carolina. For both Scales and Louise, segregation was a sort of fascism, not that different from the German variety the world war had been fought to defeat. They both rebelled against what Scales called "the dominance of the know-nothing, bigoted, hateful brutality" they observed firsthand.[3]

Following the news helped distract Louise from the nerve-wracking wait until her first book would be published. She knew immediate acclaim was rare, and rarer still for the author and illustrator of a children's picture book, but it never hurt to imagine. And such things did sometimes happen. Look at *Eloise*. Neither Louise nor Sandra had anything to contrast with the ease of their experience writing, illustrating, and selling *Suzuki Beane*, and they had high hopes.

Then, as if the cosmos were reminding Louise (and Sandra) that nothing, especially first books, glide to the finish line without some real-world disruption, Alixe and Louise's apartment was burglarized—twice. The first time, early on a Saturday morning in the spring of 1961, Alixe awoke to see a man sneaking out of their bedroom. It seemed unbelievable, and by the time she'd screamed and followed him to the door he was gone, leaving the door unlocked. She and Louise reported the break-in to the police, but the burglar hadn't taken anything but a kid's bank with quarters in it. No one had been hurt, and the cops assured them it was just a one-time thing, disconcerting but over. Not true, Louise told Jimmy Merrill's partner, David Jackson, in a letter. The first man had just been casing them out: on Monday, when Louise and Alixe were out of the apartment, they were robbed of their hi-fi, all their jewelry, a Polaroid camera, a suitcase, Louise's typewriter, and her flute and trumpet. The thieves upended every cabinet and desk into a chaotic mess on the floor. Louise and Alixe felt disgusted and exposed, and Louise felt a simmering anger toward everyone and everything. It was likely that the police would never catch the thief, and she'd never again see those stolen things she loved. She might have stayed in bed and wallowed if not for the saving grace of learning that her new car had arrived at the dealer's. Feeling like an exile with one last possession, she drove her new red Volkswagen around for a while, then stashed it in a secure garage. "Louise loved her cars," Alixe said.

In 1961, when *Suzuki Beane* was published by Doubleday and Company, a copy cost $2.50. Louise was thirty-two years old, and Sandra was twenty-five. Their book came out during an age of novelties, when sophisticated take-offs and spoofs were all the fashion. (*My Son the Folk Singer*, Allan Sherman's Borscht Belt–type interpretations of classic songs, and Vaughn Meader's jokey impersonation of John F. Kennedy, called *The First Family*, would be hit albums within the year.) In the book, seven-year-old Suzuki uses beatnik slang to relate her adventures with her uptown friend Henry Martin. Their comic encounters with parents and other adults result in a cascade of cultural and generational misunderstandings. In the end, Henry and Suzuki conclude that they don't fit in either uptown or downtown; they go on the road to found a Utopian kids' village "where a square could be a square and a swinging cat could swing in peace—and kids could feel things because they do."

It's a truly good-natured work, like a Beatles song. Its message of love and tolerance is expressed in an unsentimental, jokey way. Everybody is relatively cool, as befits the age. Henry's people are society types with cigarette holders fused to their fingers. His mother, Cynthia, calls her child "dah-ling" through clenched teeth, and his father is rakish with malevolent eyes. Suzuki's parents, a downtown arty couple, are lank haired and sallow with disturbingly dark circles beneath their eyes. Suzuki sleeps on a mattress without sheets, which seems taken for granted, as Fitzhugh's drawings play on assumptions about the unwashed masses. Poetry seems a universal interest: Suzuki attends Cynthia's weekly WAETCPPA (Wednesday-Afternoon-Evening-Tea-and-Cocktail-Poetry-and-Prose-Advancement party), at which "an absolutely enchanting young poet" has been persuaded to read his new work, "Summering Seed." (Sandra admits to satirizing Jimmy Merrill's poem "Wintering Weed.")

Another character taken from life is Louise's childhood nurse (here named Helen), who works for Henry's family. She hugs Suzuki, who typically suspects all adult affection but in this case find herself surprisingly comforted. The illustrations all have an ardent joy. Suzuki dancing, rolling, and soaring in her solo dance scene is a rapturously uninhibited, unhinged, happy cupid free of everything—including gravity.

The reviews were excellent, with much praise for its story. Many critics wrote affectionately, tongue in cheek. "Does for the kindergarten set what Jack Kerouac's *On the Road* did for their (slightly) elders," wrote one. Some took the opportunity to luxuriate in beatnik slang: "Suzuki is a hip chick age of six, who mukluks her way around a pad in way-outs-ville. Dig This"; "Kookie, Suzuki"; and "Like, for Youngniks." Almost all the reviews were short on analysis, but at least one reviewer got in one. The book, it said, acted "like children are people."[4]

Jimmy Merrill didn't appreciate seeing himself (or "Wintering Weed") mocked in the poetry-reading party scene. He wrote to Louise in protest: "I do not think one can ridicule a friend's work without hurting the friend."[5]

Louise replied in a long, discursive letter with the feel of something written and rewritten in fits and starts. First, she puts the blame on Sandra, whom Louise claims did not say whose poem she was spoofing until the book was finished. Then she flatters Jimmy, reminding him how much she's loved him and admired his poetry, and for how long, and how amazed she is that he would be anything less than amused by the book's gentle satire. How *could* he think that she would deliberately ridicule his work? The letter takes another unexpected turn as she reminds him that she understands how an artist *might* be hurt by mockery, because of the time he'd said someone in one of her paintings looked like Mr. Magoo, but that was a long-buried grievance that she hardly remembers. Had she but an inkling he'd react as he did, she'd have done anything—stopped the presses, pulled the book if necessary. She was sorry she'd realized too late how hurtful the experience had been for him. She apologizes for causing any offense. Then, once more, for good effect, she assures him that the whole idea was Sandra's.

Louise's apology to Jimmy is an uncomfortable, squirming performance. Very likely it was something she hated to write, since she fudged what she knew and when she knew it. Sandra would confirm that "Summering Seed" was always meant to be a deliberate take-off of Jimmy's "Wintering Weed." Perhaps Louise didn't recognize the specific poem, but she certainly knew its author, since her illustration of Cynthia's scintillating protégé was true to the young James Merrill, down to his flashing eyes.

After a little chill, Jimmy forgave her. When Louise moved uptown with Alixe to 524 East Eighty-Fifth Street, she invited Jimmy and David to dinner as soon as they had a rug down and chairs for guests to sit in. Their new apartment provided new rooms for Alixe to renovate and redecorate, a hobby she continued to enjoy, using it to unwind after her long hours as the casting director of a new weekly TV drama called *The Defenders*. Louise was proud that Alixe was getting recognition at last, and told Jimmy, somewhat defensively, that the show was pretty good—not as bad as it could be, given that it was a boob-tube sensation.

Later that summer, when Louise's mother came from Clarksdale to visit her in New York, they took a celebratory road trip to the Hamptons. Mary Louise was justifiably proud of her daughter, the published author and artist. If Louise didn't reciprocate the intensity of her mother's affection, their adult relationship was improving. Given the earlier obstacles to it—starting with the Fitzhughs' success at separating them, and later, Louise's adolescent coolness toward her mother—this was real progress. Mary Louise had made a happy second marriage and was surrounded by her extensive family network in Clarksdale. Her own mother had died in 1958, but Mary Louise remained close to her sisters and was a devoted aunt to her great-niece Glenda. Mary Louise was "an adventurer, not scared of challenges . . . who was always talking about Little Louise," Glenda later said. When she saw that her daughter had dedicated *Suzuki Beane* to her, Mary Louise was moved to tears. She and Glenda, then seven years old, had read it aloud together.

In October, Louise turned thirty-three. She announced disconsolately to Jimmy that youth was over and their glory days were behind them. She said she was suffering recurring melancholia and often fantasized about running away to Paris. Her greatest complaint seemed to be that she and Alixe had fallen into a routine. She blamed herself for not appreciating her success or her domestic happiness, and realized she was in as much a loop as a rut. Alixe worked very hard, and Louise had started to find their domesticity irritating. Alixe was reluctant to invite guests for dinner before all their renovations were complete, which Louise suspected would never be the case. Writing to Jimmy about her former boyfriend, Fabio, seemed to cheer Louise up; she joked that Fabio, like almost everyone else they knew, was writing a novel. She wondered if they might work together in the mural-making business again if she ever got back to Paris. New York City seemed to have her in a vise—she was finally receiving some public attention and appreciation, but she knew she had to build on what she'd started. But what she really wanted was a holiday break where she didn't have to think about all the projects piling up.

Alixe suggested they go to Monhegan Island off the coast of Maine for two weeks, a brainstorm that probably added months to their marriage. Louise found it a sort of nirvana. The island had no cars or electricity, and Louise loved walking on the beach and sampling the wonderful food at the little town's restaurants, especially the lobsters and blueberry pie. It had been a warm fall, and the maple trees were at the height of their beauty. There was a tranquility on the island that Louise said gave her new energy. She did a lot of drawing in her sketchbook and began to jot down some ideas about another new play. They stayed up late and slept in. In one late-night conversation with Alixe, Louise wondered whether she had abandoned too much in a rush to the front lines. She wanted, in the future, to try to move more slowly, act more conscientiously, and preserve the calm they'd found on Monhegan Island.

Such peace was soon defeated by the energy of New York. It was the height of the fall theater season, and Alixe and Louise fell back into their metropolitan routine. That included going to shows on Friday nights. They saw almost everything in 1962, every style—except things with puppets, which Louise had forsworn at age ten. They saw *A Funny Thing Happened on the Way to the Forum*, revivals of *Miss Julie* and *A Long Day's Journey into Night*, *Tan-Tan*, and a play Louise particularly adored, called *The Days and Nights of BeeBee Fenstermaker*.

Surrounded by theatrical people, Louise began to write plays. After some of her actor friends staged a reading of her first one-act farce, she reported the event to Jimmy. Her audience had enjoyed the play, she said, which surprised her, since she personally despised farces. Under the impression that Louise always needed cheering on, Alixe had been encouraging her to show her work to other writers for feedback as well as to producers. However, the more Alixe enthused, the more it seemed Louise resisted. When the young director Andre Gregory asked to read Louise's comic one-act for a little theater production, she reluctantly sent it, but soon after fell into a funk.[6] She wrote to Jimmy, "I can't seem to rid myself no matter how I try, of an intense feeling that everything I do stinks."[7] At any rate, she told Jimmy, the audience had laughed at her jokes.

Louise also tried to write some commercial scripts for television and film, but she had little appetite for the form. So she continued to tinker with one-act plays, two of which, *The Butcher Shop* and *The Luncheonette*, were also the titles of paintings she'd shown at the Hudson Park branch of the New York Public Library back in 1956. She continued to meet with Sandra to brainstorm new projects, but not much except hangovers resulted from their lunches together. They celebrated when they learned that *Suzuki Beane* had been optioned for a television series by Desilu, Lucille Ball and Desi Arnaz's production company, but negotiations caused new quarrels. The copyright for the words belonged to Sandra, while Louise owned the illustrations. Although they agreed that Sandra had officially written the book, Alixe believed that Louise should have pursued coauthorship credit for her contribution of some words and phrases. Louise wanted Alixe to let it go, but Alixe believed Louise was not standing up for herself.

The writing project that finally absorbed Louise the most was an autobiographical three-act play that she eventually called *Mother Sweet, Father Sweet*. It is full of "honest misery," she told Alixe. She wanted to write about her Uncle Gus, her grandparents, her father, and the Black staff who worked for their family, so she set herself the task of staying on schedule and writing a set number of scenes daily to complete it. Her devotion to this play, with its themes of wealth, delusion, and madness within a segregated culture, became even more conflicted when, on March 8, 1962, her Uncle Gus died. Louise had spent many years thinking about the myths surrounding Uncle Gus, and she had written various versions of plays in which a character based on him, to a greater or lesser extent, was the tragic hero. The play raised questions: Had he been unloved by his father, loved too much by his mother? Schemed against by his siblings? Metaphorically castrated? Having explored these fictional tributaries with zeal in her writing for theater, she found that her uncle's death suddenly made him real again. As she mourned him, Louise told Alixe that she worried about having inherited the family madness: perhaps it was dormant, but might someday leave her "not all there," like her Uncle Gus.

At the center of the unfinished *Mother Sweet, Father Sweet* is a little girl and her eccentric, very rich grandmother. Louise wrote at least fourteen versions of this story. In some versions, the grandmother is more endearing; in others, she is more abusive. In every version there is a Black nurse or maid or nanny who is the little girl's advocate and most reliable champion. Louise believed that her play was at its best when recounting the tragic story of the Gus-like character's inability to resist stronger personalities, comfort, and wealth. She thought it failed in its third act to honestly convey the relationship of the little white girl and her Black nurse, but she kept trying to make it work.

After Jimmy Merrill and David Jackson read the script, while it was still in progress, Jimmy praised her work, saying it was beautifully written. He said he enjoyed the first part very much. But he gently criticized her for manufacturing tragedy in the second half and for punishing the characters she did not like. He said he and David had wondered, "Louise . . . aren't you rich enough to afford a happy ending?"[8]

Toward the end of 1962, Louise met Lorraine Hansberry, the playwright of the masterful *A Raisin in the Sun*. They had friends in common, and both attended readings at the Playwrights Unit at the Actor's Studio. Lorraine was two years younger than Louise, married, a celebrated writer, and an outspoken civil rights activist. They visited each other's homes and exchanged affectionate letters. Louise's are flirtatious and full of flattery for her new friend's work and character, and they alternate between serious social criticism and campy storytelling. In one letter she dishes fellow writer Edward Albee, whom Louise thought a childish bore but a brilliant playwright. In another, she describes the scene after their neighbor's pregnant cat had kittens on the pillow next to Alixe's head. The bloody afterbirth had made the bed resemble nothing as much as a "murder room at a wax museum."[9]

In a sober voice, Louise's letters to Lorraine also reflect on race and politics. The two friends had many conversations comparing segregation to fascism. In one letter Louise refers to the segregated South of her youth as a "cesspool," later comparing its white segregationist population to fish gasping in toxic water that they're too oblivious to sense is coming to a boil. In the same letter, she writes that she knows "it is stupid to hate all Germans, to think them all fascists, because the greatest antifascists in the world were also in Germany, and that's true in the South today."[10]

After Louise and Alixe visited Lorraine's upstate New York home, Louise wrote to say she'd decided to look for a quiet place to write outside the city. New York was wearing on her, she said. "There's nothing this city really has to offer except theater, women, places to get drunk in and people who take up your day telling you inanities over the telephone." She told Lorraine that since she was at last in a monogamous relationship, the city routine didn't hold the allure it once had.

Louise continued to work on *Mother Sweet, Father Sweet*, and at Alixe's urging she submitted her script to Kermit Bloomgarden, who had produced *The Little Foxes* and *The Crucible*. He saw promise in it and wanted to meet with Louise to discuss rewrites.

Rewrites! Louise scoffed at the idea and acted as if she'd been rejected outright. Alixe later said, "It was a biographical play and so intensely personal that Louise said she couldn't bear to change it."

Alixe, who had charged herself with supporting Louise's genius, was bewildered by Louise's resignation in the face of minor obstacles. Alixe believed *Mother Sweet, Father Sweet* was a very good play and was frustrated when Louise wouldn't take it to another producer. Alixe didn't understand whether Louise had run out of steam because she wasn't sure how to revise her play, or if she just didn't want to. She thought Louise might have persuaded herself that however she finished it, her play would flop. Alixe tried, but Louise filed the script away in a drawer.

Around that time, Louise's psychiatrist suggested that she start a therapy journal as a way of tracking her dips in confidence and fear of failure. At first Louise wrote quickly about the various things that bedeviled her. On one page she wrote of her fear of rejection by an art gallery; on another she worried that she wasn't sufficiently vulnerable, and maybe a little mad. She felt driven to extremes and defiance. She kept her journal sporadically over the year, but started doodling on blank pages and eventually dropped the practice. In fact, Louise didn't much like writing about herself. When it came to autobiography, she always preferred the camouflage of plays and fiction.

Louise was experiencing a sort of whiplash, alternating between the society of lively, gregarious theater friends and her own periods of solitude, intensely writing autobiography; guided by Dr. Slaff, she was also studying her own psychology. After a time, she felt cramped by the whole business and craved the physicality of painting again. She didn't want to isolate herself in her studio and told Alixe she wanted to meet more women artists.

It was Sandra Scoppettone who introduced Louise to Frederica Leser, a tall, handsome painter whose brusque, suffer-no-fools attitude Louise found appealing. Frederica had grown up in the Adirondacks in a wealthy, adventurous family, which, for a time, kept a private zoo. (They had been waiting for delivery of an elephant when the United States entered World War II.) Her first impression of Louise was of someone "very small, tiny . . . who had an androgynous quality, neither boy nor girl. She looked and dressed like a young boy, and could be mistaken for one." Frederica thought Louise an "immensely sensitive person, whose youth and smallness made many people mistake her for a child and completely misjudge her."

Once, an exasperated Louise had asked Frederica to help her rent a loft to paint in. "The rental agents thought Louise was underage and refused to take her seriously and wouldn't rent her anything," Frederica said. Louise, in her thirties at the time, had been incandescent with anger. It was an experience that bonded the two artists, and Frederica never forgot how much Louise particularly hated to be underestimated.

Frederica's social circle included the couple Barbara Phelan, who worked in advertising, and Lois Morehead, a switchboard operator who would study to be a nurse. All three had grown tired of the lesbian dating scene. They were impatient with discreet lunches, polite drinks parties, and carefully curated dinners, and tired of the trashy bar scene with its femme-butch dichotomies, thugs at the door, and Mafia bagmen. As an elegant alternative, the three friends decided to throw a costume party with the sophisticated theme of "After Mayerling," set in late nineteenth-century Vienna.[11]

They sent out beautiful invitations to their soiree, hired musicians to play Viennese waltzes, and put crates of champagne on ice. In the days before the gala event, a hundred guests and more browsed the costume shops of New York for swords and lace fans. On the day, they moved the furniture out of Frederica's brownstone on Twelfth Street and rented twelve golden chairs, like those at a dancing school.[12] Lois came dressed as Consuelo Vanderbilt, Duchess of Marlborough; Frederica was an archduke in full military regalia, including a sword. Their friends came dressed as Sigmund Freud, Gustav Klimt, Adele Bloch-Bauer, Egon Schiele, artists' models, and aristocrats. Louise dressed as the Prince of Something von Something. The party was such a success that more followed. At one, Louise and Sandra attended together as Scott and Zelda Fitzgerald. At another, themed "Tyrants and Revolutionaries," Louise came as Memphis's Boss Crump in a white suit. Sandra came as God and won first prize.

Frederica's parties were the only place where the various circles of Louise's women friends would regularly intersect. A partial guest list might include Alixe's cohort of sophisticated, professional women, like Lorraine Hansberry, literary agent Pat Schartle, attorney Helen Molly Leeds, publicist Patty Goldstein, agent Gloria Safire, anthropologist Mariam Kreiselman, celebrity journalist Liz Smith, and Kaye Ballard, the comedienne. Sandra's crowd of artists and writers included actress Connie Ford and Jane Wagner, a writer from Tennessee. Wagner, a young artist and writer, didn't have much money and used to bum Dunhill Light cigarettes from Louise.[13] She characterized the company as mostly "successful, creative, pleasure-loving, ambitious, knowledgeable lesbians." A third group, from Louise's earlier days in New York, included the actress Lilyan Chauvin, photographer Gina Jackson, and her former friend and art teacher Jean Sherman.

Frederica, Barbara, and Lois always particularly wanted to invite Louise. She was attractive, high-spirited, charming, and a wonderful dancer. After a few drinks, she could also become fiery. Alixe, Sandra, and Frederica all spoke of her very sharp tongue, particularly when defending her left-wing political positions. Frederica saw Louise as a rebel who wasn't an ideologue or doctrinaire. Louise welcomed a battle: with a trial lawyer's perspicacity, she wore out several sparring partners on the subjects of politics and literature. At their parties, topics under debate included the revolution in Cuba (*Wait and see*), whether huge demonstrations, like the "Ban the Bomb" march in London, could actually affect policy (*Yes!*), Jackie Kennedy's style (*Hell, yes!*), and whether *The Flintstones* really was funny (*Alcohol helps*).

Some of Louise's best-remembered arguments were with Professor Mariam Kreiselman, whose politics were not that different from Louise's, but who liked to play devil's advocate. Their occasional shouting matches apparently didn't diminish Mariam's admiration for Louise's art. She bought Louise's paintings and declared, on more than one occasion, that she thought Louise a genius.

Sometimes, in a heated mood, Louise liked to shock people. It annoyed her particularly that northerners were so ignorant regarding segregation, and she'd talk frankly about the brutal treatment of Black Memphians that she had observed firsthand. One story she told "in horrified remembrance" to Alixe and others was about white teenage boys and girls of her acquaintance who would go on dates to one of the Black neighborhoods of Memphis and "throw rocks at the heads of young Negro boys and girls."[14]

Louise had started to draw images that reflected her childhood in the segregated South and her family history as slave owners and cotton factors. Her new pieces were done on a larger scale than previous work (for instance, one drawing was sixty by thirty-four inches, another fifty-three by fifty), and she was using water-based Italian inks. To some extent, she attributed the changes in her work to an offhand comment Jimmy Merrill made on a visit to her studio. He'd said, "There are other things in the world to be loved and painted besides the human face."[15]

Those words ignited a spark of inspiration just as she'd been feeling stuck. She began to turn away from portraiture to a set of surreal, intensely colored dream paintings. In one, a small, screeching birdlike figure hangs like a puppet from wires. In another, a streetcar is tipping over amid a crowd of screaming angels. She painted a series of staircases as well as her grandmother's grand piano, imagery harking back to her grandparents' mansion, Samarkand, as well as a series featuring a little boy with half his face in mist. While as a painter Louise was becoming increasingly interested in surrealism, her drawings were more and more overtly satirical and political. She was drawing cowboys and pioneers to comment on the national infatuation with violence and acquisition.

Louise would show some of these new paintings and drawings at the Banfer Gallery on East Sixty-Seventh Street in May 1963.

Her former Bologna boyfriend, Fabio Rieti, would be exhibiting his new work there at the same time. Others were included in the show, but a whole room would be dedicated to Louise's work, so it was in essence her first solo show. Fabio arrived back in New York from Paris, where he'd been living with his new wife, Laurence Aillaud, who was also an artist. Laurence didn't speak English, so Louise served for a time as her interpreter. Over drinks one night, Laurence urged Louise to find a compatible man like Fabio, who neither interfered with nor judged Laurence's romances with women; in turn, she left him to his own affairs (one of which had been with Louise). Fabio and Laurence loved one another, she assured Louise, and at its core their marriage was a great success.

The subject of lasting relationships was weighing on Louise. Over their six years together, she and Alixe had routinely flirted with other women. She'd had a brief dalliance with Sandra, but afterward she and Alixe had sworn to be faithful. Then, around New Year's 1963, Louise had discovered that Alixe had been having a long affair—a serious one—and suddenly, they were in deep trouble. Louise was bitterly angry. Alixe was contrite. They patched things up, but there were still tensions and suspicions, and Louise felt that whatever they might try would only be temporary. Moreover, she had begun to see herself as single again, and the prospect didn't seem as horrible as it once had.

One night, by way of apology—and hoping they might start fresh—Alixe proposed a Christmas vacation in Paris. Alixe had never been to Paris, as her demanding work had always kept her in New York. Instead of being pleased, Louise said Alixe didn't understand what it was like for an artist to work in isolation, and she'd been looking forward to the upcoming season's parties. When Alixe said it was selfish of Louise to deprive her of a trip she so longed to take, Louise encouraged her to go alone. Their argument escalated, and days passed until they made peace. Alixe agreed to move out in early June. Meanwhile, they'd share the house and sleep separately. The only cure for their relationship, Louise told David Jackson, would be to take a break from one another and hope for some reconciliation down the line.

In mid-March, with six weeks to go until her opening at the Banfer Gallery, Louise was anxious about the reception of her new drawings and paintings and her father's failing health. Separated from Alixe, she also worried constantly about money. Her allowance had become an embarrassing symbol to her of failed promise, despite all advantages, to succeed on her own terms. She was counting on the Banfer Gallery show being the kind of turning point that would catapult her into the upper echelon of artists, that elite caste who could sell their work and live on the proceeds.

Two of Louise's colored ink drawings were selected for the Banfer catalog, both American regionalist images in a satirical style. One is of a pouty lipped cowboy in a carnival booth. A sign at the level of his crotch invites players to shoot him, five chances for a dime. The other is of a captive giant Black woman giving birth to a miniature Victorian-era white family. The captive's arms are outstretched and she is tied by her wrists to stakes. From between her open legs rises a fully dressed nuclear family. The husband and wife have self-satisfied expressions on their faces. The man wears a Van Dyke beard, a stylish collar and tie, and a bowler hat. His legs are crossed, one toe on point. His lady wife's hair is dressed in a high-top bun. Her tightly fitted pioneer dress, with a high neck and mutton leg sleeves, is transparent, making the bones of the captive's pelvis visible.

Two children are perched on the giantess's left breast. The little boy wears a white jacket and short pants, along with socks and white shoes with straps—which look like tap shoes. The little girl has on a flouncy white pinafore, black leggings, and black ballet-like shoes. She wears a large tam o' shanter, tilted to the right, as large as her head. The boy looks concerned, and the girl looks avid. There is a very dim caul around the family and a thin stream of umbilical cord drifting upward. The captive's complexion is many shades darker than the family's. Her feet are splayed like fins. Her furious eyes are difficult to isolate in a face that runs like molten iron from crown to torso.

France Burke and Frederica Leser attended the Banfer opening. Frederica noted Louise's distinctive style and found many of the new pieces "beautiful and quite disturbing." In her journal, France noted, "Fine lines, color seeping or exploding all over the place, highly psychoanalytical. But can she draw!!" Reviewing Louise's show in *Art News*, Ti-Grace Atkinson wrote that "Fitzhugh . . . has a painter's feel, a satirist's eye, a comic's hand. She depends substantially on line and montage technique, assembling images, one memory overlying, giving way to another. *Two Salesladies Discussing God* in colored inks and synthetic resins resembles Mother ripened to vintage state in the cellar."[16]

Immediately after the exhibit, Louise basked in what seemed to have been a success. The reviews were good and she'd sold eighteen pieces. But a few weeks later, she was declaring the episode a catastrophe. She felt the gallery owners had cheated her, withholding money owed for the sale of her work. A solo show in a gallery was an experiment Louise told Jimmy she wished never to repeat. All of this was happening at the same time that her relationship with Alixe was continuing to crumble. Their breakup unexpectedly returned Louise to her autobiographical fiction. She wrote a draft of a novel she called *Crazybaby*, using the same foundational material she had relied on for her play *Mother Sweet, Father Sweet*.

In this more comic iteration, an eponymous eight-year-old orphan has been rescued by Teacake, a proto–Ole Golly figure.

Teacake is housekeeper and factotum to Mrs. Birdsong (the Grandmother Fitzhugh character), and her son, Byron, is a poet who speaks in rhyme. Mrs. Birdsong, an eccentric, throws money out the window to the birds and dresses bizarrely. In the style of magical realism, the little girl heroine believes she can cause a person's death by completing their portrait. At one point, she tests her theory, finishing her picture of a cruel, duplicitous white man who then dies at the final stroke of her pen.[17]

Louise put the unfinished novel aside temporarily as other projects took precedence. Frustrated by the lack of movement in her career, she fired her agent, Gloria Safire, and hired Patricia Schartle, whom M.J. had recommended. In June, Louise wrote to tell Jimmy that she still hadn't received any payment from the Banfer Gallery show. She had returned to writing and had been trying various freelance strategies to earn some money. She had also started a new children's book, which her agent had been showing to publishers. Harper had indicated some interest. Louise wrote to Jimmy, "It is called *Harriet the Spy* and is about a nasty little girl who keeps a notebook on all her friends."[18]

Walter and Josie Perkins, Louise Fitzhugh's maternal grandparents, around 1900.

Photograph courtesy of Glenda McCoy, Perkins family collection.

Mary Louise Perkins, Louise Fitzhugh's mother, dressed for the May Festival, around 1912.

Photograph courtesy of Glenda McCoy, Perkins family collection.

Sally Taylor, Louise Fitzhugh's stepmother, was married to Millsaps Fitzhugh.

Courtesy of Taylor collection. Permission of Ross Taylor.

Ed Thompson around 1949. Louise Fitzhugh eloped with Ed Thompson in August 1947. Their marriage was annulled the following month.

Photograph permission of Rebecca Jacks.

Painting Class, 1949. Louise Fitzhugh is the model for artist and Bard classmate Fred Segal.

Permission of Bard College Archives and Special Collections.

Louise Fitzhugh and her friend, photographer Gina Jackson, around 1952.

Collection of Sam Shea. Photo by Lilyan Chauvin. By permission of Julie Ann Johnson.

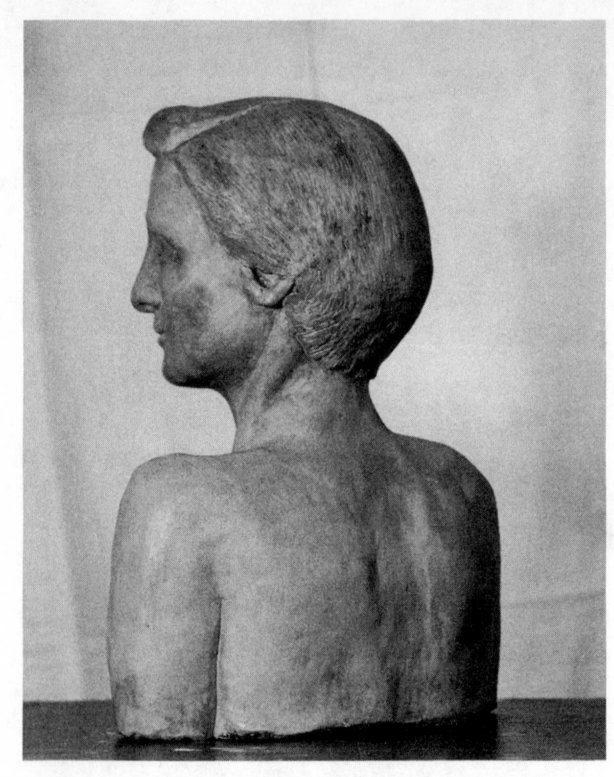

Clay head of Louise Fitzhugh by France Burke around 1954.

Collection of Sam Shea. Used by permission.

Louise Fitzhugh and France Burke in the attic garret they shared at 7 Leroy Street. Around 1955.

Courtesy of Sam Shea.

Louise Fitzhugh and friend and fellow artist Fabio Rieti in front of a mural they painted together in Bologna, Italy, 1956.

Handwritten commentary by Fabio Rieti. Photograph permission of Fabio Rieti.

Two studios. Top photo is in Louise Fitzhugh's studio in Bologna, Italy, 1956. Bottom photo of Louise in her New York City studio, around 1963.

Photographs by Fabio Rieti. Permission of Fabio Rieti.

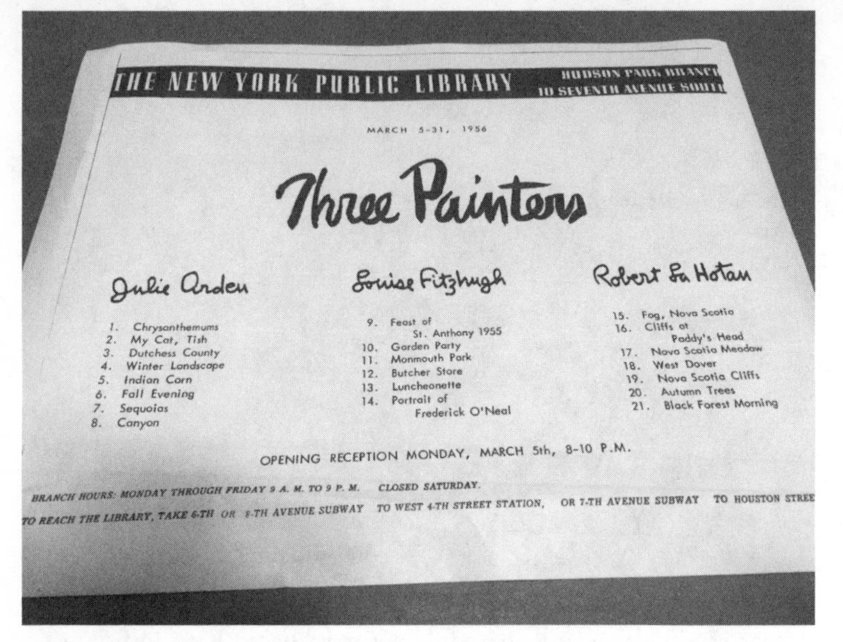

THE NEW YORK PUBLIC LIBRARY
HUDSON PARK BRANC
10 SEVENTH AVENUE SOUT

MARCH 5-31, 1956

Three Painters

Julie Arden	Louise Fitzhugh	Robert La Hotan
1. Chrysanthemums	9. Feast of St. Anthony 1955	15. Fog, Nova Scotia
2. My Cat, Tish	10. Garden Party	16. Cliffs at Paddy's Head
3. Dutchess County	11. Monmouth Park	17. Nova Scotia Meadow
4. Winter Landscape	12. Butcher Store	18. West Dover
5. Indian Corn	13. Luncheonette	19. Nova Scotia Cliffs
6. Fall Evening	14. Portrait of Frederick O'Neal	20. Autumn Trees
7. Sequoias		21. Black Forest Morning
8. Canyon		

OPENING RECEPTION MONDAY, MARCH 5th, 8-10 P.M.

BRANCH HOURS: MONDAY THROUGH FRIDAY 9 A. M. TO 9 P. M. CLOSED SATURDAY.

TO REACH THE LIBRARY, TAKE 6-TH OR 8-TH AVENUE SUBWAY TO WEST 4-TH STREET STATION, OR 7-TH AVENUE SUBWAY TO HOUSTON STREE

Louise Fitzhugh's first gallery show was at the New York Public Library, Hudson Branch.

Permission for use granted by NYPL.

Louise Fitzhugh and Alixe Gordin. Happy days, around 1962.

Permission of Richard Glas.

Drawing of Louise Fitzhugh by Fabio Rieti, around 1963.

Permission of Fabio Rieti.

Louise Fitzhugh, around 1970.

Permission of Richard Glas.

twelve

AGENCY

It was Charlotte Zolotow, then a forty-eight-year-old senior editor in the Harper Books for Boys and Girls division, who first saw the earliest version of *Harriet the Spy*. In her department, any editor could open submissions that came in the mail, and if an editor found a manuscript she liked, and the higher-ups approved, that book was hers to edit. Charlotte knew that the literary agent Pat Schartle, who was a consummate professional, would only represent something of quality, so she wasn't surprised that she found Louise's pages delightful. She was, however, surprised by how brief the submission was: only around four typed pages, and most of it summary, with very little sample writing. What was there was a very funny introduction to an eleven-year-old and her notebook, in which she wrote brutally frank impressions of her neighbors on New York's Upper East Side, where she lived with her sophisticated, affluent parents.

Charlotte had admired Louise's illustrations for *Suzuki Beane* and knew she was a painter, but since there were no illustrations included with the proposal, she presumed the book was for readers around the age of its heroine. Instead of asking for clarification, Charlotte took a leap. The note attached to the brief reader's report she delivered to her boss, Ursula Nordstrom, read, "You have to get this writer to come in and talk. This isn't a book, but it could be."

In 1963, Ursula was the head of Harper Books for Boys and Girls, and she knew that her lieutenant, Charlotte, had a brilliant instinct for finding and drawing out great children's books from new and incipient writers and illustrators. Charlotte also wrote successful picture books. Among these was the charming *Mr. Rabbit and the Lovely Present*, published in 1962, with illustrations by Maurice Sendak. Charlotte and Ursula agreed that Louise's original story was sketchy and unfinished, but it did have an interesting heroine, and on that basis they invited her in to talk about the book she hoped to write.

On the day of their meeting, Louise arrived with another manuscript—this time an illustrated notebook, which Charlotte said contained no dialogue. Ursula and Charlotte loved the pictures, but they still were unsure whether Louise intended to write another picture book, like *Suzuki Beane*, or something for older children. Louise didn't seem to know either. As the two editors read the short synopsis out loud, guffawing at their favorite lines, they made it clear they were enthusiastic about its possibilities but couldn't yet see the book-to-be.

Louise, who never liked having her work scrutinized, sat slumped in a chair, arms crossed defensively. Charlotte thought she looked like somebody spoiling for a fight. (In later years she would say of Louise, "She was resentful of almost every adult she ever came across.") At last, Louise spoke up: "So you're not really interested, are you?"[1]

Ursula assured her they were very interested, but they still had lots of questions. Charlotte asked, "Why is Harriet so angry?" Louise wasn't ready for that one, and it woke her up. Until then, and despite their reputations, neither woman had really impressed her. Still, she wasn't ignorant of the fact that this was a rare opportunity, one not to be squandered. Louise shot back, "She's angry because her nursemaid went away and deserted her. She never wrote and she never came back."

From that point, Ursula and Charlotte subjected Louise to what Alixe called a harrowing barrage of follow-up questions: Was she angry because she had dearly loved her nursemaid and didn't want to be left behind? Had Harriet felt rejection in the suddenness of her nursemaid's departure? How did she feel about being left behind with her parents? Was she angry because she recognized that as a paid employee, her nursemaid had just been doing her job? Or was it all about her helplessness as a child—never being told the truth and being left in the dark when a beloved friend disappeared? Was Harriet angry at the nursemaid, or was she angry at the world?[2]

Most importantly: "There is no nursemaid in the story that you've shown us," Charlotte told Louise. "Put her in."

Then, for about an hour more, Ursula and Charlotte asked questions about Harriet's school friends, her relationship with her parents, and her diary.

"Why is she keeping a diary?" Ursula asked.

"Because she wants to be a writer," Louise replied.[3]

The editors told Louise to go home and finish writing her book. If her audience was ten-year-olds, the book needed to be *at least* twenty thousand words. They encouraged her to keep it as funny as it was starting out to be. Furthermore, there were no restrictions on its vocabulary. When Louise asked if she could say people are finks, Ursula didn't object. She liked Louise and wanted to give her every encouragement. She also gave Louise a "small" but "decent" advance.[4]

On the day she received a completed version of *Harriet the Spy*, Charlotte brought the manuscript home in the old canvas tote she used to carry manuscripts to and from work. She asked her eleven-year-old daughter, Ellen, to read it, and waited impatiently for her verdict. Ellen zipped through the book—and happily reported that she loved it.

It was a lucky break for Louise to work with Charlotte Zolotow and Ursula Nordstrom. In 1963, Ursula was one of the most influential book publishers of children's literature. Louise had not begun *Harriet the Spy* with the idea of writing a long book, but Ursula and Charlotte guided her to writing one book divided into three sections that, at 298 pages, was longer than the novels then typical for middle-school children. But Ursula knew her readership, and she was confident that *Harriet the Spy* would find its audience.

Ursula was respected as a hands-on editor. She famously cultivated long, supportive relationships with her stable of authors and illustrators, including Margaret Wise Brown, who wrote *Goodnight Moon*; E. B. White, author of *Charlotte's Web*; Laura Ingalls Wilder, of *Little House on the Prairie* fame; H. A. and Margaret Rey, creators of *Curious George*; and Marc Simont, Tomi Ungerer, and Garth Williams, among other great illustrators. Around the time Louise and Ursula met, Harper Books for Boys and Girls had swept the year's highest awards for children's literature, including the Caldecott for Maurice Sendak's *Where the Wild Things Are* and the Newbery for Emily Neville's *It's Like This, Cat*.

Louise was revising very quickly to meet a spring deadline and came to rely on Ursula's experience. They shared a dry sense of humor, a progressive political perspective, and a love of music and dance. Louise told Jimmy Merrill that in short order, Ursula had become someone she truly admired. This was saying a great deal for Louise, who had few heroes. She thought Ursula decent, truthful, and droll. Ursula recognized Louise's talent and set out to develop a rapport between them, as writer and editor, that she hoped would result in a lasting professional relationship. This meant encouraging her to trust that Harper's commitment was to all of Louise's writing, not just her books for children. In one long afternoon meeting, Louise sat down with Ursula and talked through all the manuscripts Louise had been working on for the past decade. This material included fragments and some finished sections of short stories and novels for adults. In a follow-up letter, Ursula wrote, "We've gone over the fascinating material you left with us a week ago, and I sort of think you might consider taking the very best things out of the various little books, and perhaps making one book of it. It really should be done as an adult book and so would you consider getting some of the things together so we can present it to an adult editor, I mean an editor of adult books?"[5]

In their meeting, Louise had told Ursula about a novel she'd begun calling *Mimi*. Ursula replied that she was intrigued by Louise's description and urged her to send the manuscript for her to read. It's a tantalizing exchange and might be a clue to one of the mysteries associated with Louise's work. Louise had been making notes and sketching a book about Amelia Brent since her friend's death in 1956. She had written various bits and pieces for years, and had shown two chapters of an unfinished novel to Alixe. Alixe thought the material was "beautiful . . . and overwhelmingly sad." It was a romance between two young women set in Memphis. The age of the characters notwithstanding, Alixe understood this to be an adult novel. Louise often changed her titles. Was *Mimi* the working title of her Amelia novel?

Louise had also sent a chapter of her *Amelia* book-in-progress to her agent Pat Schartle, whose reply was disappointing. According to Alixe, Pat was "quite terrified . . . horrified because it was about lesbians." Pat herself was bisexual, so it wasn't the lesbians who terrified and horrified her, but perhaps she was frightened of the possible damaging effects such a book might have on Louise's reputation as a writer for children. Alixe considered this episode a tragedy for Louise, saying, "She could've been a very successful [adult] novelist, and wasn't, because Pat Schartle was fearful of its subject matter."

It isn't apparent that Louise shared Alixe's view. Louise didn't care for criticism, and she didn't much like being told what she could or couldn't do, but she didn't fire Schartle as she had her previous agent, Gloria Safire. Neither Sandra Scoppettone nor M.J. Meaker, two writers with whom Louise was most likely to discuss her work, heard her mention a book-in-progress about Amelia. They were also unaware that Pat Schartle had refused to represent the book because it was a coming-of-age lesbian love story. Pat was a pragmatist. It is very possible that it was not the subject matter that dissuaded her. Two chapters are hardly enough to tell what a book will become, or, from an agent's point of view, how to sell it. Louise had written one picture book for children, and *Harriet the Spy* was still months away from publication. Pat might have deliberately discouraged Louise from switching gears until she had built a dependable readership. She also might have asked Louise to show her more of the book when she had a more complete manuscript.

According to Alixe, Louise's reaction was to put the manuscript away, perhaps intending to return to it at another time. In her subsequent letters to Louise, Ursula asked if she had made any progress on *Mimi*, but Louise didn't reply to the query. She apparently never sent Ursula any pages from that novel or anything else about Amelia. No book called *Mimi* was ever published, and it didn't show up in the inventory of unfinished works made after Louise's death.

By the summer of 1964, Louise and Alixe's romance was over, but they were determined to stay friends. They shared a vacation rental on Swan Creek, which fed into Mecox Bay in Water Mill, Long Island, with Susanne Singer, a textile designer, and Constance Ford, an actress. Alixe had known Constance since she had auditioned for a *Studio One* episode. The four friends paid $1,500 for the season, and, come the weekend, would pack up their cars—Sue had a 1962 Corvette convertible—for the five-hour drive to the end of the Long Island Expressway, around Patchogue. Then they would drive backroads for another hour to their place. In addition to the sensory pleasures of being in nature, stepping away from routines, from crowds, from bosses, they escaped the ubiquity of disapproving straights and conventional roles to a land beyond the closet where they could be themselves without hiding or lying. "We were all young, carefree, and gay," Sue Singer would say. "It was a wonderful scene out there. You could express yourself without going crazy." Anyone with the assets or the ingenuity to get to the Hamptons was going.

Their rental house had a deck above the water and a wraparound porch. There, women from Louise's literary and artistic circles mingled with the theatrical types among Alixe's friends. The Hamptons were crowded with summer visitors, many of them artistic, fashionable, and gay. "Everybody," Sue said, "searching for something great and something wonderful." The weather was hot and the weekenders lived in bathing suits, T-shirts, and shorts. Sometimes they cooked in the kitchen together when it rained, or barbequed when the weather was clear. Other times, they would eat appetizers for dinner in a cocktail lounge, or head to a favorite seafood shack on the beach for fried clams. Most nights, they went dancing at house parties or clubs. There were several gay bars where society people would come to slum, bringing lots of booze and city drugs.

Betty Beaird, an actress known to her friends as Dutchie, visited on several weekends that summer. "You had to be very special to be in that group," she said, and she felt lucky to be among them. Dutchie was devoted to Alixe, whom she felt had changed her life by encouraging her to branch out from the advertising agency for which she had been working. Dutchie had felt stifled there, and with Alixe's help began to audition for roles in episodic TV. Eventually she was cast as Diahann Carroll's white next-door neighbor in the TV sitcom *Julia.*[6] The show, an early, mainstream attempt to portray a middle-class, African American family, tried to avoid the customary racist tropes and stereotypes.

For Sue Singer, it was Louise who inspired her. Louise encouraged her to make the leap from commercial art (fashion textiles) to photography. "Come on," Louise said. "You can take my photograph." Sue shot rolls of film of Louise as the two of them tore around at the beach, and later in Carl Schurz Park. The picture Sue took of Louise on a child's swing, holding her Yorkie (Peter), became her author's photo, landing on the jacket for *Harriet the Spy*. Sue was a little in love with Louise, who in her estimation was a true artist and a Renaissance woman. Louise liked spending time with Sue, whom she treated as a protégée. There would be other young women over the next few years who would sing Louise's praises because of how she had encouraged them: she was empathetic and generous with her time (and sometimes with her money). Louise discovered that when her mood and circumstances aligned, she had a talent for teaching. She liked being the older, wiser one for a change. She tried to be thoughtful when she critiqued her friends' art and writing, and she did not lie.

Although her writing life was more disciplined and her professional relationships unexpectedly stable, Louise's relationship with Alixe was still in tumult. They had separated earlier that summer and were doing their best to mend their friendship, but

Dutchie thought Louise seemed extra testy and argumentative. In contrast to seeming like the tiny or fragile person others tended to underestimate, to Dutchie Louise was confident and powerful, a woman who liked to be in charge and who went her own way. She could be generous and funny, but a mercurial temperament made her a frustrating housemate. Sometimes stomping around in a bad mood, she would disrupt everyone's holiday. "You didn't mess with Louise," Dutchie said. Sue saw Louise's demons reflected in the portraits she painted, which seemed to her more contorted, anguished, and surrealistic than her earlier work had been.

Mary Louise's visit that year coincided with the 1964 Freedom Summer project in Mississippi, where civil rights workers were drawing attention to the inequities and violence of daily life for African Americans.[7] It would be hard to underestimate the reputation that Mississippi held for brutality and backward thinking in a New York City liberal's imagination. The same year that *Harriet the Spy* was published, Louise and others in her circle were listening to Nina Simone sing "Mississippi Goddam," which captured the moment's tension and violence. They also had likely heard Phil Ochs, one of the troubadours of the protest and folk generation, sing "Here's to the State of Mississippi," recorded in 1965. In eight verses Ochs excoriates the laws, judges, schools, churches, and people who perpetuated the state's racist and brutal system. He concludes with this directive: "Mississippi find yourself another country to be part of."

Indeed, Ku Klux Klan doctrine held sway in the state, and racist cops and politicians provided no protection. It was a dangerous place for dissidents. Canton, Natchez, New Albany: all were places of lawlessness and Klan control, and all were within a few hours' drive from Mary Louise's home. In the Clarksdale library, where Mary Louise still worked, real change came slowly.

Required by the 1964 Civil Rights Act to integrate, the library invited African Americans to enjoy the books—but they removed chairs from the library floor so no reader would mistake duty for hospitality.[8]

At the end of the summer, Alixe and Louise finally divided their household. Louise invited Constance Ford, one of her housemates in Water Mill, to move into an apartment with her at 10 East End Avenue. Their building was close to Seventy-Ninth on a short street running along the river. Sue Singer and Louise's other friends heard the news with relief. Connie was one of the few people who seemed able to influence Louise, who might help keep her from drinking too much and on track to finish her book.

Connie Ford, born in the Bronx in 1923, was an actress who began her career as a model for Victory Red lipstick during World War II.[9] She had acted on Broadway, notably as Miss Forsyth in the original production of *Death of a Salesman*, as well as in movies and television. She mainly played character parts: prisoners, society ladies, saloon girls, witnesses, clients in legal dramas, and patients and nurses in medical programs. When she moved in with Louise, she was playing Eve Morris, a homicidal playhouse proprietor, in the soap opera *The Edge of Night*.

If Louise was worried that she was falling into an early, stodgy middle age, Connie was an immediate antidote. They had fun going to bars and parties together. Connie was lighthearted and their love affair a confection after the Sturm und Drang of breaking up with Alixe. Connie was also a good influence when it came to work ethic. She had her own demanding career with morning costume and make-up calls to meet, which encouraged Louise to discipline herself and write or revise several pages every day.

As an actress, Connie was always watching her weight, and Louise joined her in a mutual dieting regime. After a lifetime as a sylph, Louise was adding pounds and newly self-conscious about how she looked. As she tried to resist the delicious biscuits and cakes that she so loved, she and Connie experimented briefly with the diet pill Dexedrine, an amphetamine that was popular among actresses and models of the era.[10] The pills made Louise feel euphoric, creative, selfish—and not the least bit hungry. "Someone should've given me some when I was two and I would never have had a problem in the world," she told David Jackson.[11]

Two was the age Louise had been taken from Mary Louise to live with Millsaps, and she sometimes wondered *what if* she had stayed with her mother. Uppers couldn't change the past; nor could they provide lasting willpower against the temptations of sugar and butter. But for a brief while the Dexies gave Louise a powerful sense of control. When their unpleasant downside produced bad moods and hungry bingeing, Louise returned to the reliable, high caloric consolation of brandy.

thirteen

AGENT HARRIET

In 1963 and 1964, as Louise was inventing *Harriet the Spy*'s world, nannies and spies were very much in the public eye. *Mary Poppins* and *The Sound of Music* were in the movie theaters. John le Carré's *The Spy Who Came in from the Cold* and Ian Fleming's James Bond books were leading hardcover and paperback bestseller lists, and *Spy vs. Spy* was a popular feature in *Mad Magazine*. Louise read these, but when it came to intrigue and mystery, she preferred the intellectual peregrinations of Dorothy L. Sayers's detectives, Harriet Vane and Lord Peter Wimsey. Her affection for the name Harriet is obvious, and Louise herself would briefly use Peter as an alternate name.

In a letter to Lorraine Hansberry, Louise listed some of the other books she was reading as she worked: *Ship of Fools* by Katherine Anne Porter; Julius Horwitz's *The Inhabitants*, about unrelenting cycles of poverty in Harlem; *Freedom Road*, Howard Fast's novel about the Reconstruction era; a biography of Eugene

O'Neill, whose tragic life of alcoholism she found both pitiful and a little boring; and Lawrence Durrell's gorgeous *The Alexandria Quartet*. These books are very different; what they all have in common is their investigation into how the powerful connive to take advantage of defenseless individuals or marginalized groups. In O'Neill's life story and Durrell's novels, there's also a sense of the fragility of the artist, which seemed to Louise much like the vulnerability of a misfit child.

The heroine of *Harriet the Spy* is Harriet M. Welsch, who lives in the Yorkville neighborhood on the Upper East Side of Manhattan with her parents and Ole Golly, her beloved nanny. She's a precocious child and is in sixth grade at the elite (fictional) Gregory School (at 100 East End Avenue), where her best friends are Janie Gibbs and Simon "Sport" Rocque. Harriet always moves fast: she bangs, bumps, bounces, and zooms on her way to enlightenment. Ole Golly, a reader of great literature, encourages Harriet to keep a notebook in which to write her impressions. Harriet takes her writing practice seriously and protests when adults discount her. She declares, "I do not go out to PLAY, I go out to work."[1] Indeed, she is dedicated to recording her observations and writes her entries in capital block letters:

OLE GOLLY SAYS DESCRIPTION IS GOOD FOR THE SOUL AND CLEARS THE BRAIN LIKE A LAXATIVE.[2]

Harriet's interplay with her nanny is exactly what Ursula Nordstrom and Charlotte Zolotow had hoped to draw out of Louise in their first meeting. When Ole Golly leaves Harriet's family to move to Montreal with her new husband, Mr. Waldenstein, Harriet is left feeling alone and misunderstood. Her crisis is exacerbated after her notebook is taken by another child in a game of tag. When Harriet's friends and schoolmates find that she has been writing unflattering (but perceptive) things about them, they shun her. Consequently, Harriet begins rampaging around like a holy terror. She curses, deliberately trips one classmate, pinches another, throws a pencil at the face of a third, puts a frog in a girl's desk, and cuts off a sizable lock of another girl's hair. (Harriet finds the ensuing chaos deeply satisfying.) She throws a shoe at her father (of whom she was otherwise fond), skips school, and says uniquely mean things at every opportunity. Her mother, an endearing but easily inconvenienced and childish diva, tries to intervene, first by banning all writing in notebooks outside of school, then by sending her child to a therapist. (Dr. Wagner is likely based on Louise's own Dr. Slaff, a practitioner in adolescent clinical psychiatry.) Harriet's meltdown continues until she receives a letter from Ole Golly, who tells her that, to put things right and regain her friends, she'll have to do two things: apologize and lie: "Little lies that make people feel better are not bad." More important, Ole Golly tells Harriet (and it is worth repeating), "Remember that writing is to put love in the world, not to use against your friends."[3]

Harriet belongs to a tradition of wise child protagonists who owe much to *Catcher in the Rye*, which had been published about fifteen years earlier. Harriet has a soul sister in Holden Caulfield's younger sister, Phoebe, who also keeps notebooks, and who becomes a dedicated novelist by the age of nine. Phoebe's novels feature the girl detective Hazel Weatherfield, whose father "is a tall attractive gentleman, about 20 years of age." Through the 1960s and into the 1970s, little boys with big mouths show up in memory plays and movies by Woody Allen. Their parents holler and are typically dismissive of their kids' genius. In *A Thousand Clowns*, by Herb Gardner, there's a wiseacre kid who wears the same kind of heavy black glasses as Harriet. His guardian, a free-spirited writer, is a case study of the many ways a childish man can fail an adultish child.[4] In the 1964 film *The World of Henry Orient*, from the novel by Nora Johnson, two fourteen-year-old girls who attend an elite girls' school (much like Gregory) are infatuated with a concert pianist, spying on him as they chart his movements in a notebook. They, too, are disappointed by parents, whose absence they first appreciate for the freedom it allows, then view as selfish or neglectful, and phony.[5]

It wasn't at all common in kids' books for a child to see a therapist, as Harriet does to good effect, but it was in the zeitgeist to talk about sending kids to shrinks. The counselor Louise dreamed up for Harriet, a fellow in thick black glasses with a therapist's couch, was a stock New York character, mocked by some and deferred to by others as the man with the answers. Those children who did not live on Manhattan's Upper East Side might not find themselves in a Dr. Wagner's office, but pairing troubled adolescents and therapy was in the air. Stephen Sondheim's lyrics for *West Side Story*'s "Gee, Officer Krupke" relate, "This boy don't need a judge / He needs an analyst's care!"[6] Children and dogs are both analysts and analysands in Charles Schulz's *Peanuts* cartoons. Starting in 1959, Lucy van Pelt's lemonade stand doubled as a therapy kiosk. When the gallant failure, Charlie Brown, asks how he can overcome "deep feelings of depression," Lucy replies briskly, "Snap out of it! Five cents, please."[7]

Like Holden Caulfield, who loves the Museum of Natural History "because the figures in the glass cases don't change," Harriet is a writer devoted to routine.[8] She loves her tomato sandwiches, her egg creams, and her spy route and notebook both because they give her a lot of pleasure and because they ground her. Like a working artist, she doesn't want to think about the mundane details. That's what a parent—and later, a partner—is for: somebody who can deal with practical things so an artist doesn't have to. When Harriet's routines are disrupted, all hell breaks loose. A thousand more writers would call that realistic.

Louise declared Harriet a "nasty" child, and she meant it affectionately. She was a little girl who cursed, lied, spied, and told inconvenient truths. While Harriet's nastiness delighted children, she alarmed some grown-ups, who decried her as a poor example. And just as a "nasty woman" may be deemed unfeminine by those whom she threatens, so Harriet was attacked as unchildlike by adults, who protested her self-awareness.[9] She is mouthy in the way that, in the mid-1960s, children were not supposed to be. Children whose parents had an authoritarian disciplinary style might find themselves threatened with a smack if they didn't watch their mouth and their manners. Charlotte Zolotow recognized early on that Harriet challenged "adult authority." The novel possessed "all sorts of political strains," she says. Louise had "definite feelings about the rich and the poor and they came out in her novel," in Zolotow's estimation. "Underneath all her books there was a value system about life and people and politics." Louise, for one thing, saw adults "as the oppressors."

In her notebook, Harriet reflects on how money works for or against the subjects on her spy route. When she notes that rich people do not necessarily have a lot going on inside, and that poorer people cannot get a break, she speaks for Louise, whose politics were to the left of liberal and had what used to be called "class consciousness." Harriet is an avatar of 1960s antiauthoritarianism, as much opposed to the tired conventions and political orthodoxies as any hippie, rebel, or radical of her generation. A few years after the book's publication, in universities across the United States, students opposing hypocrisy, materialism, and the Vietnam War would hear the same kind of response in defense of the status quo. *You don't know what you're talking about*—or, the worst one of all: *Grow up*. Like Harriet, they did not listen.

Louise held a reverence for tools, and she deliberately created Harriet as a capable child. She straps on her tool belt, which carries a flashlight, pens, a canteen, and a knife, before going off to work. (The belt idea was adapted from an actual belt that Louise's friend Dutchie wore over her farmer's overalls during her Texas childhood.) Harriet's spy clothes included an old, dark blue hoodie, her beloved ripped blue jeans, and blue sneakers with holes. Her pièce de résistance is a pair of heavy black-rimmed glasses without lenses that she wears to make herself look cool and clever, more like the writer she was. This unisex outfit endears her to other resourceful kids who like to tinker and experiment and who resist limits imposed on their adventures by gender conventions, pigeonholing, or profiling. Harriet, like Louise, wasn't very interested in people telling her who she was or what she could do.

When Louise first proposed *Harriet the Spy* to Harper, Ole Golly was just a vague idea without a character arc or backstory. In subsequent drafts, Louise drew on her own experience with nannies and nurses to add more where Charlotte pushed. Ole Golly was a *femme sérieuse* who entered the Welsch family orbit in Harriet's infancy. Louise's illustration of Ole Golly is a person of indeterminate race and ethnicity whose outstanding characteristics are intelligence, penetrating eyes, and an index finger raised mid-admonition. She has a mother who lives in Far Rockaway, Queens, who is as dim as Ole Golly is brilliant. Despite clues like some pronounced southernisms in her speech, Ole Golly's history remains a mystery. Why would such a well-read, confident, and self-possessed woman work as a child's nurse for eleven years? She is presumably not a convict on the run, since even the neglectful Welsches would have asked for some references. For all the reader knew, she appeared out of the blue, like Mary Poppins to help the Bankses, or Hagrid to invite Harry Potter to Hogwarts.

In the book's early chapters, Ole Golly is an aphorism machine, spitting out quotes for every occasion. Harriet, recognizing the consoling effect they have upon her nurse as she delivers them, listens attentively, absorbing their primary lesson, which is *read, read, read.* (Or, as Louise's Uncle Gus would say, *write, write, write.*) It is cheering to think of a young reader casually passing on Henry James's helpful adage that "there are few hours in life more agreeable than the hour dedicated to the ceremony known as afternoon tea," or Keats's observation that "beauty is truth, truth beauty,—that is all / Ye know on earth, and all ye need to know."

When Ole Golly decides to accept a marriage proposal, Harriet is angry at her nurse for abandoning her. A good deal of Harriet's confidence has been predicated on having a receptive audience for her ambitions to be a spy and a writer.[10] At eleven, she has a healthy ego, common in young geniuses who otherwise might not make it out of childhood alive—either smothered by adoration, crushed by rejection, or left to flounder in indifference (coincidentally, this is also the unhappy fate of many thwarted women artists). Confidence was a quality Louise herself often struggled to embrace, and—like the good witch she is—Ole Golly inculcated confidence early on in the child. Later, when Harriet finds herself, as in the Shakespearean sonnet, "in disgrace with fortune and men's eyes," a letter from Ole Golly reminds her to dig for this submerged resource. And while Louise attributed the doubts she felt regarding her own talent to a competitive father, Harriet's father seems fed up with the rat race. Mr. Welsch is in the television industry. He gives the impression of being a workaholic, but just to keep up, not necessarily because he's ambitious. Alixe Gordin believed she inspired the character of Harriet's father—which is interesting, given how often their mutual friends referred to Alixe as being like a mother to Louise.

Mr. Welsch is also Louise's vehicle for a further discussion on the incompatibility of art and money. He has a liberal philosophy, and "iniquity" is one of his favorite words (along with "fink"). While on her spy route, Harriet confronts the iniquities associated with class distinctions; in her home, her father rails against the iniquities associated with artists who must by necessity bow to mammon. He seems to have reconciled the compromises he has made in his own life, but he still has to deal with plenty of finks who think only of money and show no discernment or taste.

This was also Alixe's frequent complaint. In contrast to Mr. Welsch, Ole Golly's suitor and eventual husband, Mr. Waldenstein, has had a documented spiritual crisis. When profits come to mean nothing to him, he quits his job as a jeweler and seeks a more meaningful life. In her illustration of Mr. Waldenstein, Louise brings back the face of the man whom she first saw on shipboard in 1956, and whose portrait she had drawn many times. Here she has drawn him as a sympathetic companion. It is typical of Louise to have given him a profession that requires superb craftsmanship and an eye for beauty. Mr. Waldenstein, regretting nothing, builds his life over from the bottom, serenely and optimistically.

For Harriet, Yorkville is like a small town. A reader following Harriet's spy route, which runs from Eighty-Second to Eighty-Eighth Streets between York and East End Avenues, might start with the Dei Santis' delicatessen (around Eighty-Sixth and York),[11] where the poorest children rely on scraps from Little Joe Curry, the Dei Santis' grocery delivery boy. The Dei Santis themselves are merchants who are trying to make their family enterprise succeed, but they are constantly stymied by obstacles, including missing merchandise, a broken-down delivery truck, and the unpredictable work ethic of their children. Down the street (Eighty-Seventh between York and East End) and at the other end of the financial scale lives the wealthy Mrs. Plumber, who spends her life in bed and has a lady's maid. In one of the novel's iconic scenes, Harriet scrunches herself into the dumbwaiter in Mrs. Plumber's building to eavesdrop. She listens as Mrs. Plumber tells a friend on the telephone that she's discovered "the *secret* of *life*."

To which Harriet can only exclaim, "Wow." Mrs. Plumber's philosophy is deliciously Pascalian.[12] Her secret is to stay in bed, surrounded by boxes of chocolates and magazines, until something better reveals itself.

Continuing down the block (York and Eighty-Eighth), Harriet's spy route takes her to Mr. and Mrs. Robinson, whose art collecting Louise regards in the same spoofing spirit she brought to connoisseurs of modern poetry in *Suzuki Beane*. These bourgeois are dull and vulgar. Although they think themselves and their taste high tone, their enthusiasm renders them speechless. Louise's illustrations capture their herd mentality and canned zest for art.

At last, Harriet turns the corner to spy on Harrison Withers (Eighty-Second and York), who represents a kind of equipoise between the sharp intellectual pursuits of Ole Golly and the transcendence of Mr. Waldenstein. Withers is an anxious and solitary artist who is resigned to living on yogurt in order to provide sanctuary to his twenty-six beloved cats, whom Louise named after literary idols, baseball celebrities, and close friends.[13] His love of his creatures makes him vulnerable, however, and he suffers a tragic loss when the animal control department cruelly removes his dear feline companions. His face shows Harriet what a lost soul looks like, and his story reflects Louise's recurring fear of powerful forces destroying the defenseless artist. Louise is so fond of this particular character that she names him after Harriet.

Harriet's best friend Janie (who lives off East End Avenue on Eighty-Fourth Street) is already a dedicated professional. Janie knows she wants to be a scientist and is practicing through trial and error to blow up the world. Harriet admires her for her tough-mindedness. Her other best friend, Sport, is an excellent housekeeper and has given himself a little leeway regarding his future occupation. He'll either be a sports star or a certified public accountant. In the 1960s, the stereotypical CPA was a reliable if nerdy breadwinner. Louise was often looking for somebody versatile like Sport, who could keep a house going, freeing her from day-to-day details. In exchange she was prepared to provide the household's main financial support. In the novel, Harriet declares her intention to marry Sport. In any vows, Harriet would surely want to protect her spying and writing time—just like Louise. Sport's position on matrimony is not documented.

Louise drew on her southern past in her depictions of hierarchies and mores within Gregory School society. Harriet's main adversary, Marion Hawthorne, plays bridge and has tea parties with her cronies and lackeys. The girls act a lot like miniature versions of Memphis club women Louise knew in her childhood. It may have seemed to young Louise a displacement of so much female power and energy for those educated women to fritter away their lives on social events that only ever reinforced the status quo.[14] Over the course of the novel, Harriet's conviction that having a profession is worth the pain of loneliness is tested, but she doesn't betray her principles. Better to live on yogurt than to be a spy-catcher like Marion Hawthorne and her ilk. That's saying a lot for a child who—like her creator—enjoys a good lobster thermidor.

For some of the twentieth century's so-called children's literature gatekeepers—librarians, teachers, and members of parents' associations, who considered themselves protectors of children's welfare and arbiters of moral instruction—Harriet was a problem child. Not because she was naughty and kept a notebook full of often nasty observations, but because—despite Ole Golly's guidance—Harriet does not change. To this portion of the reading public, she was insufficiently contrite, never really chastened, and stayed mean. She does not, in the words of the McCarthy-era HUAC witch-hunters, many of them still active as Louise was writing her book, recant. Harriet thrives in the last chapter, intellectually engaged, fully capable of making friends and of being one. It was particularly irksome to the gatekeepers of yore that Ole Golly, an adult who should know better, encourages Harriet to get herself out of a jam by lying.

In fact, Ole Golly offers Harriet contradictory advice. "Always say exactly what you feel. People are hurt more by misunderstanding than anything else." And while some circumstances might demand a fib, Ole Golly affirms, "To yourself, you must always tell the truth." Agent Harriet's mission is to decipher *what* situation matches *which* aphorism—and to regain the trust of her assets—all in time for summer vacation.

Harriet agrees with Ole Golly's assessment that a little lie is a sort of social lubrication. A little lie is a little mask, useful for hiding all sorts of secrets. As an adult, Louise Fitzhugh was unapologetically out of the closet. She was also well aware of the trials a gay adolescent had to endure in hostile territory. A little lie to preserve your identity and self-respect can be a soul-saving measure. When you are alone, and it looks like your cover is blown, a spy uses all the weapons at her disposal.[15] When Louise said she wrote on behalf of kids in this lousy world, she meant, among many other things, this bigoted, homophobic one.

Harriet doesn't make a sudden shift from principled truth-telling to deceit and deception. She's already a proficient liar, and it's not really that big a deal. She lies from the start about her spy route. She knows it's dangerous, especially scrunching into that dumbwaiter at Mrs. Plumber's. But a reporter must be fearless in pursuit. Harriet is perhaps rather more an instinctual than a deliberate liar until her notebook is taken; with Ole Golly's encouragement, she apologizes efficiently in order to get her schedule back on track.

Although Harriet considers the art of compromise, that was not really something Louise often practiced. For instance, in a letter to her friend Fabio Rieti (written at the same time she was writing *Harriet the Spy*), she's as forthright as they'd always been with one another and as he expected her to be. They couldn't be the comrades they were, she said, if they didn't tell each other the truth about their art. In that spirit, she urged Fabio to take more risks, and to show more of the pain she knew he felt on his canvases. She encouraged him not to care so much about causing offense or pleasing people: "Painting should shock and burn and hurt and fly right off the walls with feeling."[16] It has to be that intense, she said, or you need to question what you've done.

There were other literary influences on Louise as she completed *Harriet the Spy*, particularly Harper Lee, and probably William Butler Yeats. *To Kill a Mockingbird*, set during the Jim Crow era of Louise's own youth, and told in the voice of Scout, a six-year-old girl, was a popular success from the time of its publication in 1960.[17] The movie, released in 1962, with its Oscar-winning performance by Gregory Peck as Scout's father, Atticus Finch, imprinted the novel's story of racism and heroism in Depression-era Alabama onto the national psyche. Harper Lee was celebrated as the author of a novel so monumental and important that it practically defined the twentieth-century South for a generation, and her book was prime material for Louise's satire. Harriet's role as an onion at the Gregory School's Christmas pageant is an homage to Scout's ham costume, which, in Lee's novel, protects its owner's life. Later, in the final pages of *Harriet the Spy*, Louise puts her own spin on Atticus Finch's famous adage: "You never really understand a person . . . until you climb into his skin and walk around in it." Harriet imagines what it must be like to walk in her friend Sport's shoes, "feeling the holes in his socks rub against his ankles."[18]

Imagining herself in Sport's socks is only part of Harriet's initiative to imagine herself as other creatures and objects. She has given a lot of thought to the subject:

> I HAVE TRIED TO BE A BENCH IN THE PARK, AN OLD SWEATER, A CAT, AND MY MUG IN THE BATHROOM. I THINK I DID THE MUG BEST BECAUSE WHEN I WAS LOOKING AT IT I FELT IT LOOKING BACK AT ME AND I FELT LIKE WE WERE TWO MUGS LOOKING AT EACH OTHER.[19]

Louise is riffing here on shape-shifters like the ones in the Yeats poem "Fergus and the Druid," a work she admired. The exhausted King Fergus has "been many things— / A green drop in the surge, a gleam of light / Upon a sword, a fir-tree on a hill / . . . And all these things were wonderful and great; / But now I have grown nothing, knowing all."[20] This is a droll rebuke to the literalists, the phonies, the finks, and the unimaginative adults who cannot see all the ways that Harriet has changed by the novel's end.

fourteen

DIVIDED LOYALTIES

When *Harriet the Spy* was published on October 21, 1964, a first, underwhelming review in *Harper's Bazaar* suggested that the novel published by Harper and Row "should provide a few innocent hours entertainment for pre-teenagers."[1] More perceptive reviewers soon recognized its charm and its power. In the *New York Times Book Review*, Gloria Vanderbilt wrote, "Harriet M. Welsch is an 11-year-old spy, partial to egg creams and tomato sandwiches, whose parents look upon her as though she were a curiosity put on television for their entertainment. We think she's delicious, but that's probably because she hasn't included us in her spy route—yet."[2] Vanderbilt was an enormously famous personality at the time, an artist, former model, and socialite, so this very positive review was a big deal. A review in the *School Library Journal* by Ellen Rudin placed Harriet "in the best tradition of literature's most anguished heroines."[3]

Soon after Ursula Nordstrom saw Rudin's review, she invited her to become an editor for Harper Books for Boys and Girls.

In the approach to the 1964 holiday season, *Harriet the Spy*'s popularity was spreading through word of mouth. Booksellers recommended it, and hip relations gave it to children for Christmas and Hanukkah. *Harriet the Spy* appeared almost exactly a year after the great social fracture that was the assassination of President Kennedy and just as the Civil Rights Act had finally been passed. It was the year the Beatles arrived in America and Sam Cooke sang "A Change Is Gonna Come." Stanley Kubrick's dystopian satire *Dr. Strangelove, or: How I Learned to Stop Worrying and Love the Bomb*, captured the comic incongruities of the era. In a December *New York Review of Books* roundup of the "Best Children's Books of 1964," Janet Adam Smith wrote that Harriet "makes no concessions and remains splendidly sour."[4] She closed with, "As I love a tiger behind bars, I love Harriet so long as she's caged in a book."[5]

In Memphis, the *Commercial Appeal* bubble machine was in full effervescence. "Gracious how these Memphis and Mid-South authors do win distinction," it fizzed, featuring a formal portrait from the archives of a glamorous, unsmiling Louise, her hair in a beauty-shop set.[6] In another, more candid photograph, taken at a Memphis bookshop called Erle Howry's Book Shelf in Poplar Plaza, Louise is autographing a book for her old friend "Der," now the stylish and pretty young society matron Ann DeWar Blecken.[7] Ann's friendly presence mitigated the general unpleasantness of Louise's Memphis homecoming: she felt judged by her family and disgusted by the white supremacist milieu. It was only a few months after passage of the Civil Rights Act of 1964, and the white establishment was for the most part still standing fast to its racist prejudices. In the snapshot, Louise and Ann are happy to see each other again. It is a tender and triumphant moment, just as Ole Golly had predicted for Harriet—that when she grew up and published books, her friends would line up to get their copies signed.[8]

Early in the new year, the blowback against Harriet began. First, in a syndicated book review published by the *New York Herald Tribune*, a critic was upset that the characters showed so little compassion.[9] Then, in February, two reviews targeted to conservative schoolteachers and librarians outside the metropolitan area called the book "pathetic." Ruth Hill Viguers wrote in *The Horn Book* that "the objects of Harriet's spying are merely depressing types. Her schoolmates, from ghoulish Janie to pathetic Sport, represent not reality but the distortion of caricature."[10] Patience Daltry's lugubrious review in the *Christian Science Monitor* was no match for its clever title: "The Cold That Came in with the Spy."[11] "Harriet is rather a pathetic figure," Daltry wrote. "Too pathetic one hopes for children to admire." Phyllis Cohen in *Young Readers Review* smeared Harriet as "un-child-like."[12] Ursula dismissed these complaints as inane; meanwhile, the novel practically flew out of bookshop doors.

The degree of *Harriet*'s popularity and attendant controversy surprised Louise. She found it at once exciting and excruciating to be in the public eye. She refused to participate in a marketing or publicity campaign, neither giving interviews nor making appearances at children's bookshops. Louise felt every criticism as a thorn and was frustrated by the few vehicles available to authors who wished to publicly defend their work. Custom dictated that writers and critics not communicate directly; those who broke protocol courted the disapproval of the literary tastemakers who policed the boundaries between art and marketing. A writer had only her advocates to act on her behalf.

In this, Louise found Ursula Nordstrom a stalwart defender. Charlotte Zolotow said she had a "whim of iron."[13] Ursula was also a diplomat and cultivated various champions, organizations, and institutions that might provide counterweights to any negative press. Louise's first novel had brought the attention and acclaim she had always wanted as a painter, but she suspected her celebrity would soon fade, as it had after *Suzuki Beane.* Ursula and Charlotte assured her that would not be the case: she had a readership now, and something to say that children were waiting to hear. Ursula was optimistic that if Louise finished another book by spring 1965, Harper could put it on the fast track for publication and provide a better marketing strategy, with better ad placement and more advance reviews in prestigious magazines.

Living in New York with Connie, Louise gradually absorbed the changes associated with being the author of a best-selling book. Her royalties, at least, were concrete evidence of *Harriet the Spy*'s success. The regular checks made her self-sufficient and independent at last from her family. Her first gift to herself was a beautiful 1965 Mercedes Benz convertible with red leather upholstery. *Harriet* also gave Louise the clout to help her friends. She introduced aspiring writer and illustrator Jane Wagner to Ursula Nordstrom, and she lent money to Barbara Phelan, who wanted to get out of the city rat race—an ambition Louise shared.

While the pro-Harriet forces were fighting on her behalf, Louise began an entirely new kind of art project.[14] She wrote to tell her friend Fabio that she was working from photographs to develop a new style borrowing from expressionist painters like Max Beckmann. She hoped eventually to paint monumental subjects, perhaps even make a painting of the Kennedy assassination. In this same letter, she counseled her old friend against falling for the seductions of pop art, which she distained as a fleeting fashion. She thought the artists and their creations alike were commercial garbage (apart from the sculptor George Segal, whom she thought superb, and the painters Robert Rauschenberg and James

Rosenquist, who each had a shot at becoming great). Andy Warhol and the rest of his crowd were just about surface style and clever packaging—about the money and not the art.

Louise grappled with her own divided loyalties as an artist. Her conflict wasn't so much between art and writing as it was about reconciling her writing for children with a sense that it wasn't serious work. It was popular, commercial, and successful. It came more easily than her other work. It wasn't risky. How could it be *art*?

One day, Louise visited her old friend Joan Williams in Connecticut. When conversation turned to their shared experience as young women artists in a man's world, Joan said she felt they had both benefited from having friends who had helped them up. They agreed that this kind of nurturing was essential for artists, and they felt it was incumbent upon them to help other artists when they could. Louise had been frustrated by an art establishment that always favored male artists, no matter how many women made art, ran galleries, or edited magazines, and she admitted she was still sometimes baffled by her new role as a children's author. She had considered her writing and illustration for children a diversion from the kind of art she still intended to produce. Surely *Harriet* was meaningful, but it was just one of the many things she'd tried in order to subsidize her painting.

Joan reminded Louise that her ambivalence about art and readership wasn't a new dilemma. Sometime after *Suzuki Beane* and Joan's first novel, *The Morning and the Evening*, had been published, they had made a joint appearance at a Memphis bookstore. The evening's hostess had introduced them as Hutchison alumnae who had gone north to conquer the literary world, and she praised both for their achievements as the writers of new books. Louise had turned to Joan at the time and mumbled, "Except mine is for children."

After Joan's sons went to bed, Joan and Louise sat up talking late into the night. Louise wondered why she had always felt so stuck in the old hierarchy, believing that painting and poetry were somehow superior to illustration and prose, and that writing adult literature was superior to kids' lit. If her experience had taught her anything, it was to resist all forms of supremacy in art and life. Joan and Louise agreed on the proposition that it was a whole lot easier and more fun to draw a character in fiction who learns from, and can *explain*, her experience than it was for a person to do so honestly in real life.

By 1965, the music of the Beatles had penetrated into even the coolest literary circles. Susan Sontag, wearing black boots, pants, and a turtleneck, discussed their influence with her publisher and patron Roger Straus. Straus played them on the hi-fi when he entertained his many lady friends. Lois Morehead, one of the triumvirate who had hosted the elegant costume parties at Frederica Leser's, and who had worked as a switchboard operator at Farrar, Straus and Giroux, was one of Straus's lovers, recruited from among his employees.[15] Frederica remembers Lois as one of Straus's "mistresses"—a quaint word that Frederica characterized as true to Straus's old-school style. Frederica liked him, she said. A lot of women did, a verity Straus parlayed in the era of free love into something of a mini-playboy empire. But that's another story.[16]

As more and more young Baby Boomers entered elementary classrooms, new public schools were built by the thousands to accommodate the unprecedented demand. In 1965, Congress passed the Elementary and Secondary Education Act of 1965. One of its provisions funded, among other things, new school libraries and the books to fill them, as well as many textbooks for children's classrooms. Barbara Alexandra Dicks, Ursula Nordstrom's secretary, said everyone knew they had caught a break when the act passed.[17] The expansion of children's education meant that children's book publishing was suddenly a booming market, and publishers embraced the windfall.

Ursula was a savvy businesswoman. If she'd been cautious at first about embracing the advent of paperbacks, questioning their sturdiness and staying power, by 1965 she had come to see the profitable mass-market paperback as the future of children's publishing.[18] Once she convinced Harper authors that a paperback book would not necessarily mean poorly produced pulp, or comic book quality, she could promise teachers and librarians affordable editions that would make classics easier to use in classrooms. Paperbacks also meant greater access to contemporary books—many of them, like *Harriet the Spy*, written in the new realistic vein. New Realism hit a nerve. An influential article published in the *New York Times Book Review* called for more children's books on socially relevant themes. It suddenly became an emerging trend, with *Harriet the Spy* in the vanguard.[19]

In 1965, *relevance* was the watchword for adult books, too. The emerging New Journalism propelled nonfiction books like *In Cold Blood*, by Truman Capote, and *The Kandy-Kolored Tangerine-Flake Streamline Baby*, by Tom Wolfe, to the best-seller lists. Open-minded readers found *The Autobiography of Malcolm X*, as told to Alex Haley, an essential resource months after his assassination. The civil rights movement—despite the kidnappings, bombings, and murders still taking place—continued its inexorable advance, juddering back and forth through protests, marches, trials, conventions, and sacrifice. In March 1965, Martin Luther King Jr. led his famous march to Selma. In New York City, complaints about police brutality toward Black and Puerto Rican people in general as well as toward antiwar protesters of any race became a common refrain.

Louise's political consciousness was adapting to the times. Like many others on the political left, she dismissed the state communism of the Soviet bloc and closely followed the resurgent human rights discussion and social liberation movements. Louise was fascinated by the idea of an incipient children's liberation movement. Well aware of reports of increasing police brutality against children, she would write an incident of prejudice against a young Black man into the third novel in her Harriet trilogy, *Sport*. In a later novel, *Nobody's Family Is Going to Change*, she condemned the murders of two African American youths, the ten-year-old Clifford Glover and the fourteen-year-old Claude Reese, by New York City police. In the same book, she would set her heroine the task of writing a children's bill of rights.

In February 1965, at long last, the review of *Harriet the Spy* that meant the most to Louise arrived. It was from Jimmy Merrill. "Your book is so good—so serious," he wrote, "as well as being funny; full of truth + understanding. I could find no fault with it (I don't mean that I tried very hard)." He wondered how the book was selling and asked, with pride and some envy, if she was getting fan mail—"from real-life schoolchildren? Governesses? Vegetables? Wonderful YOU!"[20]

Louise was able to say that it had become a best seller among children's books. Her publishers were happy, but as usual, she was full of doubt. She was starting another Harriet book, but she also wanted to finish *Mother Sweet, Father Sweet*, the play she'd been working on for years, and her novel for adults based on the same biographical story, *Crazybaby*. Success made it easier to accept that writing for children was a significant art form, but she also hadn't given up the idea that she could do everything.

Despite Louise's misgivings about being a children's author, she went ahead and wrote a second novel, first called *The Watermill Mystery*, then *The Long Secret*. Ursula read Louise's initial draft and returned it with a letter to reassure her that "marginal notes are to be IGNORED until you have finished the whole book. . . . Most of them are utterly complimentary."[21] Ursula especially loved reading the section of *The Long Secret* concerning the onset of a twelve-year-old girl's first period. "I plotzed!" she said.[22] To her knowledge, menstruation had never before been mentioned in a trade book for children.

In a comic and absorbing scene, twelve-year-old future scientist Janie Gibbs, familiar to readers from *Harriet the Spy*, undertakes to inform Harriet and her schoolmate Beth Ellen of the practical consequences of their natural biological cycle. Every thirty days or so, she explains, the mucousy endometrium that lines the uterus falls out if it hasn't been implanted with an embryo. Her audience is fascinated and disgusted by such facts of life. When Harriet, who has yet to get her period, declares she will not willingly participate in such a disgusting exercise, Janie has no sympathy. Every woman, even Nobel Prize winners like Madame Curie, suffer the same fate, she informs her friends.

In her letter to Louise, Ursula says, "I think you have handled this beautifully and we are grateful."[23] Louise, for her part, was grateful for her editor's composure and advocacy, especially when upper management became nervous about the passage, fearing the discussion about periods might cause controversy, "My God," Louise said to Frederica Leser, "What do they think women do?"

Ursula cheered and coaxed Louise through the revision of *The Long Secret*, as she had when they had worked together on *Harriet the Spy*. Louise's friend Marijane Meaker, who had observed Louise's writing process, said, "She was an editor's dream." M.J. had marveled at Louise's discipline and dedication to writing or revising at least ten pages a day.

Over the course of the next year, though, Louise had become a considerably less reliable author. She missed deadlines and did not return many of her editor's phone calls. She argued extensively with Ursula regarding one character's membership in the right-wing John Birch Society, which at that time was active on Long Island where *The Long Secret* was set. Indeed, it was a presence nationwide in the 1960s. Ursula didn't think Louise should give her character any particular affiliations, arguing that because her books would still be selling well into the future, "generalization will make more sense than 1965 specifics. I think the Birchers will be forgotten by then. But the respectable, cruel bigots will still be with us."[24] Louise acquiesced, but afterward she seemed less interested in Ursula's guidance on form and content.

While *Harriet the Spy* had come in as a rudimentary manuscript, Louise's manuscript for her second novel was complexly plotted and written in a distinctly idiosyncratic style. Louise told Jimmy that she'd decided to stick her neck out, and in this book she knew exactly what she wanted. Meanwhile, Ursula considered Louise to be "brilliant, erratic, moody, often extremely thoughtful and endearing." She said, "I loved her—through the bad times as well as the good."[25] Ursula kept trying to figure out how best to support Louise as an author, but fond as they may have been of each other, their working relationship was in a downward spiral. Once Ursula believed that Louise had become unreceptive, and more or less unyielding, Charlotte stepped in to edit *The Long Secret*.[26] Then, for reasons Charlotte says she never fully comprehended, Louise also began to doubt that Charlotte believed in her work as she once had.[27] At last, Ursula asked Ellen Rudin, the young editor who had written an early, glowing review of *Harriet the Spy*, to work with Louise and see the second book through to publication.[28]

The Long Secret, published in the fall of 1965, picks up twelve-year-old Harriet and her friend Beth Ellen the following summer, when their families are on vacation in Water Mill on Long

Island, New York. Harriet, still spying, is determined to discover who is sending around anonymous notes that ask their recipients to confront hard, personal truths. At the same time, Beth Ellen, who lives with her extremely wealthy grandmother, Mrs. Hansen, receives the surprising news that her jet-setting mother, whom she has not seen for seven years, is returning to Water Mill with her new boyfriend. Beth Ellen's subsequent tailspin is exacerbated by the onset of her period along with a confusing crush on Bunny, a dissipated fortyish pianist and lounge singer at a local hotel. Beth Ellen joins Harriet's spy team, and as in *Harriet the Spy*, spycraft becomes the medium for a girl's deeper understanding of herself in society.

The Long Secret is also to a great extent about the creative process. Harriet shows the reader how to pick up a sketchbook and start to draw, and how to solve a literary mystery. She is now a more mature and artistically confident writer who has graduated to carrying two notebooks, one for spying and another for storytelling. There is an unexpected digression in which Harriet demonstrates how a poem is made when, over four pages, she wanders through the alphabet (with increasing anxiety) trying to find the perfect word to rhyme with "rain." In one of the novel's several themes, religion and identity, the pianist Bunny, pursued by Agatha Plumber (in a return appearance after *Harriet the Spy*), categorically rebuffs an offer of marriage, claiming that his religion makes such a match impossible. He is a practicing Catholic and she is not, and he tells her in no uncertain terms that there will be no marriage: he will stay faithful to his religion. He says, "That is my life; that's just the way I am." Judging by the social cues and inferences, Bunny is a closeted gay man who is also an artist, not a parasite like Mrs. Plumber, who presumes far too much. He is always going to prefer men. That's his life. That's just the way he is.

In the course of their spying activities, Harriet and Beth Ellen (and later, their school friend Janie Gibbs) meet the Jenkinses, a family of evangelical grifters from Mississippi who are making toe medicine from watermelons—a kind of snake oil—to sell to gullible Long Island locals. The witchy and uncouth Mama Jenkins, who "walks like a truck" and drives a "white Maserati," is Louise's sly tribute to her grandmother on the Perkins side.

Mama Jenkins's daughter, Jessie Mae, also joins the spy team, and in the course of their surveillance the girls encounter "the Preacher," who is something of a prickly bodhisattva, and the only African American in the cast of characters. (Early on in the editing process, Ursula and Louise had clashed over the character of the Preacher, who Ursula thought veered too close to caricature.) The Preacher is one of only two adults in the novel—Harriet's mother is the other—who comes to rational conclusions after thoughtful examination of a societal problem. Mrs. Welsch's fields of expertise are class, status, and romance, while the Preacher's are spiritual and political matters. He tells the girls that he can no longer sit by while his people (the poor, Black population of the South) are drugged by religion. Instead, he believes in action, and by inference, the civil rights movement, which is shaking up the old ways. Over the course of the summer, Beth Ellen begins to consider becoming an artist someday, thanks to Harriet's conviction that everyone needs meaningful work. Harriet, meanwhile, under the Preacher's influence, agrees to become an agent of change. She is in the right mood for the rest of the sixties, when the most imaginative, restless, and curious youths of America would also refuse to sit by.

On October 7, 1965, Louise's father, Millsaps, died of pancreatic cancer in Memphis. He was sixty-two years old, and the doctor signing his death certificate noted significant other conditions: cirrhosis and diabetes. Over the following days, newspaper obituaries described a dedicated Republican loyalist and politician, a city booster, and an activist in charitable and social organizations. Millsaps had succeeded his father as attorney for the *Commercial Appeal* newspaper, and its editor, Frank Algren, was one of his pallbearers.

In her father's house after his lavish funeral, Louise went directly to her room and locked the door. She slept and then read through the obituaries and condolence cards. They recalled with sympathy Millsaps's radical break from the Democratic Party in 1936 and the reasons he gave for it: revulsion at Roosevelt's effort to pack the US Supreme Court with Democrats and concern for the health of the two-party system in Tennessee.

Distrusted and in many quarters reviled for his apostasy, Millsaps would later be recognized as something of a visionary for remaking the Tennessee GOP as a party where white people were comfortably in leadership again. He was a driven and intense campaigner for Dwight D. Eisenhower, served as western Tennessee's United States Attorney for six years, and from 1960 to 1963 had been chairman of Shelby County's Republican Party. He collected rare coins and was remembered for his love of tennis as well as for his polish. He was certainly debonair. Millsaps's confident, cutting, argumentative style was something Louise had long since absorbed and adopted to protect herself during their quarrels.

One of the articles Louise came across revealed an unexpected side of Millsaps in which he confided his dream of becoming a matador: "donning his suit of lights, and lifting curved sword against the proud charging beast."[29] Millsaps and Sally were apparently frequent visitors to the bullfights across the Mexican border from their Arizona winter home. Sally, the article relates, sometimes tossed a rose into the ring. It was a romantic scene. When Millsaps died, he and Sally had been married for thirty-two years. To the casual observer, they looked like a successful and powerful couple. But Louise knew their marriage had been tempestuous and that Sally had suffered from Millsaps's violent temper. There were rumors of his philandering.[30]

After the funeral, Charles McNutt visited the house on Lombardy where he and Louise had seen each other almost daily for a time as kids. Charles knocked on Louise's bedroom door, where she had retreated, and whispered some words of consolation through the wall, but Louise wouldn't see him or anyone else who came to pay their respects. Louise had rarely visited Memphis in the fifteen years since she'd gone north, and in all that time, she'd mostly disparaged her father. She had told several friends that she hated him, and she had drawn complicated and sometimes malign versions of him, both in her paintings and in her biographical plays and stories. At his funeral, Louise was sad, confused, and angry. She'd be depressed for some time to come.

After the funeral and the goodbyes, there was still one piece of business she had left to do in Memphis. Visiting a new car dealership, Louise paid cash for a brand new Jeep Wagoneer. And then she drove herself and Millsaps's rare coin collection back across the Mason-Dixon line.

The Long Secret was published on October 27, 1965. The reviews, despite their impressive placement in prestige publications, were not particularly enthusiastic or encouraging. Most of the interest surrounded Harriet's return: *The New Yorker* reviewer was disappointed that she wasn't as prominent in this follow-up. The book "is not as good as its predecessor, because Beth Ellen is not as interesting as Harriet, but it still has a degree of life and honesty that is well outside the mold."[31] Other reviewers agreed. *Kirkus Reviews* said, "*The Long Secret* is not as good, or perhaps cohesive, a story as the first one, partly because Harriet is subsidiary to her friend Beth Ellen."[32] The reviewer for *Book Week* quickly dispenses with *The Long Secret* and—apparently happy to get a second shot at Harriet—calls her "one of the most fatiguingly ill-mannered children imaginable."[33]

There is some discussion of religion in the reviews, but few of the reviewers took the evangelical Christian Jenkins family seriously as more than local color; most reviewers gingerly avoided direct discussion of the scenes depicting Beth Ellen's first period at the age of twelve. *Book Week* offered that "the girls' clinical discussion of the physical changes of maidenhood . . . will make squeamish parents blanch." *Kirkus Reviews* suggested, "There are however occasional sequences which make the book, rather than Harriet, vaguely (very vaguely, by our standards) liable to censure."

Carolyn Heilbrun in her *New York Times* review is the only one who discusses the subject of fulfilling work, to which Harriet is dedicated. Heilbrun, a feminist scholar known for her studies of Virginia Woolf, wrote mystery novels under the pseudonym of Amanda Cross. She praised *The Long Secret* for "allow[ing] its children, though they are girls, to know that work one really likes to do ranks alongside love as life's great experience." Employing the style of the fractured quotations sent as anonymous notes to people in the book, Heilbrun directs a message to the book's author: "Before Harriet turns into Eloise or Holden Caulfield or gets too involved with her father's old girlfriends, Miss Fitzhugh might care to devote herself to the proposition that novels of adults, by adults, and for adults shall not perish from the earth. I can't say nicer than that."[34]

To Louise, those were fighting words. Who was any critic to tell her who she should or should not write for? She had found, as she once vowed to Ed Thompson, a way to try to do something about the "rottenness of the world." Joan Williams said Louise told her that "writing for children gave her a wonderful sense of doing good."[35]

PART THREE

If I turned out to be a woman who lived in a way you didn't like, would you still love me?

—*Nobody's Family Is Going to Change*[1]

fifteen

LUCK, SPECULATION, WINDFALLS

In 1966, the journalist Nat Hentoff interviewed Maurice Sendak, the author of *Where the Wild Things Are*, for a *New Yorker* profile.[1] Among the items in Sendak's home studio—paintings, a classical record collection, and first editions of books—was a grand array of pens and brushes that Sendak said had minds of their own. "Some of these pens are with me, and some are against me," he told Hentoff. Sendak was not alone in anthropomorphizing his tools. Louise jokingly said she believed her typewriter was imbued with a creative power that helped her write for children.[2] Her friend M.J. Meaker—by then a successful crime novelist—said she and Louise had a long running joke about how exchanging their typewriters would give each instant mastery in the other's style and genre. Louise may have once wished to write a witty detective story for adults, but after publication of *The Long Secret*, she put those plans aside. By the mid-1960s, Louise and

Maurice Sendak were two of the most popular and successful authors of children's books.

They had much in common. Both belonged to the same playwrights' group; they shared a wicked and theatrical sense of humor; and they wrote and drew stubborn, antiauthoritarian children. Louise agreed with Hentoff that Sendak's drawings were so "intensely, almost palpably alive, they seem to move on the page and, later, in memory."

Louise knew Maurice was also gay—a detail not mentioned in Hentoff's article, where he is coded as a "bachelor"—and she considered him a Renaissance man, the highest compliment in their circle. After reading *The New Yorker* profile, Louise told her friend Sue Singer that Sendak was her hero, and she did not have many of those. Louise was particularly struck by Sendak's acknowledgment of the responsibility he felt in reaching so many children and his struggle to keep on good terms with the child inside. Resigned acceptance of a writer's former self was territory Sendak shared with the essayist Joan Didion, whose essay "On Keeping a Notebook," written that same year, counsels writers to keep on "nodding terms with the people we used to be, whether we find them attractive company or not. Otherwise they turn up unannounced and surprise us, come hammering on the mind's door at 4 a.m. of a bad night and demand to know who deserted them, who betrayed them, who is going to make amends."[3]

Louise didn't have a problem staying in touch with her younger self. Her friends were fascinated by how easily she fell into conversations with the girls and boys she met in passing, most of whom were the progeny of acquaintances. Her own childhood often occupied her. But although sometimes themes from her early years found their way into the pages of her books, her novels were hardly autobiographies. She may have wondered about the convergence of events that had made her a children's author, but she was practical enough to recognize that the first impulse had been commercial. When her painting career had faltered, she had needed to make money. Unexpectedly, she'd had really good luck conveying the character, comedy, and emotions of some imagined middle-grade children. She'd met Ursula and Charlotte, and alongside them she had come to feel like an advocate for the eleven-year-old mind.

Fame in itself didn't really interest Louise. When Ursula encouraged her to attend conferences and dinners to increase her readership, as authors commonly did, Louise demurred. Her decision was based in part on her suspicion that celebrity was fleeting, and in part it was because of her shyness with strangers. Alixe said Louise was always gregarious with friends but "intensely shy" otherwise. Since she was usually surrounded and protected by friends, her reserve hadn't ever been a problem before. But when asked to become more of a public personality, Louise balked. Even the *idea* of touring or giving talks made her nervous. The thought of having to dress for the occasion made her angry. She told Alixe she wasn't interested in squandering her time on self-promotion. It would only keep her from the work she wanted to do.

Jimmy Merrill was one of the few people Louise really trusted to tell her the truth about her life and work. She sometimes worried that he would tell her she was frittering away her talent or wasting her time, but he never did. He wrote from Athens to say he loved *The Long Secret*. Jimmy did not pull punches, and, to Louise's delight, he said he wished he could write such vivid and fully drawn characters. He asked, "Would a teen-aged Harriet enroll at Bard, in the sequel?"[4] Louise replied in the same comic tone, wondering at how naïve her own college shenanigans had been in contrast to the current gang of LSD-taking teenagers. She agreed that it would be funny to see an older, wilder Harriet at Bard, perhaps seasoning a tomato sandwich with pot.[5]

That spring, Louise tried to write another novel about Harriet. In one manuscript of a hundred pages, the twelve-year-olds Harriet, Janie, Beth Ellen, and Sport all attend dancing school, where Harriet falls for twelve-year-old Willie, an African American boy whom Louise would feature at length in her later novel *Nobody's Family Is Going to Change.* That manuscript's other themes are infidelity, divorce, and money—all sophisticated topics—but in 1966, an interracial crush in a comedy of manners for kids would have made this plot an even more radical harbinger of change than its predecessors.[6]

Louise kept trying to shape the same material and characters. In another false start, Mr. Welsch decides to drop out of his job, become a writer, and move with his reluctant wife and child to Connecticut. Louise only wrote fifty pages of this story before she put the draft away. Finally she settled on a comic, fast-paced story line featuring Sport that was set primarily in New York's Plaza Hotel. It helped that, in between her acting jobs, Connie took over all the cooking and household duties they usually shared. Once again, Louise had someone looking after her while she looked after her art.

Louise zipped off a first draft before intervening events forced *Sport* to the back burner. Her father's death had hit her harder than she had anticipated and her life seemed awry. Sandra and Alixe had both heard Louise say how much she disliked Millsaps, and that she had disliked him since childhood. Nevertheless, her friends in Memphis said he spoke of Louise with pride and affection. Joan Williams told Louise that once when her mother had run into Millsaps they'd talked about their daughters, and Millsaps's eyes had filled with tears. Josephine Walt, a Fitzhugh first cousin, later said, "Millsaps never minded her going north. He wanted to remain in a good relationship. . . . It was she who left us, not we who left her."[7]

Louise had left Millsaps and Memphis without regret and with the intention never to return. The force of her grief now caused a welter of unexpected emotions, including frustration that even in death Millsaps was somehow thwarting her. She was having a hard time focusing on new work or much of anything, and she was also suffering a bad case of wanderlust. (She and Connie might have jetted off to visit Jimmy and David in Paris and Athens had Connie's acting not kept them in New York.) Louise wrote to Jimmy about how hard it was to keep going on her book. There was something like a death pall around it; whenever she got up a head of steam, she was called back to Memphis to attend a funeral. It was not only Millsaps who had died. Sally Fitzhugh's father had also died in the past year, along with one of Louise's uncles, Andrew Owens Holmes, Mary Fitzhugh's husband, who had been a judge on the Tennessee Supreme Court.

When Connie found a job on the soap opera *Another World* (a character she would play for the next twenty-five years), Louise shifted her base of operations to her summer rental in Quogue, Long Island, where Connie visited on weekends. Still unable to focus on new work, querulous, and in low spirits, Louise found new distractions and ways to fritter. Pot was suddenly available and abundant on the end of Long Island. Head shops, with their hippie aesthetic of beads and feathers, were popping up in surrounding towns.

In a letter to Jimmy, Louise wrote that the Hamptons suddenly seemed to be overrun by affluent teenagers taking LSD. She was not unsympathetic to the hippies, who camped on the beaches and drove around in gangs of twenty or more, but they were noisy and unconcerned with cleaning up after themselves. She and friends like Sue and Alixe started calling them a race of giant babies. When Jimmy wrote back to ask Louise what she wanted him to bring her as a gift from Carnaby Street, the fashion hub of Swinging London, Louise told him, "As to Carnaby Street my dear I *am* Carnaby Street. Bring me anything as I love it all."[8] Given her size, she continued, she was hard to fit, so a tie was probably the wisest choice.

When it came to what to wear, Louise had style. Her work outfit was typically a pair of paint-covered overalls, but sometimes she would dress like a preppy boy. She often mixed her fashions: she would wear combat boots with a Brooks Brothers gray suit, for example, sometimes with a cape. She loved capes. She was always a petite person, and capes gave her increased mass, presence, and substance. She had some stylish three-piece suits made at a tailor's. One black cashmere suit made of heavy wool included a fashionable matching cape lined with water repellent taffeta, reversible in bad weather. Periodically, Louise would weed her closet and Sue Singer would inherit a pile of beautiful but barely worn button-down Brooks Brothers shirts.

That summer, Louise's mother came from Clarksdale to visit her in Quogue. Unlike Alixe, who had clashed with Mary Louise, Connie got along relatively well with her. For her part, Mary Louise had made peace with her daughter's world. There would not have been any reward in discussing Louise's choice of friends or lack of a husband. She surely must have been aware of her daughter's sexuality. Louise slept in the same bed as Connie, just as she had with Alixe. In any case, it was not a subject that mother and daughter discussed. Perhaps on occasion Mary Louise thought back to her marriage to Millsaps, who had been so passionately vocal about insisting that it was improper for girls to sleep together.

Mary Louise reveled in her daughter's success. For a librarian to have a child who was a best-selling author was an unmitigated pleasure, affording unexpected status. That Louise's books were so interesting and funny was an added happiness. She'd defend them to any old crank who said a word against them. And although money was another subject they did not normally discuss, for Mary Louise, who had been denied custody of her daughter and had been turned away at the Fitzhughs' door, enjoying her adult daughter's largesse was sweet revenge. Millsaps had tried his best to keep Mary Louise from getting one dime of his money, but Louise was generous and would treat her mother to New York holidays and vacations in the Hamptons.

During Mary Louise's visit that summer, Louise introduced her mother to her publisher, Ursula Nordstrom. They got on well together and later, from Mississippi, Mary Louise wrote Ursula a charming note, which Ursula related to Louise. She "loved meeting some of your friends . . . and loved being introduced as your mother and Harriet's grandmother. Said she'd never been so proud in her life."[9] For her part, Louise found there were unexpected benefits to her mother's visits. In one letter to Jimmy she wrote that after one stay of four days, her mother's Mississippi accent still reverberated in her ears. Her turns of phrase were so vivid and syrupy that she could almost pour them onto the pages of her play. The play under discussion was *Mother Sweet, Father Sweet*. She had returned to it while her work on the *Sport* manuscript stalled.

In September, back in the city, Ursula urged Louise to show her some part of the *Sport* manuscript. The outcome was not good. Ursula considered the book underwritten, and in return, Louise ignored most of her suggestions for revision. Charlotte Zolotow again stepped in as editor, but Louise was not prepared to work agreeably with her either. Louise may just have become bored by the prospect of another sequel to *Harriet the Spy*. She didn't need the money, and she never liked repeating herself. She confided in Alixe that since Ursula and Charlotte had not liked what she had written so far, she was putting *Sport* aside again. Ursula and

Charlotte tried to coax Louise out of what seemed like petulance, but she ignored their phone calls and letters. Instead, she began to work on an adult novel called *Christmas Dinner*. In this, she returned to her biography, perhaps looking to Flannery O'Connor for inspiration. She was trying to tell the story of her own southern childhood as dark comedy. O'Connor had died about two years before, in 1964, but her reputation had continued to grow, and Louise admired her work. Despite its festive title, *Christmas Dinner* was not a happy experience. Louise was depressed, still struggling in the wake of Millsaps's death, and the words would not come. She described it to friends as something like a moldering fowl. It was hard to gain momentum, and she kept expecting to be called back to Memphis for yet another funeral.[10] Her stepmother, Sally, was suffering from end-stage emphysema.

Sally died in March 1967. There had been a time, not long after Louise had left for Bard, when, as part of the story she spun about escaping a Southern Gothic childhood, she had described Sally as a mythically mean stepmother. At the time, when her childhood friend Ann DeWar Blecken caught wind of this, she thought Louise must have misremembered. Ann believed that Louise may have had to demonize her parents, including Sally, in her own mind in order to break away from Memphis. "It took a lot of grit for her to leave. But she could not convince *me* she disliked Sally; I was there," Ann later said.

When she had the chance, Ann had confronted Louise. "I just looked at her and she backed down." Ann was one of the few people who could ever say that she got Louise Fitzhugh to back down. Louise admitted she had been out of line, exaggerating Sally's character for effect. Nevertheless, it was true that she had mixed feelings. It was not until her stepmother was dying that she realized she had really loved Sally.[11]

As for Sally, she had no mixed feelings toward Louise. In her will, she wrote, "I referred to LOUISE FITZHUGH as my daughter. While she was not the child of my body she was in every other respect my daughter. Her father and I were married when she was an infant and she has been as dear to me as though she were of my own blood."[12]

With her inheritance from Sally, Louise fulfilled her longtime ambition to live in the country. She bought a lovely old house in Cutchogue, on the North Fork of Long Island. It was on a bluff overlooking Long Island Sound, with a ladder down to the beach. The neighborhood was quiet and rural, and half an hour away from the fashionable Hamptons. The house had a big attic that Louise used as a storage area, keeping some of her unfinished manuscripts there. She hoped to make progress in the quiet of the country. Among the papers she brought with her from the city was an untitled manuscript she had begun some years before: a fictionalized version of her relationship with Amelia Brent.

One late night in the summer of 1967, Louise telephoned Alixe, who could hardly hear her friend on the other end of the line. Louise murmured, in a sad little voice, "Someone has stolen my manuscript. It's gone." According to Louise, her Amelia manuscript, composed of several chapters and notes at that point, had simply disappeared from the attic. Alixe wondered, "Who could have done such a thing?"[13] They discussed possible culprits, but there was no proof and no way of saying even when such a theft might have occurred. Louise did not want to call in the authorities. She scoured the house looking for it. All her other manuscripts, journals, and paintings were still there, but the Amelia book did not turn up. It felt to her as though she had lost Amelia all over again. It would be too painful to re-create. Many times, Alixe encouraged Louise to tell the story another way, perhaps in a play, but she never would.

Over the years, rumors accumulated that the Amelia manuscript had been a completed novel and that it might have made history as the first lesbian love story marketed for a young adult audience. The piece may have been stolen. Or Louise may have misplaced it, somehow losing it in the move from Manhattan to Cutchogue. Perhaps she accidentally burned it in a bonfire on the beach. She could have somehow trashed it in a hundred different ways for a hundred different reasons. Whatever the case, it was gone.

Meanwhile, *Harriet the Spy* had proved to be a durable sensation. Fans wrote to ask for more news about Harriet and her friends, and Ursula continued to urge Louise to write another sequel. The two women didn't socialize much, and Louise rarely attended events where she was likely to run into other writers, especially ones she didn't know. But around Christmas she accepted an invitation to attend a party at Ursula's United Nations Plaza apartment. Ursula would have invited most of the Harper Books for Boys and Girls office staff and editors, along with some journalists and columnists, to mingle with her authors and illustrators. E. B. White, for one, liked to come to Ursula's when he was in town. Louise would likely have dressed for the occasion in something mod, à la Carnaby Street, perhaps her blue velvet pantsuit beneath a black cashmere cape.

A literary holiday gathering that season would have had some cool jazz playing in the background and assorted guests who looked like they'd walked out of *New Yorker* cartoons: thin men with bangs flopping over horn-rimmed glasses and young women with beehive hairdos chain-smoking cigarettes. The holiday fashion demanded canapés like mini-quiches and pigs-in-blankets, and drinks like Tom and Jerries, hot buttered rum, and mulled wine. Conversations would have swirled around the Vietnam War protests, draft-card burning, women's liberation, underground newspapers, and, of course, the year in books. It had been a strong year in literary fiction, led by translations of *One Hundred Years of Solitude*, by Gabriel García Márquez, and Mikhail Bulgakov's *The Master and Margarita*. Everyone was talking about Marshall McLuhan's *The Medium Is the Message*, and some breakout books were attracting a new "hippie" audience. The latter included *Trout Fishing in America*, by Richard Brautigan, and Angela Carter's *The Magic Toyshop*. The second volume of *The Diary of Anaïs Nin*, covering 1934 through 1939, was securing an expanding and passionate readership, and the mass-market publication of Jacqueline Susann's *Valley of the Dolls* was impossible to ignore for its sales and salaciousness. But the big story that year was S. E. Hinton's book *The Outsiders*, published by Viking. Written by a teenager for teenagers, it didn't really fall into any established genre. It would soon become the keystone of a powerful new commercial force called "Young Adult books."

Later in the evening, as the party wore down and Motown music replaced Miles Davis on the record player, Ursula came upon Louise dancing by herself. "She was marvelous—such rhythm, and on her face a rapt inner contemplation of the music and the beat, and the general pleasure she was experiencing." When Ursula complimented her performance, Louise replied, "Well, my mother was a hoofer."

In February 1968, George Woods and Margaret F. O'Connor of the *New York Times Book Review* staff selected the paperback *Harriet the Spy* as one of the "Best in the Field" for children. In their commendation, they described Harriet as a "slightly zany child" who reports her "shrewd observations . . . in a secret notebook." The book was "vigorously original in content and style."[14] This was high praise indeed from the New York establishment. Louise might have felt encouraged under other circumstances, but she was still grieving the deaths of her father and stepmother. She felt stuck and unable to write; for the first time she found that even her drawing, which had always flowed effortlessly, was stalled.

Ursula, who had coaxed writers through writer's block before, sent Louise the following quote from the choreographer Martha Graham:

> There is a vitality, a life force, an energy, a quickening that is translated through you into action, and because there is only one of you in all of time, this expression is unique. And if you block it, it will never exist through any other medium and it will be lost. The world will not have it. It is not your business to determine how good it is nor how valuable nor how it compares with other expressions. It is your business to keep it yours clearly and directly, to keep the channel open. You do not even have to believe in yourself or your work. You have to keep yourself open and aware to the urges that motivate you. Keep the channel open.[15]

Louise kept the paragraph typed on a sheet of paper folded in her wallet as a talisman. The words were consoling but little defense against the forces unsettling her life. While getting out of town had become Louise's abiding passion, Connie, now a leading actress in a Monday-through-Friday television series, was not interested in a permanent home outside New York. Louise had hoped they would travel together to Europe, but Connie's schedule hardly allowed for a Hamptons weekend. Wanting a less constrained life, Louise felt low and let down. When Ursula heard that Louise and Connie might be on the rocks, she conceived a grand, rather desperate idea to lift Louise's spirits and keep her involved at Harper. She wrote to Charlotte proposing that Louise illustrate Charlotte's next picture book:

> Dear Charlotte Please please please take up this challenge. I know you cannot write to order, but you can be galvanized by this opportunity to come up with something terrific. Louise will

> be very difficult for any editor . . . but if the text is by you, she will be more reasonable than she would be otherwise. She has great regard for you as a writer, as a person, and she raved about you as an editor to Maurice Sendak as recently as a year ago.

Charlotte agreed to send Louise the text of her picture book *My Friend John*. Louise's silence in reply seemed at first an indication that she had not rejected the idea outright. In fact, Louise liked the story very much, and she may have made some preliminary sketches. But she never showed these to Ursula or Charlotte. As her grievances hardened against Harper, she put them aside unfinished.[16]

Like a lot of other people in the year in 1967, Louise sometimes felt as if the whole world were going crazy. The quiet of Cutchogue offered some peace of mind, but no place was far enough away to escape news of the escalating war in Vietnam, the draft, and news of dying soldiers. Louise was deeply troubled by US policy, which seemed unhinged. She feared that the war would expand and continue indefinitely, a horrible prospect. To Jimmy, she wrote, "That cowboy in the White House [meaning President Lyndon Johnson] will then mobilize us all, I suppose." In the jargon of the sixties, "mobilize us all" meant that everyone in their circle would end up joining the growing protest movement. Connie and she were bickering, meanwhile, and over the next few months they would break up. Connie moved out and Louise struggled to focus on the things that had been most important to her—art, writing, and old friendships.

Louise's relationship with her friend and writing partner Sandra Scoppettone had often been quarrelsome, but they agreed on at least one thing entirely: their opposition to the escalating war in Vietnam. Pat Schartle sold Harper on the idea of a new picture book illustrated by Louise Fitzhugh that would speak to kids and adults alike. Louise and Sandra reassembled their team to co-write a book with an antiwar theme. They called it *Bang Bang You're Dead.*

When Louise and Pat met in Ursula's office that spring to discuss Louise's works in progress, Ursula made a note that Louise seemed rundown and gloomy. Ursula reassured Louise that Harper and Row believed unreservedly in her talent and held her in high regard as one of their finest writers. Louise wanted to talk about the new picture book for children that she was writing with Sandra, and became frustrated when Ursula steered the conversation to Louise's Harriet trilogy. Was Louise making any progress on the latest Harriet story set in Connecticut? Was there anything her editors could do to help move *Sport* forward?[17] Louise suspected that Ursula was not fully behind *Bang Bang You're Dead*, and she was disappointed that her publishers seemed to consider the picture book's potential commercial success or failure more important than its artistic and social value.

Ursula was at a considerable disadvantage, as she had not yet seen any of Louise's preliminary sketches or even the text for *Bang Bang You're Dead.* She asked Pat to please send these items to the book designer so they could at least start selecting type. She also urged Louise to trust that they knew their business when it came to picture books. Even Maurice Sendak—Louise's hero, as Ursula knew—still stopped by to show Ursula the early mock-ups of his new books.

Ursula also asked Ladislav Svatos, a book designer in her division, to answer Louise's questions about the design and production of picture books, especially as they related to her ideas for *Bang Bang You're Dead.*[18] Louise wanted the illustrations to be printed in full color, and Svatos's explanation—that full color was particularly expensive and complex—only reinforced Louise's sense that her book would not receive the budget and attention it deserved. She suspected he was patronizing her, which only served to harden her position. Worse, she suspected Ursula of humoring her. Ursula assured Louise that no one at Harper and Row wanted to foist their ideas on her or constrain her freedom, and they would do their best to give her everything she wanted. In fact, while practical Ursula and perceptive Charlotte supported the book's antiwar stance, neither considered *Bang Bang You're Dead* a commercially viable project. They valued it mainly because it was important to Louise.

Louise then brought her coauthor, Sandra, along to what turned out to be another disappointing meeting. Ursula, who hadn't expected Louise to bring her coauthor, was caught off guard. It was an awkward situation, and Ursula, at her most imperious, handled it poorly. She invited Louise into her office first, while leaving Sandra to sit in a waiting area. Louise reacted angrily at Ursula's lack of courtesy. She argued that "Sandra as co-writer had every right to attend their meetings and express her own opinion."[19] Eventually, Sandra was called in, and she met both Ursula, whom Sandra described as "mean and heavyset," and Charlotte, "the opposite of Ursula, extra sweet and thin." It seemed clear to Sandra that Ursula wasn't interested in hearing what she had to say. For Louise, this was further proof that Harper no longer had her best interests at heart.

On April 4, 1968, Louise was shattered when Dr. Martin Luther King Jr. was assassinated in Memphis at the Lorraine Motel, a location Louise could see clearly in her mind's eye. The subsequent violence and anxiety, and the riots and protests, in cities and on college campuses across the country exacerbated Louise's own restlessness and loss of heart.[20] The illustrations she drew for *Bang Bang You're Dead* capture that era of social unrest as well as her own discontent.[21]

Stress was wearing Louise down, so she was not at all surprised when her doctor warned her to take her high blood pressure more seriously. He advised her to radically cut back on her drinking, to lose weight, to exercise more, and to stop smoking. Connie had moved out by then, and Louise was lonely and finding life hard to manage. She had many friends, but for the past twenty years she had almost always been in one meaningful relationship or another. After Connie left, Louise made what Frederica would call "a rather brutal painting—but an interesting one . . . two stubby vaguely childlike figures . . . being ripped apart. Literally dismembered by their separation, with only the tips of their fingers still entwined. The dull canvas is splattered with a thin blood-like red."[22]

In June, living alone in her Cutchogue house, Louise was doing all the things she had been advised against. She was stressed and smoking cigarettes; she was bingeing on steak, pizza, fried clams with tartar sauce, and rich desserts; and she was drinking a lot of expensive brandy. She had fallen in with the crowd that hung around Patricia Hemingway, a lean, sporty, charismatic, and disreputable perennial on the summer circuit. M.J. Meaker called Hemingway "the most famous lesbian barkeep in New York" and described her "as having a kind of Garbo look, feminine but with a masculine, aggressive aura," adding that she "cut a swath through the lesbian world. A lot of people found her extremely irresistible, including Louise, for a time."

Whatever Pat Hemingway did, she did with style. She was a mesmerizing talker, had an encyclopedic knowledge of fashionable cocktails, practiced transcendental meditation, and was a notably good car mechanic. She could, if she wished, divulge the secrets of any number of indiscreet summer visitors, advise on the appropriate outfit to wear to a job interview, and provide directions to the closest auto junkyard (A&B Wrecking in Speonk, Long Island).

Louise's new association with Pat was a turn-around from the summer before, when she and Alixe had mocked her as "that terrible Pat Hemingway" and "Bat-cunt." Hemingway and her boon companions—including the rich and notorious society diva and DuPont heiress Francis Carpenter, who purportedly was the model for Mrs. Plumber in *Harriet the Spy*, and Hugh Shannon, a lounge singer like Bunny in *The Long Secret*—were like characters out of Maupassant crossed with Flannery O'Connor. Maybe that's what attracted Louise to them: there was something sinister and Southern Gothic in their plotting assignations with married women and men, the threat of outing someone fecklessly, and their habits of rubbing shoulders with mafiosi, gambling, crashing fast cars, and overindulging in cocaine and champagne. They were louche, profligate, licentious, and debauched, and the population of the Hamptons was helplessly fascinated with their shenanigans.

Pat and Louise's affair began soon after Louise temporarily lost her driver's license. She had been alone, speeding in her Thunderbird convertible, when the cops pulled her over for reckless driving.[23] For someone who loved her cars, as Louise did, and who had never before been punished for such a transgression, this was a shock to the system. There was no other way to get around in that part of Long Island; trains were infrequent, buses slow, and taxis required booking in advance and were still unreliable and expensive. You needed friends if you did not have wheels. Although Pat worked nights as a bartender, she always seemed available to drive Louise anywhere she wanted to go. For a time, while she was not writing and not drawing, Louise found Pat bewitching company.

Pat's employer, Francis Carpenter, liked to have beautiful people around. Her coterie of amusing gay men and witty, useful women attended her at lavish parties and at fancy dinners in exclusive clubs.[24] She often invited famous personalities from the intersecting worlds of film, theater, or fashion to stay at her Southampton mansion. Liz Smith, the New York gossip columnist whose modest summer rental was nearby, used to sit on her roof with friends and watch through binoculars as Greta Garbo or Oscar de la Renta took a morning walk on Francis's private beach.

Francis's beach, with its white sand dunes and ideal swimming conditions, may have served as the location for that summer's jamboree of Dykes on Bikes. They were not yet the incorporated motorcycle organization they would become later in the 1970s, just sundry motorcycle enthusiasts who rode their Harley-Davidsons to converge for a festive weekend. They were not drifters, deviants, or violent gang members, but a utopian tribe for whom the term "dyke" was a compliment, representing self-respect and power. They camped in tents, cooked over campfires, swam, drank, played music, made love, and performed some light motorcycle repair. Mostly, the idea was to spend a few days of freedom without a straight man in sight. They had camp names like Pacifica and Raven and Tyke. Louise may have introduced herself as Willie, one of the sobriquets she'd been test-driving.

Louise's friends had seen her sample various male identities over the past few years. She had occasionally called herself Peter when Sandra first met her. Connie called her Sport. Ursula confirmed that in the years after *Harriet the Spy* was published, Louise still could look like a twelve-year-old boy. M.J. agreed, but not a sloppy boy: "Louise was very well tailored. She wore nice clothes, male clothes," M.J. said. "She was like a wonderful-looking little Victorian boy, running around in her boots and suits."

It may have been the weather turning. Louise may have just been ready to trade in her T-shirts and shorts. It may have been the morning after another bacchanalia on the beach, or just after one party too many. For whatever reason, Louise decided to pack up her house. Her friends agree that her fling with Pat did not end well. M.J. said, "I know that they were very happy for a time. . . . But any kind of a barkeep doesn't have a normal life." Their fling was brief, but Louise had fallen hard. By autumn, she was back in New York, again brokenhearted, with hardly a new word written.[25]

sixteen

TRADECRAFT

Not long after Richard Nixon won the presidential election of 1968, his Republican administration began to chip away at the domestic largesse of the Lyndon Johnson years. The Department of Defense was sucking up the greater part of the national budget for the war in Vietnam, leaving little for educational programs like those mandated under the Elementary and Secondary Education Act, with its benefits for libraries and schools. Children's publishing might have suffered more than it did if not for the success of paperback trade and mass-market editions. Dell Publishing, led by George Nicholson in its juvenile division, purchased the paperback rights to books for children in the lower grades that they predicted would become classics. In 1967, Dell launched its first list of Yearling Books, "Tasteful paperback editions that were faithful to the originals." Their catalog included E. B. White's *Charlotte's Web* and *Stuart Little*—and Louise's *Harriet the Spy*.[1]

As Ursula Nordstrom had anticipated, these less expensive paperback versions reached children far beyond their initial readership. In many schools they were added to core reading lists. Paperbacks published a year or so after a hardcover version were an industry-wide boon. In addition to all the suppliers of paper, ink, and offset printing costs, a new paperback edition required editors, new book designers, publicists, and marketers. Many magazines and newspapers began publishing "New in Paperback" columns for children's books. For Christmas 1968, Louise's two Harriet novels were repackaged as part of an omnibus volume.[2]

As *Harriet the Spy*'s reach and influence grew, so did new and recurring criticism of it.[3] Harriet's lying, spying, cursing, and general antiauthoritarianism appealed to many young readers, but its critics would cite the same factors as evidence of muddled ethics. If early reviewers in mainstream newspapers and magazines evaluated *Harriet the Spy* mainly for its literary merit and social impact, subsequent reviews by teachers and children's librarians in industry journals looked rather for the book's so-called usefulness to children. The controversy growing around *Harriet the Spy* would not be about *banning* the book, but about *buying* it. Banning a children's book was not like a public burning. But it was still significant. Children's librarians who opposed the book for any reason simply did not order it—or later might tidily weed it from a shelf. If *Harriet the Spy* were to reach children and secure its reputation, it would be because enough librarians advocated for it and included it in their budgets.

The argument over the book's value divided children's librarians into two main camps. Those opposing it were bothered by its urbanity and wickedness; there was recurring criticism from librarians who said that Harriet and her friends were unnatural, dishonest, and immoral. One librarian worried that the book's readability made it "dangerous in a child's hand." Those who supported the book did so with equal passion. One advocate wrote that Fitzhugh "brushed away the cotton candy cobwebs." Another declared that if her library refused to purchase copies of *Harriet the Spy*, she would supply copies herself.[4]

On April 3, 1969, the *New York Times* published an appraisal by its cultural reporter Harry Gilroy, who noted that children's books were moving further into realism.[5] Louise Fitzhugh was recognized as a forerunner of the trend—in *Harriet the Spy*, for its awareness of adult matters like divorce and alcoholism, and in *The Long Secret*, for its practical and comic discussion of menstruation.[6]

Several months after Gilroy's article, and under Ursula's guidance, Harper and Row would publish John Donovan's *I'll Get There. It Better Be Worth the Trip*, the first gay novel for adolescents. Many librarians and teachers welcomed the book. Others called it "inappropriate" (a word becoming ubiquitous and useful for many occasions), arguing that such portrayals robbed children of their innocence.[7] Then, in 1970, Bradbury Press (later acquired by Macmillan) published Judy Blume's *Are You There, God? It's Me, Margaret*. Blume's book explored the kinds of problems that advocates of the New Realism had hoped to see featured. Louise Fitzhugh may have breached the wall with *Harriet the Spy*, but time would prove it a distant relation to the rush of problem novels that followed.[8] These books, addressing topics like identity and self-respect as its characters overcame sorrow, emotional distress, and physical pain, were mostly welcomed by a newer generation of gatekeepers as refreshing developments in children's literature. Many of these issue-driven novels were the advance guard in what would become the new and commercially successful Young Adult genre that *The Outsiders*, published the previous year, had foreshadowed.[9] Those initial Young Adult books fed a hunger in kids for characters who resembled them and exhibited feelings—joys and worries—similar to their own. In short, young people wanted to read about characters they could relate to.

A reader can draw a line from the teen-oriented fiction of the 1970s back to the adult pulp of previous decades. There is relatively less costume drama than in the earlier pulp books, and many more heart-to-heart talks, but the pacing is similar. They share an emphasis on galloping dialogue and narrative twists and turns. The typical hard-boiled prose of pulps is replaced in Young Adult books by slangy but earnest language, although cynics and sarcasm still abound. As in the pulps of yesteryear, even antiheroes have their day—but there is at least one sensible adult, and good is eventually rewarded. Louise's versatile friend M.J. Meaker would become a leading author in this genre, publishing her first Young Adult book, *Dinky Hocker Shoots Smack*, under the pen name M. E. Kerr.[10] Sandra Scoppettone would also publish successful kids' books as part of her diverse portfolio, starting with *Trying Hard to Hear You.*[11]

By 1970, another literary trend, that of *journaling*, began seeping into the mainstream. The publication, since the mid-1960s, of Anaïs Nin's diaries led a generation of bold young women, inspired by Nin's poetic ethos, to forswear "ordinary life" and "seek only the high moments . . . searching for the marvelous."[12] Even for less fabulous practitioners, journal writing was becoming a popular exercise. It was considered helpful for focus and concentration, and aspiring and working writers alike started recording their *pensées*. This trend was good news for Harriet. For the younger set, Harriet's notebook was a generally recognized cultural artifact. In a 1970 advice column for adolescents, called "Ask Beth," a reader with the pseudonym "Bored" complained that her friends were allowed to carry notebooks in which they wrote "all kinds of things about the people they see," but her mother told her to keep hers at home, "because someone might read it and get mad at me." Beth advised "Bored," "Carry scratch paper and read *Harriet the Spy* by Louise Fitzhugh—it tells what happens to girls who write personal comments in notebooks."[13]

Many devoted young writers dismissed such agony-aunt advice and took the risk. Over the next decade, children (mostly girls) would form *Harriet the Spy* clubs. Sometimes they'd dress like Harriet.[14] Sometimes they'd share their writing, but more often they regarded their journal entries as sacred and private. They were well aware of the trouble associated with unintended (or unappreciative) readers. Like Harriet, these kids were dedicated to firsthand experience. Knowing everything is not an uncommon ambition for an eleven-year-old—and while Harriet was fortunate to have had a nanny to help her connect the art of spying to the craft of composition, these fledging writers had Harriet. Independently, they went to work noticing details, characterizing emotions, and imagining histories. In some cases, they converted their impressions into stories. From such experience, thousands upon thousands of reporters, novelists, and poets have been wrought. Theirs was an apprenticeship in ways of seeing, which meant, in most cases, writing rather than espionage—although at least one CIA operative did cite Harriet as an inspiration.[15]

Louise's illustrations for *Bang Bang You're Dead* capture the era's atmosphere of suspicion and simmering violence. The picture book, which she co-wrote with Sandra Scoppettone, features two racially integrated gangs of kids costumed as warriors. The first gang is led by a child named James who is dressed as a Wild West cowboy. His companions include a child in an oversized coat with World War I–style epaulettes, another in a World War II–era helmet, and another in a fantastic, floor-sweeping, eagle-feathered headdress. These four play a game they call *Bang Bang You're Dead*, switching roles between being bad guys and good guys in the fight for a hill. They shoot each other with toy guns, then fall down and pretend to be dead. Later, they share a life-affirming ice cream.

A second gang comes along led by a child who goes by Big Mike, who wears a sort of ragtag police uniform. This group includes a girl who looks like Sandra, or a slightly older version of Suzuki Beane; a little boy, taller by a head than the others, who carries a spear; and another child in a sailor suit and hat. They hurl epithets and then challenge the first gang to a battle for the hill. At the designated time and date, the two sides arrive with rocks and sticks and beat the hell out of each other. There is a double-page spread of hurt and bleeding children. Everyone is on the ground.

The adversaries, concluding there are no clear winners, decide to share the hill so there will be more friends to play with. On the last page, they're standing together for a group portrait. They look tired, proud, and something else—perhaps *avid* best sums up the expression in their eyes, as well as Louise's theme for the illustrations. All of them are craving more experience, even after rolling and writhing in self-inflicted pain. The battle scenes are a direct attack on an adult reader's sensibility: how unnecessary it all seems, and how brutal. Although the book's ending is aspirational, even utopian, it was not sufficiently persuasive to adult book buyers.

Louise's illustrations for *Bang Bang You're Dead* were more like the satirical grotesques she had shown at the Banfer Gallery than those in her *Harriet* books. The gargoyle faces of the kids in *Bang Bang* were not popular even with parents who appreciated the book's message. *Bang Bang You're Dead* was uncategorizable, its illustrations pitching it into the realm of social commentary. It caricatures the costumes and masks that boys (and one girl in this case—so 12.5 percent female participation) put on to portray those who harm others for duty, pay, and enjoyment.

As Louise's publishers had feared, the book's reception was disappointing. An antiwar statement in a time of divided sentiments, even in a children's book, was likely to be rejected and attacked as propaganda and subversion by proponents of the opposing view. Some critics found its antiwar position clumsy and overstated. *School Library Journal* said it was "a literary ABM [antiballistic missile] that overshoots its mark." *The Horn Book* objected to use of the expression "puke face." Ursula Nordstrom, who had predicted this reaction, took the heat and tried to calm the clamor. She wrote apologetic letters, even offering to exchange free copies of alternative picture books to some outraged readers. The book also had its fans. The rock-fighting scene on the double-page spread was a big hit with some bloodthirsty children.

"It was a big bomb," Sandra said. "A failure. The people most important are the librarians and they did not like it. It did not get good reviews and kids did not like it either. It failed because it's fun to play war. We really did not make our point somehow. It was a different audience than *Suzuki*."

Louise had particularly wanted her illustrations to be printed in full color and gory detail, to give the book's antiwar message its full visceral impact. Ursula had written to assure her that no one at Harper wanted to inhibit her artistic freedom, so Louise was surprised and disappointed when Ursula later explained that their budget would only cover black-and-white reproductions. Later, after the reviews began to come out, Louise felt undermined by her publishers, misunderstood by her critics, and certain that if she had only been able to publish their book in living color, it would have found a more receptive readership.

When a *New York Times* article about picture books recognized *Bang Bang You're Dead* as an example of how, "as a sign of the times, Negro children now appear unobtrusively," Harper and Row, Sandra, and Louise might have been pleased—if not for the insulting phrases that followed: "if somewhat mechanically, with white children."[16] Neither Sandra nor Louise believed their commitment to racial justice was *mechanical*: none of their art was *mechanical*. It was a cheap shot, and Louise blamed her publishers for exposing her to it and all the other bad reviews that followed. She felt galled that Harper had, despite Ursula's assurances, sabotaged her project by penny-pinching production and giving it halfhearted support. Louise felt let down, and she held it against Ursula.

Plowing ahead, however, Louise finally submitted a version of *Sport*, her third in the *Harriet* series, after years of sporadic work. She was caught off guard when Charlotte returned *Sport* with unexpected criticism for its title character. In *Harriet the Spy*, Sport was appealing and real; in *Sport*, Charlotte thought, his personality had changed. He was tougher and harder to understand.[17] His character needed more work, she told Louise. That kind of editorial advice hardly seems out of the ordinary, but Louise felt misjudged and no longer wanted Charlotte to edit her work.[18] Ursula tried to mend fences to keep her own friendship with Louise intact, and she also encouraged Louise to keep revising *Sport*. But Louise was not listening to Ursula's advice anymore. Louise phoned Alixe to say, resentfully, that since Harper did not like her new book, she was putting it aside.

Disgusted by the publishing world, Louise returned to her painting. She had grown used to struggling with her success, but failure—unsurprisingly—felt a whole lot worse. On her own, she sunk into melancholia. She had hypertension and was putting on more and more weight. She cut back on smoking and drinking, as her doctor suggested, but she wasn't particularly dedicated or consistent about it. Her friends thought of her as a phenomenally talented artist—but one who kept undermining herself.

For Louise, the life of an artist was an all-in proposition, not for amateurs or the faint of heart. She loved the feeling of being fully immersed in her work, and she cursed anything, animate or inanimate, that interrupted or thwarted her. She didn't suffer from all the obstacles to mastery (and, by extension, the creation of masterpieces) that women in earlier generations faced. She wasn't doomed like Virginia Woolf's Judith Shakespeare, the bard's talented sister—whose passion to be a poet in the sixteenth century was "so thwarted and hindered by other people, so tortured and pulled asunder by her own contrary instincts, that she must have lost her health and sanity to a certainty."[19] Louise had a room of her own as well as money and education. If by chance she wanted birth control or needed an abortion, she had the money to pay for one and the wherewithal to procure the other. Louise's wealth insulated her against many banal demands. But it did not insulate her against the demons of writer's block and lack of confidence.

And she was lonely. Louise had cycled through all kinds of relationships—from the youthful passion she had felt for Amelia; to the love of equals she knew with France Burke; to Alixe, who had tried to create an environment conducive to Louise's creativity. With Connie, there was an easy friendship followed by a swift decline. After her affair with "that terrible Pat Hemingway" ended and Louise was on her own again, she came to the conclusion that solitude—despite its occasional benefits—did not suit her.

Enter Lois Morehead. Lois was a friend who had been around for a while, but Louise had perhaps underestimated her, and certainly she thought her unavailable. Lois had a great deal of style, a lovely laugh, the husky voice of a longtime smoker, and a twelve-year-old daughter from a brief marriage. Louise knew Lois as Barbara Phelan's girlfriend of several years. Of the two, Louise had always been closer to Barbara. Like Louise, Barbara, who had a high-pressure job in advertising, dreamed of escaping to the country. She told Frederica she wanted to drop out of the New

York rat race to live someplace like Vermont, and maybe grow mushrooms. Lois didn't seem to share that dream. Her family in New Jersey hadn't had much money, and she wanted her young daughter to have an easier life. Lois told friends that she wouldn't sacrifice her daughter's future to Barbara's back-to-the-land hippie dream.[20]

One afternoon in the spring of 1969, Louise ran into Barbara and Lois at Frederica Leser's Manhattan apartment. Barbara, who had been drinking, was fantasizing to Frederica about leaving her job. Meanwhile, Lois caught up with Louise. Lois was charming and amusing and easy to talk to, and Louise was not at all averse to a little flirting with a beautiful woman. Louise, at forty-one years old, and Lois, thirty-seven, were each on the verge of making major changes in how and where (and with whom) they lived. They both wanted more settled lives.[21]

"I can't abide all this calling and making dates and wondering where your next bed is coming from," Louise had written to Jimmy some years earlier, when she'd been single and fed up with the city's social whirl.[22] After her unhappy summer, Long Island was losing its glamour; she felt tempted to move to Connecticut, which had proved a refuge for Jimmy and David. Lois and Barbara had been living in Ridgefield, Connecticut, but if Barbara left, as she dreamed of doing, it would be an expensive place to live for a single mother on a nurse's income. Lois turned to Frederica to explain that her daughter's father had remarried and had other children. Private school tuition was expensive, and she needed a lot of money to raise her kid. Frederica was sympathetic, but she couldn't offer much help. It seemed that Lois was asking for more than a loan, and she recalled laughing at her friend's chutzpah.

Lois pivoted to Louise. "I need to send my kid to private school," she said. Barbara, still laughing and joking and drinking, seemed oblivious to the turn the conversation had taken.

Louise gave Lois's proposition due consideration. Within a week, in Frederica's words, "everything changed." Lois left Barbara for Louise, and "Barbara went off the rails." Soon, "her drinking got so bad it was hard to be around her." Louise needed an anchor, Frederica observed:

> And Lois was very attractive. . . . This was not just a sort of quid pro quo. But I think Louise was very vulnerable. . . . Lois was very vulnerable and angry about what Barbara Phelan had decided to do, basically stranding herself and her daughter in the sticks somewhere to raise vegetables. . . . Lois needed somebody to take care of her financially, which Louise could easily do. And Louise needed someone to take care of her in another sense . . . to be loved and cared about. . . . Lois had a lot of warmth. It just happened at that instant. It was a strange thing and I've never forgotten it. I remember where we were sitting.[23]

Alixe and Barbara thought Lois was an awful gold digger. Although the general consensus was that Louise had made a reckless move and a terrible error, Louise didn't care what anyone thought. She and Lois had as much of a shot at making it as a couple as anyone else. They were comfortable with one another. They made each other laugh. Louise wanted to distance herself from the company she had been keeping, and to get out of the city at last. She wanted somebody who would care for her physically and emotionally.

In short order, Lois helped Louise reorganize her life. Lois was an excellent cook, and under her care Louise's health improved. She began to paint and write again. Ursula, who had tried in various ways to coax Louise back into working on *Sport*, heard this news through the grapevine. Her strategy continued as before, sending flattering and gossipy letters, but Louise did not answer

Ursula's phone calls or letters.[24] She had not entirely abandoned *Sport*, but she was finished with Harper.[25]

If Louise's relationship with Lois had started as a transaction, it was soon established in love and affection. In the summer of 1969, Louise returned to Cutchogue, this time with Lois. Sue Singer visited, and in July they watched the Apollo moon landing together. Sue saw a rejuvenated Louise who was devoted to Lois and her daughter. Louise had started to relax. She stopped seesawing between dessert binges and starvation diets. With Lois cooking and helping her in other ways, Louise began to manage her weight, which also quelled her long-held terror of becoming obese. She stopped drinking, practiced keeping her short fuse under control, and started writing regularly again. Lois called Louise by the nickname Willie, and that's how her new friends would come to know her.

Writing to Jimmy in a euphoric mood, Louise announced that she'd moved to Connecticut with Lois and her thirteen-year-old daughter, and for the first time in years, she declared, "Jimmy I'm happy." In his reply, Jimmy said he was glad to get these "glimpses of domestic bliss" from her: "It's not every day one hears only good news for my dear friend, but this time you have set a flawless example to the writing public. . . . Personally I think the giving up of the civilizing glass of wine is going a shade too far. However, it was always all or nothing with madcap you."[26] Jimmy was right. It was all or nothing with Louise. In a defiant mood, asserting her control of her estate, and demonstrating her love for Lois, Louise made a will on September 14, 1970, in which she named Lois as her principal heir. She remembered Alixe with a large bequest as well, but she left nothing to any of her relatives—not even her mother, who would only inherit her daughter's estate if she outlived Lois, Alixe, and Lois's daughter.

Louise bought a beautiful old colonial house in Bridgewater. It was large, square in the Federal style, and painted brown with a white front door. Louise and Lois threw themselves into interior decorating and planted side gardens all around. Frederica came out from the city to help them put in trees. They joined their new neighborhood's resident circle of artists, writers, and theater people, visiting each other's studios, dining at one another's homes, playing marathon card games, and acting in original plays staged in a local barn. Louise became good friends with the town librarian, Kay Edwards, after she walked into the library looking for a novel by Joseph Conrad.

They often had evening cocktails and canapés with their friends Francis Hines, a painter and commercial artist for B. Altman and Company department stores, and Joan Hines, an aspiring children's author. Joan's daughter from a former marriage, Joanna, idolized Louise. She was a schoolmate of Lois's daughter, whom she would visit hoping to catch a glimpse of Louise at work.

That first summer Joanna helped Lois weed their gardens and volunteered to bring messages and sometimes lunch—a tomato sandwich and iced coffee—upstairs to Louise's attic studio. The Louise Joanna saw was "a very disciplined person, always sitting at her drawing board, always very serious," she said. "She wore magnifying glasses on her eyes when she would draw her very intricate pencil drawings." Joanna thought Lois and Louise were wonderful parents, and she was slightly envious of their close, affectionate relationship with Lois's daughter.[27] Joanna's own family life was more bohemian and less secure, and she sometimes felt like an outsider in Lois's ordered and affluent world. She found most of her parents' other artist friends outrageous, arch, and sarcastic, but she always respected Louise, and she adored Lois.

If unhappiness had narrowed her world and left Louise feeling slow and cramped, love expanded her life in every way. She became the beguiling tomboy Jimmy had met at Bard again, and the inventive, super-creative artist Jane Wagner first knew. As her curiosity came out of hibernation, she wanted to learn everything about everybody. She loved driving the back roads around Connecticut and imitating the local Yankee accent. They threw parties with smart, interesting guests and hosted lively dinners in restaurants.

Louise lived by the philosophy that money was to be spent. Some of her friends, including Joan Williams and Sandra Scoppettone, remarked on how little she paid attention to her expenses once her income from her inheritance and royalties as a best-selling author seemed assured. She was generous to friends and strangers alike with money and time. When the librarian, Kay Edwards, told her about a neighborhood family with financial woes, Louise anonymously paid their bills. Louise advised Joan Hines on writing children's books, handed around the number of her literary agent, and lent her expertise to other local writers and artists in various stages of their careers. She enjoyed her new status as a parent of an adolescent and involved herself in Lois's daughter's education at Wykeham Rise School, an elite private school. (Its motto was *For the good and the beautiful*, which sounds like a program starring Connie Ford.)

On at least one occasion, Louise, having become a local celebrity, acted as mentor to a young poet who was in the same grade as then sixteen-year-old Joanna Hines. Joanna had begun to think about also becoming a writer, but she was cautious about revealing this secret ambition. When Joanna's older stepbrother, Jonathan, who wanted to be an artist, asked Louise for her advice, she told him, "Just keep going. Don't give up."

When Joanna herself summoned her courage to tell Louise that she hoped to become a writer, she thought that at worst her idol would throw out a kind platitude, as she had to Jonathan. Not that day. Happiness hadn't softened Louise's dedication to the truth, and she wasn't going to lie to the kid. "You're too wishy-washy," Louise said.

"I am not!" said Joanna. She was mostly surprised that Louise—who had never appeared to notice her—had rendered a judgment on her character. It meant that even as Joanna had darted around, covertly glimpsing Louise at work, Louise had been spying too.

It was an old habit. Louise, whom Alixe said "never enjoyed being looked at," had her own gatekeeper now: Lois politely kept most fans at bay, making an exception for Joanna, of whom she was fond. Louise still declined interviews, and the publicity and biographical material provided by her publishers were minimal. The jacket flap photograph Sue Singer had taken of Louise on a child's swing, holding her Yorkie, Peter, in Carl Schurz Park, had for years been the only portrait of her in circulation. Being a popular and successful writer had not been particularly conducive to Louise's work, and Joanna had been fortunate to observe her idol working at speed to regain lost time.

It was all coming together. Louise was more productive than she'd been in years, happier than she had been in recent memory, more in love than she had been since she'd first met Alixe. In the earliest days of her relationship with Lois they'd tried out more or less traditional roles: Louise, the husband and provider, and Lois, her companion and caretaker, both mother to the teenage daughter they both adored and housekeeper of their beautiful home. Louise, in love, had extolled her partner's domestic successes. She adored their peaceful home, so conducive to making art. And without doubt, she enjoyed the affection Lois lavished upon her. Lois became the latest custodian of Louise's genius.

After about a year, as their honeymoon period ended and they slid into a more realistic routine, they became more interdependent and more equal. Louise may have paid the bills, but it was Lois, who'd given up nursing, who was head of the household. Louise, by then deeply immersed in writing a new book for children, began to encourage Lois to look for her own fulfilling career. All of Louise's former partners had been artists, writers, or professional women, and she believed that satisfying work was necessary to a person's happiness (a philosophy so central that it's embedded in *Harriet the Spy*). Louise was well aware that combining motherhood and career, in 1971, was not going to be easy, and it was not something she'd ever expected to do herself. Ten years earlier, while conscientiously pet-sitting a friend's cat and two kittens, Louise had complained to Alixe that she hadn't painted or written anything for days. All the meals and playtime and changing of litter had made her feel like she was running a Borscht Belt resort for felines. "How can women with children also have careers?" she'd howled. "It must drive them crazy!"

The difference now was that she and Lois had each other. She wanted Lois to feel as fulfilled as she did, engaged in purposeful work. Also, according to M.J., to whom she still spoke regularly, "Louise enjoyed being a stepfather," and by all accounts, she was doing a dandy job.

seventeen

SURVEY THE LOCALITY

Litchfield County, where Bridgewater was located, was serene, light-years away from the urban chaos of the early 1970s but still close enough to the city to commute home with a bag of still-warm bagels. Every town had its colonial-era cemeteries, white churches, horses, and estates that had remained in families for generations. There was so much wealth in the area that it naturally attracted entrepreneurs, whose businesses—modestly fancy restaurants, art galleries, auction houses, and little theaters—fit snugly into the village milieu. Many of the merchants and those they employed painted, wrote, danced, and composed. They lived in prettily renovated barns and in cottages tucked among the mansions. Their artistry added color and excitement to the tidy, venerable villages and to the lives of the more affluent residents, whose hair and clothes they styled, houses they cleaned, and children they taught.

The villagers were a discriminating population, in that they knew what they liked and believed they knew what was correct; but in another sense of the word, they were not a particularly discriminatory lot. Most residents generally respected artists and were tolerant of their gay friends. During the Joseph McCarthy years, some of the blacklisted writers from television and film who left Los Angeles founded a sort of colony in Litchfield County. Through the mid-1960s, there was an increasing migration of celebrities. Among their ranks were top-tier artists like Alexander (Sandy) Calder, Walter Bernstein, Maurice Sendak, Mike Nichols, and Norman Mailer. Even that terrible Pat Hemingway lived in Bridgewater for a while. Their world ran parallel to the elite WASPish world, intersecting at public events and on children's sports days.

Rachel Chodorov, a painter and daughter-in-law of one of the blacklisted pioneers to Litchfield County, met Louise in 1973, soon after she separated from her husband, Stefan Chodorov.[1] Rachel never saw the dark Louise and she thought Louise and Lois made a lovely, affectionate couple.[2]

On the afternoon Louise invited Rachel Chodorov up to her attic studio to see her new work, they talked about being painters, about style and craft and the various materials they used. Louise was working on a series of oil paintings of dolls and on perches around the studio had posed her doll models: old-fashioned ceramic faces, straw dolls, floppy Raggedy Anns, and fashion dolls with plasticized bodies and improbable breasts. The paintings Rachel saw were very realistic and richly colored, but disturbing. Frederica Leser would later write about these doll paintings, which she saw on a later visit to Louise's studio.[3] There were some with very big heads and empty eyes, which Frederica read as Louise's social commentary on fake, lifeless beauty and the way society reduced women to their appearance, judging them by their appeal to men. Joanna Hines also caught glimpses of the beautifully colored doll paintings, but she was more fascinated by the highly detailed pen-and-ink illustrations Louise was drawing, probably for *I Am Five*, her final book. Louise was not painting many portraits anymore. She was more interested in grotesque and surreal imagery, though sometimes she would still take her easel to the beach to paint landscapes of shadowed sand hills, ocean, and sky.

Living in Bridgewater, Louise started to socialize more with Lois's friends. Evelynne Roberts Patterson, also a nurse, was bringing up two daughters, Alice and Pat (known as Pippy), in Greenwich Village. Louise met the family just as she was completing the manuscript of a novel called *The Changelings*, about an African American family in New York divided by competing perceptions of art and status. The Patterson girls may have served as models for some of the children Louise invented in her books. Alice, Lois's goddaughter, was a fan of *Harriet the Spy*, and she and Louise shared an affection for the urban picture books of Ezra Jack Keats. As a Black child growing up in the seventies, Alice had particularly loved *Whistle for Willie* and *Apt. 3*. Once, Louise brought over a small projector to show the Patterson family a short film she liked about the legend of John Henry, and they watched it together while sitting at their kitchen table.[4]

In the summer of 1973, Kay Edwards, Louise's librarian friend, brought Louise and Lois to visit a local farmhouse where Norman Mailer had previously lived.[5] Its young tenants were Jan Buckaloo, a journalist, and Sloane Shelton, an actress, who were painting the house in lieu of paying rent.[6] Jan had grown up in Texas, and Sloane in Georgia, and when Louise found out that Sloane was a good southern cook, she didn't wait long to invite herself over for dinner. The friends began sharing meals. Some of these were Friday night chicken and biscuits; others were grander affairs. For one dinner party, Lois made a delicious crown roast.

On that night, Sloane and Jan were the youth contingent among other extraordinary guests. They included Eleanore Pettersen, an architect who'd studied under Frank Lloyd Wright. Miss Pettersen (as everyone courteously called her) was then in her late fifties and subject to narcolepsy. She fell asleep at the dinner table with a cigarette in her mouth, but awoke before her head hit the salad. Jan was impressed at the way nobody seemed overly concerned. Apart from Miss Pettersen, it was a lively party. Their conversation ran from local gossip—who was divorcing, who had bruises, who had been seen drunk, who was seen in her nightgown walking to the mailbox—to a raucous discussion of the ever-expanding Watergate scandal.

Sometimes, after the other guests left, Louise, Lois, Kay, Sloane, and Jan would play card games long into the night. They particularly liked Onze, which was played with two decks, with the winner holding the fewest cards after seven hands. Whenever they gathered, they would sing together, harmonizing on songs like "Cool Water" and "Ragtime Cowboy Joe" ("He's a hifalutin', rootin', tootin' son-of-a-gun from Arizona, Ragtime Cowboy Joe"). Louise occasionally talked about wanting to write the script and lyrics for a Broadway musical. In the past, she had considered adapting a Fellini movie, then a book about the Reconstruction era (Howard Fast's *Freedom Road*). She once even completed the first act of an original three-act play called *The Brownstone*, a musical about how the tenants of a Manhattan apartment building respond to the news that their landlord is selling the building.[7] Just recently, she'd begun working on a new idea: a children's book about the US Bicentennial, which was coming up in 1976. She asked Jan to help her with some research. Louise was always thinking up new ideas for paintings and plays and books. "She was like a fountain," Jan said.

Around the time of the crown roast party, Louise had sent the finished manuscript of *The Changelings* to her agent, Pat Schartle

Myrer (Pat had married Anton Myrer in 1970). In conversation, Louise told Pat she didn't want to work with Harper and Row (or Ursula Nordstrom) again. Pat was confident that Harriet's fame as a groundbreaking character, the controversies surrounding Louise's novels (which only sold more books), and the loyalty of her fans would ensure a great deal of interest in any new work, and that publishers would come calling. On June 15, 1973, a Friday, Pat sent letters to several leading publishers simultaneously to pitch the book. In a brisk tone, she invited bids and made clear that Louise was not interested in meeting editors in advance, "but simply to have offers made on her new book." She asked for publishers to reply by the following Wednesday. One of these letters made its way to a young editor named Michael di Capua, who offered $25,000. As the highest bidder, he purchased *The Changelings* for Farrar, Straus and Giroux.[8]

Louise, who found the schmoozing and business aspect of publishing almost intolerable, said she would only meet Michael di Capua if Pat came along as moral support. As Louise later told Alixe, almost as soon as the young editor introduced himself and his ideas, Louise was put off by his air of pedantry. She wasn't at all sure di Capua (as she always referred to him) was the right editor for her book. Pat assured Louise that her relationship with her new publisher included her right to influence and oversee the look of her new novel.

In an interview twenty years after this meeting, di Capua told the journalist Karen Cook from the *Village Voice* that his first impression of Louise was of "a sort of semi-invalid—very frail, withdrawn, interior, drawn in on herself, not comfortable in the world."[9] She seemed more than usually dependent on her agent to explain her work. He attributed her apprehension and awkwardness to the stories he had heard about her difficult childhood and many years in psychotherapy. He told Cook he'd heard that one or another of her parents had "flung her against a wall."[10] Louise and di Capua didn't have an easy editor-author relationship, according to Alixe, who often spoke to Louise during the months she was preparing her manuscript for publication. Louise felt exhausted by di Capua's hectoring during their editing sessions and didn't trust him, either as an expert editor or a sympathetic person. She had not realized how lucky she had been to work with Harper and Row when she started out. She told Alixe that di Capua was too intense. She thought he drove her too hard and that he failed utterly to understand her work, particularly in comparison to Ursula and Charlotte.

Louise made changes to the book as she agreed to do, but di Capua's seeming lack of confidence in the quality of her writing was discouraging. Louise's patience with di Capua hit its lowest point when he criticized the dialogue she had written for her African American characters. Di Capua had told her, "You don't know how to write Black people," Alixe said. "And it was so painful for her."

Louise told Alixe, "I know perfectly well how to write dialogue. I know how I want my characters to sound, and what I want them to say." Reporting this exchange, she was as upset as Alixe had ever seen her.

When Karen Cook asked Michael di Capua to respond to Alixe's claim that, as Louise's editor, he had criticized the dialogue she wrote for her Black characters, he defended his editor's prerogative. "I think that's a comment that would be commonplace in the editing of any manuscript. . . . The most careful writer in the world slips a little in getting dialogue to sound true to that particular character," he told Cook.[11]

By October 1973, the book was under production and had been sent to designer Jane Byers Bierhorst with a new title: *Nobody's Family Is Going to Change.* Over the next few months, Louise weighed in on everything from choice of paper to the plastic coating on the book's cover. She was often concerned that di Capua was not listening to her, and her letters to him showed an overexplanatory, patronizing impatience. Several times, she wrote to object to the quality of the book's cover, but it seemed he didn't heed her or take her seriously enough. Eventually, she wrote him a scathing letter reminding him that she'd told him five times before how much she disliked the cover. "Each time I was ignored. For future reference, I am always angry when ignored."[12]

Louise didn't try to make it easy for him. Di Capua, who was expected to keep the book on schedule for publication, was stymied again when, in the spring of 1974, Louise held up production to insert Alice and Pippy Patterson's names into the final typeset text (as members of the Anne Frank Brigade of the Children's Army).

At home in Connecticut, Louise was insulated by wealth and friends. Bridgewater was tolerant in a Yankee way, but it was still a small town, and small minds would have their say. Louise, along with every other resident, was subject to gossip and speculation. When the writer Jan Buckaloo had first met Louise, she was "a little taken aback because she was totally dressed like a guy and very different than the [*Harriet the Spy*] book jacket." Rachel Chodorov described Louise as "very butch. . . . She wore jeans, Frye boots, and vests." When Fabio Rieti met up again with Louise around that time, he thought "she looked somewhat ravaged: I recognized her sparkling behavior but not the facial features I had known."

In public, Louise seemed to channel the divine disinterest she had so admired in Gertrude Stein. As Jan saw it, Louise's indifference about how she was viewed made her "dangerous," particularly to those who feared lesbians, as France Burke's relative

Henry Hart had, as "moral degenerates," and to closeted lesbians who felt threatened by association.

Bridgewater villagers were tolerant in their fashion, but it was not unknown for some mean guy to mutter imprecations, or a rude kid, skidding past on a bicycle, to demand to know, *You a man or a woman?* Louise was obviously out of the closet. Her friends admired her authenticity and self-respect, but sometimes they speculated about whether Lois (like Alixe Gordin before her) had occasionally tried and abandoned asking Louise to dress in a less mannish style. Most of their friends supported the gay liberation movement that was just then emerging after Stonewall, but being out and proud in the quiet Connecticut town of Bridgewater was not in Lois's interest—no matter how many of their neighbors were allies.[13]

Lois never publicly came out as Louise's lover, partner, or wife. She presented as a wealthy, privileged, white lady who lived with her friend, the famous writer. "Lois dressed in tailored clothes, silk blouses—she was really a beauty," Rachel Chodorov said. In M.J. Meaker's opinion, "Lois Morehead was not pleased being gay." In 1973, "Don't Ask, Don't Tell," though not yet labeled as such, was the most common attitude in straight liberal society. Long after Lois's death, a friend who still wished to preserve Lois's privacy said that Lois and Louise had been "very, very good friends."[14] There was not yet a commonly accepted expression to describe Louise and Lois's partnership. Thirty-two years would have to pass before a lesbian couple would have the right to marry in Connecticut.

Living with Lois in Bridgewater, Louise saw less of the artists and writers who had composed her society in the city. Frederica visited, as did M.J. on occasion, but Louise's continued relationship with Alixe Gordin was a point of contention. Lois did not like Alixe trading on her long history with Louise, and Louise did not care for Lois telling her whom she could or could not see. In the summer before *Nobody's Family Is Going to Change* was due to be published, Louise drove to the city from Connecticut so Alixe could cut her hair, as she often had in the past. Louise said Lois had been unhappy that she had gone to Alixe's when she might have had her hair cut in Connecticut. As Louise sat on a stool in the bright kitchen, and Alixe trimmed her friend's very light, very fair hair, Louise told her that her publisher wanted her to go on the road to promote her book, something she had never before contemplated. Now she was considering taking a public speaking course. Alixe joked that she felt under pressure to give Louise an especially good haircut if she was going to be in the public eye. Louise asked about a painting she'd given Alixe, one of a series of Long Island landscapes. "Do you like it?"

"Of course, I love it. Why do you ask?" Alixe said.

"Lois was a little upset that I gave it to you."

Alixe was admittedly biased, but it seemed to her that Louise's relationship with Lois was not as secure or stable as it had once been. Louise told Alixe she was thinking about getting a second house separate from Lois, or a studio closer to the city. Louise asked Alixe, who had just begun seeing someone new, "Are you happy?" Alixe thought Louise may have been fishing to see if Alixe wanted to resume their former relationship. She said she was content with her new girlfriend.

Louise did not have to tell Alixe that Lois despised her. She could see that well enough for herself during one particularly unpleasant encounter. Louise asked Alixe, as a favor, if she could help Lois try to find another fulfilling career, perhaps in the arts. Alixe was doubtful. She didn't have a high opinion of Lois's intelligence. Alixe later said,

> Lois was not untalented. She was *a kind of wife* married to a successful man, and she was a superb hostess, a wonderful cook. I mean she made me feel like some kind of a little grunge. So

> inadequate next to her socially. She was very charming and very funny. And, as I say, a lovely hostess. I think she played the piano. It seemed to me she could sing and play the guitar and do everything that a wonderful hostess could do, and yet she was very unhappy.[15]

So an appointment was set, and it wasn't until they arrived at Alixe's New York apartment that Lois discovered she was there for vocational guidance. Alixe later said, "I don't remember what we suggested. We sat talking about what would make Lois happy, and it must've made Lois miserable, when I think about it, that Louise brought her here." The visit was a catastrophe; it was particularly mortifying for Lois, who felt she had her hands full caring for her daughter and Louise, and didn't think she needed more fulfilling work. Afterward, Lois was even more resentful of Louise's phone calls and periodic visits to Alixe.

Some of Louise's old gang, who were also armchair shrinks, analyzed Louise as looking to be mothered (as she had been by Alixe and Connie). The maternal, warm Lois, who had also studied to be a professional nurse, filled the bill. Even if Louise played the child with Lois in private, in public she seemed the dominant half of the couple. A new friend, Lucille Stoffregen, meeting the couple for the first time, noted, "It was clear Louise considered herself the boss." In Sandra Scoppettone's words, "She used to push those mothers around."

That fall, Sandra had dinner out with Louise and Lois on Long Island. "It was not fun," Sandra said. There was an uncomfortable moment at the end of the meal when the check came. Louise customarily paid the bill for everyone, but on this occasion, when Lois handed her the check, Louise snapped back, "I don't need to be told how to act." Frederica, who also witnessed quarrels between Louise and Lois, said, "It was not easy for Lois, believe me.

Louise was not easy to live with. She had high blood pressure and had been told by doctors to take care of herself, to eat carefully, and exercise. She was not supposed to drink, and she did."

As 1974 went on, despite a new book and other projects on the horizon, Louise was restless. She missed the city. Living in a Connecticut village—no surprise—was getting boring, or maybe it was just dawning on her, as her city friends had sensed for a while, that Louise was stuck in an uninspiring marriage to a rather conventional woman.

There were a couple of unexpected bright spots that autumn. For one, Louise's mother never gave up on her relationship with her daughter, even when Louise seemed remote or uninterested. That year their relationship seemed to become even more equal and consequential. Mary Louise was excited about the approaching publication of her daughter's new novel and wanted to celebrate with her. She visited from Mississippi in the summer, as she normally did, and hoped to persuade Louise to come down to Clarksdale, which was changing slowly, starting at last to come to terms with the advances the civil rights movement had forged. She had retired, but she hoped Louise would give a presentation someday at Clarksdale's library.[16] Even among the legions of *Harriet* devotees, it would have been hard to find a more devoted fan of Louise's books than Mary Louise Perkins Trevilion.[17]

Then there was a happy reunion between Ursula and Louise. Thirty-four years after becoming director of Harper Books for Boys and Girls, twenty years after she had first been appointed to the Harper and Row board of directors, and thirteen years after she had been made a company vice president for the children's book division, Ursula Nordstrom retired to her own house in Bridgewater, not far from Louise's. Ursula had accomplished many great things during her span of employment and fostered many wonderful books, though it was always more difficult than it should have been because of the glass ceiling she routinely encountered. Her assistant Barbara Dicks recalled one meeting during which an editor from the adult section asked Ursula to get him a coffee. "He did not get very far with that one, I'll tell you. She made mincemeat of him. You go do it. I'm a vice president of this company!"[18]

In October 1974, entirely by accident, Ursula ran into Louise at a Bridgewater restaurant. They had "a rapprochement [with] happiness and emotion on both sides. We were both moved," Ursula wrote. "All past silly hurts and misunderstandings disappeared."[19]

eighteen

WITNESS

Nobody's Family Is Going to Change is the most political of Louise's novels and her most personal. The Sheridans are an African American family living comfortably on the Upper East Side of New York in 1973, well aware of what it took for them to arrive at that place in that time.[1] Emancipation Sheridan, called Emma, is eleven years old, a fiercely intelligent and competitive girl attending the Gregory School. She wants to be a lawyer. Her father, William, a New York district attorney and humorless male chauvinist, discounts his daughter's ambitions on the grounds that women lawyers are ridiculous and inadequate. Mr. Sheridan has designed a strategy to protect his family in a racist culture, but despite his good intentions, his children see him as willfully misunderstanding them and unjustifiably controlling. Emma bridles at the injustice of his position and at the absurd limitations to which she is subject.

Emma's mother, Virginia Sheridan, has a good heart and a great deal invested in being an upper-middle-class housewife. She is satisfied with the status quo. Her son, seven-year-old Willie, whose ambitions are as high as his sister Emma's, wants to follow in the footsteps of their Uncle Dipsey, a Broadway hoofer. To his cautious father, Willie's wish to become a dancer seems both retrograde—a throwback to a time when dancing was one of the few careers available to a Black male adult in the United States—and uncomfortably, transparently gay. He insists that Willie must follow him into the law, an idea that revolts his young son.

The two children deal with the situation differently. Willie believes that charm might persuade the grown-ups, while Emma, with more experience of her father's obduracy, feels unloved and frustrated. As a result, she eats obsessively. She has her father in a nutshell: "Willie wants to do a girl's thing, and I want to do a boy's thing, and our father hates both of us."[2]

Emma's eventual resistance begins as a logical objection to her father's irrationality, but it moves toward active rebellion when she joins an uptown Children's Army that tries to rescue kids who are at risk for abuse and exploitation. When Emma discovers that the Children's Army's leadership is also mired in misogyny, she and her girlfriends split off to found a more harmonious faction. Although Mrs. Sheridan eventually asserts herself in defense of her children, Mr. Sheridan is intransigent. His dilemma is that he knows just how bad things have been and could be again. To save his children from suffering, he tries to suppress their imaginations, an effort bound to fail.

Louise originally called the novel *The Changelings*, and she plays with the various ways children can feel alienated from the parents who love them. In folklore, fairies who steal human infants from unsuspecting parents will leave one of their own in exchange. A changeling child is sometimes subtly—sometimes extravagantly—different, and typically at odds with their foster family. Emma feels like a changeling child who has been deposited at the wrong address, while Willie, also feeling misunderstood, dreams of an unknown rescuer who will arrive out of the blue to lead him away to somewhere among dancers and singers, and not disapproving lawyers. The novel builds to a propulsive reckoning as Emma, overcoming crushing self-doubt—becomes a brilliant advocate for her little brother just as she is realizing her own power of self-determination.

Harriet M. Welsch wants to know everything. Emma Sheridan, although the same age, is more discerning and aware of consequences. Both girls attend the same elite Upper East Side private school. In Emma's life outside her home, issues of race exist as something of a delicate nimbus, surrounding her but not imposing on her—until they do. For instance, in one passage, Emma, strategizing uninhibitedly with three friends, suddenly realizes that everyone in the conversation is white except for her. She instantly becomes more self-conscious of every word she says and even more scrutinizing of how her friends reply.

In *The Long Secret*, Harriet declares that she and her generation will be the ones to "fix" things, and Emma Sheridan takes up the torch. Through her heroine in the new book, Louise managed to address women's liberation, racial equality, and class consciousness as well as issues surrounding a young woman's body image (anticipating the body-positive movement, which would not come into its own for another half-century). As in all of Louise's books, art has a liberating quality.

Around the time she was creating the Sheridans, Louise spoke to Alixe about her newly concise philosophy of life and work: "Sometimes," she said, "it just comes down to life is funny."[3] *Nobody's Family Is Going to Change* has a funny, restless tone, oscillating between anxiety and satire. There are some moments when joy breaks out, mostly associated with Willie's dancing. Emma stomps around, unable, even when she tries, to hide herself. The misogyny that thwarts her ambition and the comic horror of family life constitute the kind of material that a million more women would ponder with their therapists, and that future comediennes would chew over in a thousand stand-up routines.

Publishers Weekly came out with a brief review of *Nobody's Family Is Going to Change* on November 4, 1974. About 125 words, the review considered the book to be mixed: there was some good and some bad. The review compliments the "brilliant" author of *Harriet the Spy*, whose new book is "in many ways a triumph—fast, funny and provocative." It then lambastes Louise for relying on such predictable themes that "one feels the clock in the author's house stopped years ago." The review concludes that the book "entertains as it inspires, but only to a degree."[4]

It was not the worst review Louise ever received—some of the *Harriet* notices were much harsher. But something in its compressed callousness—and its accusation that Louise, at age forty-six, was already out of touch with the zeitgeist—pierced her to the heart. She had a couple of brandies, and then a few more. She drank a lot that week. Although her friends assured her that better reviews would come, Louise felt vulnerable and under siege. This was her first novel to be published in almost seven years. Michael di Capua later told Karen Cook he thought it "the nastiest meanest review"; it implied that Louise had "completely lost whatever talent she ever had."[5]

On Saturday, November 16, Louise phoned M.J. Meaker at her home in East Hampton. "What's the matter? My God, you're not drinking brandy, are you? You know the doctors told you you're not supposed to drink brandy," M.J. said.

"I'm drunk because of the review," Louise told her. "I started drinking when I read the review. You would too. I'm doing everything I shouldn't do."

The next night, November 17, Louise and Lois had dinner with Sloane Shelton and Jan Buckaloo at Kay Edwards's small colonial house in Bridgewater. Afterward, they played Onze. Louise drank a lot of brandy that night, too. She was still miserable about the review, but conceded that it was good to have her friends around. They toasted Louise's new book, then cursed *Publishers Weekly* and the anonymous reviewer who did not know her ass from her elbow, agreeing it was monstrous to inflict so much pain in so few words. A person could spend years working to create a meaningful work of art, and then some apprentice writes a casual dismissal and doesn't even comprehend how crushing it might be! They discussed writing letters to the editor on Louise's behalf, reassuring her that once the book was released a few days later, everyone would see what that *Publishers Weekly* idiot had missed.

After dinner, Sloane and Jan had to drive home to the city, but first they walked Louise and Lois back to their house from Kay's. It was a very cold, clear, dark night with the constellations sharply defined. Sloane and Lois were up ahead. Louise was animated by the beauty of the night sky. "Look at all those shooting stars," she said. Jan was perplexed. The sky she saw was unremarkable. "Don't you see them?" Louise asked. Later, Jan wondered if Louise had been hallucinating.

On Monday morning, Louise woke with a brutal headache. She often had painful headaches after a night of drinking, but this was worse, a slamming pain into the back of her skull. Lois was out somewhere, and Louise didn't think she could drive herself to the doctor. Once she started to cough up blood, she called the town ambulance, which raced her to the New Milford Hospital. She was conscious when she arrived, but soon, by the time Lois showed up, Louise had fallen into a coma.

Lois phoned Kay, who phoned Sloane and Jan in the city. Jan had just returned from work and was entering their apartment as

Sloane was hanging up the phone. Kay had called to say Louise had an aneurysm and was in the hospital. Sloane threw some things in an overnight bag while Jan ran to pull the car up.[6]

Before setting out for New Milford, Sloane phoned Alixe to tell her what she knew about Louise. Alixe said she would take her own car and meet them in Connecticut. She had never driven to Bridgewater or New Milford before, and in her nervous state she kept taking wrong turns and getting lost. It wasn't until late Monday afternoon that she joined Louise's other friends in the hospital's little waiting room. Alixe had been practicing what to say and immediately demanded that Louise be airlifted to a better facility with specialists.

Neither Alixe nor Lois had legal standing or any way to influence Louise's end-of-life medical care, and both felt possessive and protective of the person they loved. Lois may have been Louise's life partner, but the law did not recognize their relationship. Neither she nor Alixe were related by blood, so they were not permitted to remain with Louise in intensive care. The nurses were sympathetic to both women, treating them as they would any close friend of a dying patient. They explained that Louise's condition was too critical for her to be moved. Over the next twenty-four hours, Alixe was permitted only three brief visits to Louise's intensive care unit, and all three times, Louise was comatose. At one point, Alixe, standing outside the door, and unsure whether she was hallucinating in her suffering, thought she glimpsed Louise opening her eyes to ask the nurse if she had a brain tumor. The nurse tried to calm her. "It isn't a tumor. You just need to rest."

Alixe regretted that she had not barged through the door to comfort Louise and urge her not to lose hope.[7] That was what Alixe had done all their lives together, and at the end she felt she had failed. She later said, "Louise didn't need to rest, she needed to fight." She tried again to get someone to listen. When

Dr. Robert Lee McDonald, the doctor who had treated Louise for four years, arrived to consult with the neurologist, Alixe argued passionately that Louise ought to be transported to a city hospital. She was furious with Lois for not being home and acting immediately when Louise's headache had begun, and she suggested that the delay had jeopardized Louise's life. Dr. McDonald told Alixe, in the time-honored way of physicians, *We're doing everything we can. We'll know more in the morning.*

Kay offered Alixe a bed to rest in for a couple of hours; Jan and Sloane went back to Lois's house. "Lois was devastated," Jan said.[8] In Tuesday's early hours, those standing vigil saw no improvement, but Louise had survived the night.

On Tuesday morning, November 19, Alixe phoned Louise's mother in Clarksdale to say Louise was in critical condition. Louise's first cousin, Regina Inez Ragland McCoy, answered the phone; immediately after hearing the news, she made arrangements for herself, Mary Louise, and Aunt Dodie to fly to Hartford that night. Inez drove the three of them to the Memphis airport. When they arrived, they discovered that Inez's husband, Glenn, had followed them, speeding all the way from Clarksdale. When he found them, he reported that another phone call had come in after they had left the house. Louise had died at 10:45 p.m. Eastern time.

An anguished Mary Louise boarded the plane with her sister and niece. As they flew through a snowstorm, she hoped at least to be able to bring her daughter's body back for burial in Mississippi.[9]

Alixe, as she had expected, was excluded from discussion of the funeral and memorial service. That conversation occurred between the Connecticut and Mississippi contingents. Mary Louise, in her grief, conceded that Louise had wished to be buried in

Connecticut. The proof was material, Lois told Inez. Louise and Lois had bought three plots at the Bridgewater cemetery: one for each of them, and the other for Lois's daughter. Inez agreed that Louise "had no intentions of ever returning to Memphis, as she had an unhappy childhood." She said, "It was just so hard the way Mary Louise had always been separated from her daughter in life and death."

Alixe had been surprised to hear about the family funeral plot, since Louise had been relatively young. It seemed like something an older person might do. She knew Louise had made a will, but knew little of its contents. There were other instructions that Louise had expressed over time to Lois and other friends: She had asked to be buried north of the Mason-Dixon line in a white suit and in a plain coffin. She had also spoken of her wish for a lavish after-funeral party at the Plaza Hotel.

Louise's funeral was held at a little Episcopal church in Bridgewater, St. Mark's, on November 21, 1974. Friends and family then went to the small local cemetery for her burial. Alixe attended the funeral, as did Lois, Frederica, and Sandra. Joanna was there with her mother and stepfather, Joan and Francis Hines. Kay came, as did Sloane and Jan. Ursula Nordstrom also attended. Louise's cousin Inez and her Aunt Dodie were there with Mary Louise. When Fabio Rieti heard later about the religious service at Louise's funeral, he thought it sounded a false note and was sure Louise would have objected. "The Louise I knew regarded religion of any kind as a means of establishing power and keeping people tame," he said.[10]

The day of the funeral was very cold, with a hazy, dim sun. After the burial, as Alixe and Frederica walked together to the small parking lot where they had left their cars, they were shocked to see a sudden burst of thunder and lightning. "It was like theater, like something in a film, so sudden," Alixe later said. Louise was storming on high. "She was angry. She was not supposed to be gone."

Lois also arranged a memorial service for December 6 at St. James' Church in New York City at Madison Avenue and Seventy-First Street. The beautiful old Romanesque and Gothic Revival church had been founded 150 years before as a summer chapel for the Edith Wharton crowd. Louise would have admired the beauty of its gilded altarpieces, gleaming pews, and Tiffany stained-glass windows, but she would also have disdained its high Anglican liturgy. To paraphrase Oscar Wilde, one church funeral for an atheist may be regarded as a misfortune, but two looks like carelessness.[11]

Before the service began, as guests milled around, Lois sought out Sandra Scoppettone to say how often Louise had spoken of her and how she had really loved her. The literary agent Pat Schartle Myrer found Alixe and suggested they get together to go over the work that Louise had left behind. Alixe later recalled that being in the church gave her a lonely feeling. She felt "as if a whole other group of people had taken Louise over," and they all kept calling Louise *Willie*. There were a few holdovers from the old days in attendance, such as Sandra and M.J., and Frederica Leser was the designated eulogist. Alixe, though invited to attend, had been discouraged from speaking during the service.

The funeral had been a private event, but the memorial was something else entirely. Lois and those advising her designed the event to build theatrically and had a souvenir program printed. Apart from a few remarks from Louise's Uncle Peter Taylor read in absentia, there would be no mention of Louise's childhood and youth in Memphis, few words about her life before Lois, and nothing whatsoever about her life as a gay woman as part of an expansive, creative circle of lesbians in theater, art, film, television, and literature.

The Reverend Willoughby Newton officiated. Newton was the headmaster of Wykeham Rise, where Joanna Hines and Lois's daughter went to school. After the invocation, he read aloud several tributes from friends who'd been unable to attend. Fabio and his wife, Laurence, were living in Paris, as was Julien Levy, a surrealist artist and gallery owner whom Louise held in high esteem. Julien sent a telegram that read, "Her painting held all the promise in the world."[12] Louise's Uncle Peter Taylor, Maurice Sendak, and James Merrill all sent written tributes (which may have mitigated the disappointment for some mourners hoping to see literary celebrities).

First, Rev. Newton read Maurice Sendak's eulogy. Maurice said he would remember Louise as a serious artist with a fierce sense of humor, someone who, in the pursuit of art and beauty, could be ruthlessly hard on herself. "She stood for everything I admire," as an artist and a friend, he wrote. "Louise—goodbye, for a while."

Next, Newton read Peter Taylor's remarks. By that time Peter was a prominent author whose stories in *The New Yorker* would have made him familiar to many in the audience. Louise, Peter had written, "was more little sister to me than niece." Together they had weathered a time of "great family trouble." He hadn't realized until later what she had suffered as a child in Memphis: "Circumstances and her temperament made Louise discover early that if she were ever to know real independence and enjoy the satisfaction of developing her special talents she would have to wage war—sometimes defensive, sometimes aggressive—against the smothering influence of a large southern family. She knew this to be the truth, no matter how much she loved members of that family and its 'connections.'"[13]

Next on the program was Jimmy Merrill, who had written an elegy.

If deceased Louise were listening, as some of her eulogists suggested she might be (surely still angry at this turn of events, and perhaps a little bored by the predictable clouds of nostalgia), hearing Jimmy Merrill's name would have snapped her to attention. It is likely that few in the audience would have another opportunity to hear an original funeral ode by a major poet. Louise's Bridgewater neighbor, Hubbell Pierce, had been designated to read the poem aloud.[14] Pierce was a cabaret performer known for his interpretation of the Cole Porter songbook. In his smoky voice, he invoked Jimmy speaking directly to Louise in her grave.

Never would there be a heaven or hell,
We once agreed, like those of youth.
Louise, if you've learned otherwise, don't tell.
Just stick to your own story,
Humorous and heartrending and uncouth.
Its little tomboy damozel
Became the figure in our repertory
Who stood for truth. Farewell.

Jimmy's poem predicted that Louise would have the kind of legacy that only one in a million writers ever achieve. She'd created an original character in a book that would become an unexpected literary classic. Harriet would join a gallery of memorable characters, including Jo in *Little Women*, Anne of Green Gables, and Scout in *To Kill a Mockingbird. Harriet the Spy*'s humor, sympathy, and defiance would be a lasting tribute to Louise's life and art. And Harriet would carry the enduring flame of truth. That's a lot to ask of an eleven-year-old—but heroines are built to bear the weight.

Then it was Frederica's turn. It was a given that nothing would be explicitly stated about Louise's sexuality. Frederica incorporated

Francis Hines's eulogy, which praised Louise as "that rarity, a successful creative writer and a painter of exceptional ability. . . . It was as though the inner pressure to express herself was so intense that a single means or medium could not satisfy it."[15] Frederica then described the Louise she'd met twenty years earlier. People underestimated her at their peril, Frederica said, recalling Louise as a "a genuine non-doctrinaire radical." Together, they'd battled the male-dominated art world. "It was a time when the Women's Movement, the gradual and grudging recognition that women could create first-rate works of art, the respect and self-respect women are now beginning to gain for themselves, were all in the future."

Frederica left it to M.J. Meaker to talk about Louise's writing. "She revolutionized children's literature," M.J. declared. "I don't think it was her love for children, particularly, nor her identification with them that made her such a natural writer. I think it was more her insistence that children were people, not to be talked down to, patronized or treated as some special group. The notion that children were people was a rare one, in those days, in our field."

As the memorial service wound down, Sloane read selected quotes from *Harriet the Spy* and *Nobody's Family Is Going to Change* aloud. She also read the paragraph from Martha Graham's biography about "keeping the channel open," which Ursula had once given to Louise to help her overcome writer's block, and which Louise had always carried folded in her wallet.

The program ended with two tributes by people Alixe had never met: Evelynne Roberts Patterson, mother of Alice and Pippy, and Elizabeth Baker Crabtree, a student at Wykeham Rise School whom Louise had briefly mentored. Then, after one more prayer, the postlude was played, a mournful rendition of *The Battle Hymn of the Republic*.

Afterward, Alixe, who was admittedly biased, said Lois had choreographed a spectacle meant to enshrine a commercially viable Louise Fitzhugh. The service had only partially reflected the Louise who Alixe knew. She thought the impression a stranger might take away was of someone conventional at her core, even if a little bit cheeky. Louise had been represented less as a Harriet than as a Beth Ellen—and just to be clear, a Beth Ellen before she got her period. It was a portrait that Alixe said she watched Lois cultivate over the next forty years: Louise Fitzhugh as a chaste spinster lady with a good sense of humor.

Meanwhile, from above, Alixe said, Louise was throwing down thunderbolts.

Given the chance to add a few things, how might Louise have wanted to be remembered? Probably first as an uncompromising painter. Louise didn't rate her book illustrations—as unique and influential as they would become—as highly as her painting. She once told Fabio of the "depth, the pain, the horror, searching, fumbling," that, in her opinion, distinguished painting from illustration.[16] Alixe said Louise used to destroy paintings that she considered not up to par. She'd have wanted her paintings to be seen. And she'd have wanted to be remembered as a writer whose work had meaning and staying power. Louise was happy with Harriet's success, but Louise's success as the creator of a phenomenon made it harder for her to write plays and novels for adults. She would certainly have been pleased at the theatrical success of *Nobody's Family Is Going to Change*, and its adaptation as a musical for Broadway, but she might have liked her own play, *Mother Sweet, Father Sweet*, to be seen. Alixe thought so, and tried to convince Louise's heirs to allow the play to be staged. Lois refused the request, and very few people have read the script.

It's likely Louise would have wanted to be remembered as someone who picked herself up, and who tried not to deceive herself or her friends. She wasn't ready to go, but that's not to say she hadn't given some thought to immortality. There is a passage in *Harriet the Spy* that speaks to memory and the passage of time, and it speaks to the eleven-year-old inside. It's in the voice of Ole Golly, the nanny who moved to Montreal:

> If you're missing me, I want you to know I'm not missing you. Gone is gone. I never miss anything or anyone because it all becomes a lovely memory. I guard my memories and love them, but I don't get in them and lie down. You can even make stories from yours, but remember, they don't come back. Just think how awful it would be if they did. You don't need me now. You're eleven years old which is old enough to get busy at growing up to be the person you want to be.[17]

After the memorial, the guests were invited to the Blue Room at the Plaza Hotel for a cocktail party—or "The Death Party," as Sandra called it. Louise had joked about having just such a gathering with Sandra, and even earlier with France Burke, who had come to the memorial with Sam Shea. Louise's relationship to the Plaza Hotel was complicated. She had viewed it as a bastion of the ruling class, snooty and snobby, but she enjoyed her brief incursions for its delicious food and soothing surroundings. She liked its old uptown grandeur and the way it stood in such stark contrast to her grittier downtown life. The Plaza was a symbol to be held in equipoise with the arch of Washington Square: they were two pieces in the jigsaw of her life. If Louise had her own bookplate, there might have been silhouettes of both monuments staring across town at each other, perhaps served on a bed of Long Island beach front, typewriters, euphoric brushes and pens, new cars, dogs and cats, and rosebuds dancing with brandy bottles. And, on a banner, a motto: *Bury Me North of the Mason-Dixon Line.*

Nobody's Family Is Going to Change was published ten days after Louise's death, and the good reviews did come. Alice Bach refuted the *Publishers Weekly* "stopped clock" comment, saying in the *Whole Earth Catalog* that "whatever subject Louise Fitzhugh writes about becomes a topic of the future."[18] The *New York Times* said the characters "seem alive—a singular achievement in this field."[19] The *Boston Globe* also praised Louise as a "master story teller," while a librarian writing for a Nebraska paper said she "liberated her characters long before it was fashionable."[20] The *Times Literary Supplement* lauded Louise's "extraordinary gift for exploring the teenage mind with its flashes of hatred and insight mingling with the absurd fantasies and other minutiae of obsessional image building."[21]

It is worth mentioning that there are no recorded objections to the Sheridan family members' voices, accents, or dialogue as sounding false, as Michael di Capua once feared. Reviewers in general paid more attention to the family's problems in the story than to the book's array of social issues. A few years after publication, however, the writer Adrienne Shirley put it all together. In a long critical essay for the British women's journal *Off Our Backs*, she looked at the way "privilege offers little or no protection against the powerlessness of childhood." Emma's story, Shirley wrote, unfolds at the intersection of "sexism, racism, heterosexism, class mobility and middle-class ethics," and at the end, she emerges with the special resilience of a hero.[22]

Louise makes the case in all her books for children's liberation, providing life-preserving strategies that children may employ in their power struggle with adults. Lying is one time-honored tactic; self-reliance is another.[23] The hardest advice is pure Louise—unsentimental and indefatigable—written for impatient young Emma, who likes to have the last word and speaks the truth: "We have to stop waiting around for them to love us!"[24]

AFTERWORD

Harriet, as Jimmy's poem prophesied, would carry Louise into the future. As executor of the estate in control of Louise's legacy, Lois would preserve the mystique surrounding the author of *Harriet the Spy*, starting with her physical image.

The reprints of Louise's books would typically feature one of Sue Singer's photographs from the summer of 1964. In one, Louise is holding Sue's Yorkie, sitting on a park swing; in another, she's at her desk in Yorkville. Articles and online sites would repeatedly reproduce the one with the swing; for decades it would be the most familiar version of the author, frozen in the year *Harriet the Spy* was published. The public Louise is a small, impish, unmarried lady, a lover of dogs, and a dedicated creator of a body of work about outspoken girls and boys. Harriet, her premier invention, is a mischievous problem child who in the end *learns her lesson*.

Meanwhile, the lesson *Harriet*'s admiring readers took was the one about being yourself, and about having friends *and* a fulfilling job. As Harriet went out to work, so did millions of young women in the second half of the twentieth century, embarking on many of the nontraditional careers and professions their mothers had been discouraged from joining. Harriet's intelligence and talent to adapt made her a role model in the parlance of one generation and an influencer for subsequent ones. If critics in the 1960s viewed her as cheeky, bratty, and sophisticated, from the 1970s on readers and writers began to recognize Harriet as a convention-flouting subversive. In articles from the 1980s and 1990s, Harriet embodies the spirit of the age as a smart-ass feminist who lets herself go and picks herself up.

In January 2005, a librarian named Kathleen T. Horning published an article about *Harriet the Spy* in *The Horn Book*, a magazine focusing on children's literature.[1] She talks about the book's influence on her own childhood and observes that there's a "queer subtext" throughout the book. Horning interprets Ole Golly's advice to Harriet—that "sometimes you have to lie . . . but to yourself you must always tell the truth"—as evidence of Louise's embedded instructions to gay kids: *You are not alone, come out when it is safe to do so.* Homophobes during the culture wars of the late twentieth century and early twenty-first fulminated about coded messages in the media meant to turn schoolchildren gay. Horning suggests that there *are* secret message in *Harriet the Spy*, benign and comforting ones that offer fellowship and reassurance to young people trying to figure themselves out.

> Not only is Harriet the quintessential baby butch, but her best friends, Sport and Janie, run exactly contrary to gender stereotypes. Sport acts as the homemaker and nurturing caretaker of his novelist father, while Janie the scientist plans to blow up the

> world one day. It was as if Fitzhugh was telling us kids back in the sixties that you didn't have to play by society's rules, the first lesson a queer kid has to learn in order to be happy. Harriet's whole ordeal—being ostracized by her friends after they invade her privacy by reading her spy notebook—sounds to me very much like a coming-out story.

Harriet is a fictional little girl. Whether she grows up to be gay, or even a spy, is a matter for theorists. In a 2006 short story, "The Insipid Profession of Jonathan Horneboom," the writer Jonathan Lethem imagines Harriet as an adult private eye.[2] A satirical 2017 article by Dahlia Lithwick in *Slate* begins with "An Open Letter to Robert Mueller from the Association of Super Secret Detectives." It amusingly recommends that Mueller invite Harriet to join his team in investigating Russian interference in the 2016 US elections.[3] If only.

As a note-taking child spy, Harriet was comic in execution. But spying was not always so quaint—or fictional—for those, like Louise, who came of age during the McCarthy-era Red Scare. Louise was aware that FBI agents were assigned to keep scrupulous notes on suspected communist sympathizers. She knew that the consequences of being accused of left-wing activism (whether a person was guilty or not) could be counted in lost jobs and livelihoods. People were blacklisted (like the actors Alixe tried to help), and they were hauled before the House Un-American Activities Committee (like Louise's young neighbor Mitch Grayson's headmaster at the Downtown Community School, Norman Studer).

As the United States Attorney for Western Tennessee, Millsaps Fitzhugh had the dubious honor of serving as spy-catcher in chief when Junius Scales was prosecuted for his role in a perceived international communist conspiracy. Harriet stands in vivid contrast to Louise's father. She never intends to punish the characters on her spy route for their conduct, however strange it may seem to her. She is not in the business of extortion or blackmail; nor does she wish to reveal the secrets she gathers. Instead, she spies to have something to write about. It's all material.

Alixe missed Louise so much that she made an appointment to see Louise's former psychiatrist, Dr. Bertram Slaff, just to talk about her. He was a serious man, and in line with his profession, he wouldn't discuss specifics about Louise. He did tell Alixe that he'd met Louise in a writers' group, and that he thought her "a trailblazer in the sense that she broke taboos in children's literature, introducing things that hadn't been written about before, like menstruation." He thought she was brave and that she "really put up a battle to write about things that ought not be ignored."[4]

After Louise's will was read, the lawyers for Louise's estate informed Alixe that Louise had bequeathed her $10,000. Lois Morehead was named as Louise's heir, and there were no additional bequests for family members. Some of Louise's Perkins relatives and other Connecticut friends were under the impression that Louise had left at least a portion of her fortune to a fund for abused children, but they were mistaken. There is no mention of such a bequest in her will. Lois and friends did list an address in the souvenir program for Louise's memorial. This "Louise Fitzhugh Memorial Fund for Child Abuse" was a temporary designation for donations in Louise's memory. By 1990, the organization handling the fiscal matters had been dissolved.

As 1975 began, Alixe still hadn't heard from Pat Schartle Myrer, who had asked her for help looking through Louise's manuscripts. When Alixe eventually called her, Pat said that Lois was upset at the idea that Alixe might have any influence over Louise's estate going forward. Lois had told Pat that she was "suspicious of Alixe's motives."[5] Alixe still tried to keep Louise's work in the public eye. She wanted readers to recognize Louise as a smart, sophisticated, versatile writer and artist. Her ambition to produce Louise's autobiographical play *Mother Sweet, Father Sweet* in an off-Broadway production was stymied when Lois wouldn't grant permission. Lois also made it difficult for Sandra Scoppettone to reprint *Suzuki Beane*, to which they held joint copyright.

In the year after Louise's death, Lois hired Cary Ryan, a young editor at Delacorte, to make an inventory of Louise's papers. Cary looked through the contents of a trunk and boxes containing unfinished plays, fiction, and illustrations for books in progress. She began her work with the understanding that Lois wanted to cultivate and honor Louise's legacy. She also recognized the estate's wish to monetize Louise's work. At first, this hadn't seemed like a contradiction. Everyone wanted the same thing: more Louise Fitzhugh books to be read by more people. Lois was pushing "to make the most of what Louise had left," Cary said.[6]

There were no personal letters, but there were some editors' notes about Louise's various books. Lois gave Cary permission to look at everything she had in her possession. Among the papers in the trunk and boxes were several journals that Louise had begun in 1962, when she was still in therapy with Dr. Slaff. According to Cary's notes, the journal describes her concerns about a troubled world and her search for peace of mind. She worries she's not sufficiently vulnerable, and maybe a little mad. She feels driven to extremes and defiance in the face of misogyny and homophobia. Louise is completely open about her sexuality and longs for unconditional love from the women in her life.[7]

Cary found Louise's play *Mother Sweet, Father Sweet* and her novel *Crazybaby*, both interesting as biography, but incomplete and unpublishable. There were also several pictures that might have been paired with text, as well as others in process. *The Owl and the Lark*, a picture book that Charlotte Zolotow had liked—and that Cary considered ready for publication—Lois peremptorily withdrew, saying Louise hadn't completed its illustrations.

Another children's picture book, *The Escape of Francis O'Toole*, which Cary liked too, was also missing illustrations. In a thick file with many notes attached, Cary discovered Louise's manuscript for *Sport*, which she thought close enough to completion to recommend publication.

Back in the late 1960s, after Charlotte had returned the *Sport* manuscript to Louise for revision, Louise had put it aside, perhaps intending to return to it someday. When Pat Schartle Myrer, on behalf of the estate, submitted this rediscovered manuscript to Michael di Capua at Farrar, Straus and Giroux, he rejected it. He believed that it lacked the vitality of Louise's other work. In a letter to Roger Straus, he suggests that if Louise had genuinely wanted *Sport* to be published, she would have told him so.[8] (Alixe rejects as preposterous the idea that Louise would have confided in di Capua, with whom she had such a vexed relationship when he was her editor on *Nobody's Family Is Going to Change*.)

After some additional editing, *Sport* would be published in 1979. Lois hired Cary to clean the manuscript up for publication. The novel is campy, cartoonish, and fun. It starts as Sport's maternal grandfather is dying: at twelve years old, he's in line to inherit $20 million. Sport's absent mother, Charlotte Vane, whom he hasn't seen since his father won custody in their divorce, lives a flamboyant life abroad. Her father's will entitles Charlotte to half of Sport's inheritance if she can behave as a proper mother and care for her son decently—and she only has to do so for a period of six months. It seems a potentially easy task, but not for Sport's mother, who is entirely undomesticated and pathologically incapable of submitting to the patriarchy. Charlotte, who shares a surname with Dorothy Sayers's detective Harriet Vane, messes up in every way, notably by kidnapping her own child—twice! There are some funny antics in the Plaza Hotel, and there are some inventive escapes. Louise may have personally loathed farces, but she was awfully good at writing them.

In the course of events, Sport recognizes his mother as somebody he can never love. That's dark, and it would be tragic if Charlotte didn't also obviously dislike her son. Meanwhile, Sport's father becomes engaged to a very accommodating but dull woman, which leaves the adultish Sport free from the responsibility of caring for his childish father. In the end, his mother skips back to Europe, having failed to satisfy the terms of the will, which, in any case, is stunningly misogynist and cruelly controlling. She flips off her father, her son, and her former husband. Everyone survives.

For an author whose early work was subtly political, this book and *Nobody's Family Is Going to Change* (written after *Sport*, but published earlier) are overtly so. In the second of *Sport*'s two kidnapping scenes, Sport, along with an African American friend, a Chicano friend, and a Jewish friend, is confronted by a New York policeman. Led by his prejudices, the officer accuses the boys of inciting an incident of which they are innocent. It is a reflection of the kind of police brutality reported in New York City in the late 1960s and early 1970s.[9] The angry encounter is one strange, brief turn in what is essentially a frothy, go-for-broke screwball adventure. *Sport* is distinctly *not* in the vein of the New Realism that *Harriet the Spy* gained credit for spearheading. Sport's mother, Charlotte, is drawn somewhere south of Cruella de Vil. In addition to insisting, long before it was commonplace, on the diversity of a child's cohort, Louise's plot allows for lots of commentary on divorce and class. And in its discussion of overpriced coffins, there is some reference to *The American Way of Death*, Jessica Mitford's muckraking exposé of the America's funeral business.[10]

The book had a flip-floppy afterlife. There is an ironic use of the *N*-word by a young Black kid during the angriest scene, and it continues to offend. Consequently, the book has been recommended by some gatekeepers for censorship.[11] It is not as well regarded as Louise's other books, and it is viewed suspiciously by some readers as not being fully Louise's. But there is a lot of

Louise in *Sport*, as much as in *Harriet the Spy*. Harriet flourished, but the quasi-orphaned Sport flailed and floundered. Poor kid, he was abandoned, rejected, and not nearly loved enough. Still, amazingly, he's in this book running through the Plaza corridors, fully alive, and rich enough to afford a happy ending.

Lois and her heirs continued as strict guardians of Louise's work. The requests of most journalists and biographers for permission to read Louise's papers have been politely declined. When Virginia Wolf, a children's literature scholar, was researching her 1991 literary biography *Louise Fitzhugh*, Lois permitted her to read Xeroxed manuscripts of *Crazybaby* and *Mother Sweet, Father Sweet*, but eventually decided against supporting Wolf's work. She informed Wolf that if she were to authorize a biography of Louise and give full access to a biographer, it would only be for an author with a contract to a major publisher. She felt that Wolf's publisher, Twayne, which published scholarly biographies, did not fill the bill.

After Pat Schartle Myrer's retirement, Lois hired the literary agent Phyllis Wender to help her market Louise's manuscripts and manage the continuing popularity of the character Harriet the Spy. Random House published two spin-offs featuring Harriet: *Harriet Spies Again*, by Helen Ericson, in 2003, and *Harriet the Spy, Double Agent*, by Maya Gold, in 2007. Both sold in respectable numbers, but no further spin-offs were commissioned. Louise had regularly discussed her work with Alixe, and just weeks before her death they had talked about Louise completing the pictures for *I Am Five*, which makes it her final book.[12]

The charming, funny heroine of *I Am Five* is full of outrage and self-doubt. Her face, a self-portrait of Louise at five years old, is dominated by a mass of untamed, circulating ringlets. She says she loves to talk and finds it hard to stop. With her body tilted at an angle, one hand at her waist and a finger at her brow, she gives the impression of a television host about to pontificate. She also dances, like most of Louise's heroines, in this case demonstrating a fancy soft shoe. Her complaints are few and common to her age. She doesn't want to brush her teeth or go to sleep. In one illustration, when a disembodied arm lifts her by the collar of her pajamas, her face registers indignation. Sometimes she gets so mad she wants to kick something. Later, at night in her bedroom, she makes a more intimate confession: in the dark, she's frightened because she's just so small. Come morning, her night fears forgotten, she's modeling her new topless bikini, with a campy, incandescent smile, ready for her close-up. In the final pages of the book, there's just something off. She seems to be impersonating an adult. She says she feels very well, but her expression isn't entirely convincing, and the book concludes somewhat enigmatically. Perhaps Louise intended an epilogue.

Two other books in the series, *I Am Three* and *I Am Four*, remained unfinished at Louise's death. These were published in 1983, both with illustrations by artists other than Louise.

One unexpected and lucrative development was the success of both adaptations of *Nobody's Family Is Going to Change*. It was first adapted into an *NBC Special Treat* afterschool special in 1978 under the name *The Tap Dance Kid*. Written and directed by Barra Grant, it received an Emmy. It was later adapted as a musical, with a book by Charles Blackwell, music by Henry Krieger, and lyrics by Robert Lorick. The show opened on Broadway in 1983. The commercial success of *The Tap Dance Kid* helped to revive popular interest in tap dancing and showcased some of its foremost practitioners.[13] The show won Tony awards for Danny Daniels's choreography and Hinton Battle's performance as Uncle Dipsy.

In 1988, I was hired as a playwright for a children's theater adaptation of *Harriet the Spy*. In 1996, *Harriet the Spy* was updated and adapted into a motion picture directed by Bronwen Hughes.[14] Alixe, whose career continued to flourish, and who became the casting director for many prestigious movies through the 1970s and 1980s golden age of film, was disappointed by the cast of *Harriet the Spy*. She thought the role of Ole Golly should have been played by Jane Wagner's partner Lily Tomlin. There was also an attempt to update Harriet in a cable feature called *The Harriet Blog Wars*. On the fiftieth anniversary of the publication of *Harriet the Spy*, in 2014, Delacorte Books for Young Readers published a special edition of the novel that includes short tribute essays by Nick Clarke, Anita Silvey, Judy Blume, Elizabeth Winthrop, and others, who treat Harriet's spying as the education of an artist, and the novel at its core as about ways of seeing.

In his essay for the anniversary edition, Gregory Maguire, the author of the novel *Wicked*, wrote of Harriet's singular influence on his childhood ambition.[15] In 2019, Maguire would also note how he still meets people "who became professional writers because of *Harriet the Spy*." He added, "It's really a single tripwire for an entire generation of writers."[16] The list of writers who consider Harriet an influence is a long one and includes literary fiction writers, children's authors, memoirists, and artists. Cartoonist and writer Alison Bechdel called the book "an excruciatingly accurate depiction of the compulsion to write . . . and draw . . . and the toll that this exacts on one's life."[17]

Lois died in 2009 at the age of seventy-eight. Her obituary states that during "the last 35 years, she was actively engaged in bringing to life the children's books of Louise Fitzhugh." She is praised as a woman with a charitable nature, and her mourners were asked to donate on her behalf to "Doctors Without Borders," an international humanitarian organization. She was survived by her daughter.[18]

Lois may have purchased a plot for herself beside Louise, but she is not buried there. There is no one buried on either side of Louise's grave, which is surrounded by beautiful low New England rock walls in a well-kept Connecticut cemetery. Her headstone is a large, roughly hewn piece of granite with an austere inscription: "Louise Fitzhugh October 4, 1928–November 19, 1974." Her other memorial, designated by United for Libraries as a Literary Landmark, is in Carl Schurz Park, near the water fountains and across from the playground. It reads as follows:

> Author Louise Fitzhugh (1928–1974) used this park and other familiar neighborhood sites in her novel. In this park, Harriet follows Ole Golly on her date with Mr. Waldenstein, gathers a frog to put in Marion Hawthorne's desk at school, and most memorably, plays a game of tag with the kids in her class. But most importantly, Harriet took her notebook over to the park and sat on a bench. She found that she enjoyed writing under the trees.[19]

AUTHOR'S NOTE

In 1963, when Louise Fitzhugh was thirty-five and writing *Harriet the Spy*, about an eleven-year-old girl who lived in New York, I was also an eleven-year-old girl who lived in New York. Harriet lived on the ritzy Upper East Side, while my family of five had migrated from the Bronx to rural Long Island, to live closer to my father's five-acre junkyard. His business, A&B Auto Wrecking, was located across the road from the Speonk train station—and, as I would later learn, about five miles from Louise Fitzhugh's summer home in Quogue. Speonk was the train stop for Louise's friends visiting from the city, a three-hour trip. Ursula Nordstrom disembarked there, as did Louise's other friends, including actors, painters, editors, and all the other glamorous denizens of her intersecting literary and artistic worlds.

Fitzhugh and I were from different sides of the tracks, but we may well have crossed paths at Mrs. D.'s diner, which served as the train station waiting room. Mrs. D. wore 1940s-style housedresses, her hair in a net, as she fried hamburgers and brewed coffee in what had once been the narrow galley kitchen of a working railroad carriage. Whenever my father took me to lunch at Mrs. D's, I'd order an egg cream and a tomato sandwich (BLT on white bread, hold the toast, hold the bacon), a combo I believed to be entirely my own invention. Now, I think it likely Mrs. D. served the same off-menu meal to others—perhaps even to a crop-haired, petite woman dressed in paint-stained overalls who was waiting for a train.

Harriet the Spy was originally targeted for children born during the end of the Baby Boom, in other words, readers then between eight and twelve, including me. But in 1964, when the novel was published, I knew nothing of its existence, and I would not learn about it for years. In sixth grade, I had left kids' lit behind. I preferred to read novels that seemed to last forever, like *The Agony and the Ecstasy*, by Irving Stone, and anything by Daphne du Maurier. I was a devoted reader of comic books and of *Mad Magazine*. To be honest, the most important literature in my life were the lyrics to Beatles songs.

Such was my tenuous and distant connection to Louise Fitzhugh, a state of affairs that would remain unaltered for another thirty-five years, until 1988, when I was hired to write an adaptation of *Harriet the Spy* for the Minneapolis Children's Theatre Company. I read it through several times, stunned at how lucky I was—after all this time, and the many ways our rendezvous might have gone awry—to find her.

ACKNOWLEDGMENTS

First, thanks to Gary Amdahl, my best editor, reader, and companion in lockdown. Thanks to Regina White, researcher, fact-checker, and literary detective, whose commitment is to excavating lost worlds and getting things right. Thanks so much to Laura Mazer for believing in this project and making it real, and to my agent, Wendy Sherman, for kind support. Thanks also to my talented editor Claire Potter. And thank you, Carolyn Levin, for your sage advice.

While researching this book I spoke to many people who had known Louise Fitzhugh, and I would like to take this moment to thank them all from the bottom of my heart. I am particularly grateful to Karen Cook, who did so many of the preliminary interviews and was so generous to me; to the erudite and intrepid Sam Shea, who shared France Burke's souvenirs, papers, and memories; to Marijane Meaker, a model of fearlessness; and to Sandra Scoppettone, whose knowledge and friendship have been indispensable and inspiring. Also thanks to the very kind Rebecca Jacks and to the brave, forthright Joanna Suero. I am so glad to have met you and thank you for sharing your history. I also want to honor the memories of Alixe Gordin, Fabio Rieti, Inez Ragland McCoy, and Charles McNutt for their generosity and honesty. Also thanks to Stephen Yenser of the James Merrill estate, who has permitted me to quote from poems and letters. Thanks to Cary Ryan for sharing her notes.

I'm deeply grateful for the friendship, advice, and editorial assistance of friends and readers, including Elena Engel, Erin Aubry Kaplan, Margaret Todd Maitland, Elizabeth Wray, Judith Tschann, Michael Wilson, Emily Wick, Karen Derris, Heather King Schamp, MG Maloney, and Sara Thompson. Thanks to these resourceful and talented student assistants: Erin Maxwell, Katy Trojano, Jonathan Ruhlman, and Willow Higgins.

Thanks are due as well to Flora, and Hasha and Jack; to Rick, Jane, Lauren, Erica, and Bob Brody; to Leonard Marcus and Kathleen Horning for invaluable resources along the way; and to Janis Krebs, Glenda McCoy, Ross Taylor, Denis Orsinger, Ezra Bowen, Nina Gold, Richard Glas, Julie Ann Johnson, Alice Yasuna, Lisa Hickman, Hubert M. McAlexander, Judy Zuckerman, Faith Jones, Henry Krieger, John Sieruta, Lyn Braswell, Elizabeth Winthrop, Margaret Warner, Denis Orsinger, Elise Harris, Bob Baker and The Village Voice Archive, the North Fork Women for Women Fund, Anita Silvey, Corky Sinks, Penny McElroy, Patricia Geary, Francesca Lia Block, Jean Schiffman, Katherine Streckfus, Kelsey Odorczyk, Kelly Lenkevich, Jennifer Richards, Virgina L. Wolf, Kim Womack, Rebeka Derris Murphy, Beverly Horowitz, Mary LaChapelle, Robin Jacks, Kristen Blecken, Julia Mickelsen, Patricia Reilly Giff, Jessie Wick, Joi Gresham, Tim Conant, Vivian Schneider, Lucy Wepfer, Josephine Walt, Meegan Lee Ochs, Michael Ochs, Judy Gumbo Albert, Dorothy White, and Suzy Staubach. Thanks to Elizabeth Hearne. Thanks to Jack Hayes, Arah Bahn, Beth Bierman,

Jay Carmona, Greg Farrell, Amy Gabriel, Dawn Gelle, Jennifer Gonnerman, John and Debby Hanrahan, Regina Kelly, Tom Koch, Patrice Clark Koelsch, Richard Dudley White, Thomas R. White, and Victoria J. White. Thanks to Centrum and the Dorland Colony for residencies.

Thanks to librarians and libraries around the country, including Lua Gregory and Sandi Richey at the University of Redlands; the Washington University Libraries; the New York Public Library; the Jean and Alexander Heard Library at Vanderbilt University; Rachel Dreyer, Special Collections Library, Pennsylvania State University; William Fason, formerly of the *Memphis Commercial Appeal*; Hansberry Literary Trust; Charles Griffith, McWherter Library at the University of Memphis; Sybille A. Jagusch, chief of the Children's Literature Center at the Library of Congress; Audrey Wilkicki, president of the Bridgewater Historical Society; the staff of the Smithsonian Center for Folklife and Cultural Heritage; Helene Tieger at the Stevenson Library, Bard College; Karen Brunsting at the Brooks Museum; and Tzofit Goldfarb at the HarperCollins archives. Thanks particularly to Ellen Keiter at the Eric Carle Museum of Picture Book Art and to the Hutchison School.

Some of the books and articles indispensable to my research include Karen Cook's "Regarding Harriet: Louise Fitzhugh Comes in from the Cold," *Village Voice, Literary Supplement*, April 11, 1995; Robin Bernstein's "'Too Realistic' and 'Too Distorted': The Attack on Louise Fitzhugh's *Harriet the Spy* and the Gaze of the Queer Child," *Critical Matrix* 12, no. 1–2 (2001); Faith Jones and Winnifred Tovey's website "The Unauthorized Biography of Harriet the Spy," which they call "a biography of the book, *Harriet the Spy* . . . composed for a course on the History of the Book at the University of British Columbia in the fall of 2010," https://toveyjones.com/harriet; Betsy Bird, Julie Danielson, and Peter Sieruta,

Wild Things: Acts of Mischief in Children's Literature (Somerville, MA: Candlewick Press, 2014); Leonard S. Marcus, *Minders of Make-Believe: Idealists, Entrepreneurs, and the Shaping of American Children's Literature* (Boston: Houghton Mifflin Harcourt, 2008); Ursula Nordstrom, *Dear Genius: The Letters of Ursula Nordstrom*, collected and edited by Leonard S. Marcus (New York: HarperCollins, 1998); David M. Tucker, *Memphis Since Crump: Bossism, Blacks, and Civic Reformers, 1948–1968* (Knoxville: University of Tennessee Press, 1979); James Conaway, *Memphis Afternoons: A Memoir* (Boston: Houghton Mifflin, 1993); Emma Kantor, "Tracking Harriet the Spy Through Today's YA," *The Airship*; Anna Holmes, "How to Be a Good Bad American Girl," *New Yorker*, March 6, 2014; Neva Grant, "Unapologetically Harriet, the Misfit Spy," NPR, March 3, 2008; and Andi Zeisler, "Harriet the Spy: Teaching to Transgress—Rereading a Feminist Classic of Children's Literature," *Bitch* 1, no. 3 (1996). Thank you also to the hundreds of other friends of Harriet who have written articles and posted comments about what Harriet means to them and why she still matters.

NOTE ON SOURCES

Louise Fitzhugh hated writing letters, and her only long-running correspondence was with her friend the poet James Merrill. There are some letters between Louise and her editors, and notably, an exchange with Ursula Nordstrom. She wrote and received a few others to family and friends, including to the playwright Lorraine Hansberry. Louise Fitzhugh's papers are not held by any public library or institution. The Fitzhugh estate has some papers, but these are not available to scholars or to the public, and no letters were included in the inventory made of Louise's materials after her death. Karen Cook, a journalist and former editor for the *Village Voice*, permitted me access to the many interviews she conducted for a feature story, "Regarding Harriet: Louise Fitzhugh Comes in from the Cold," *Village Voice, Literary Supplement*, April 11, 1995. Sam Shea provided France Burke's journal pages as well as the history of the Burkes. The Fitzhugh divorce transcripts were provided by Vincent L. Clark, the Shelby County, Tennessee, archivist. Most dialogue in the book's early chapters comes directly from the court transcripts. Where dialogue has been added, the intention was to re-create the essence of conversations rather than verbatim quotes. The Fitzhugh estate is protective of information regarding Louise's life. Therefore, in my commentary about Louise's work, I have relied on the Harriet doctrine: THAT SOME PEOPLE ARE ONE WAY AND SOME PEOPLE ARE ANOTHER AND THAT'S THAT.

All quotations from the following people dated before 1930 are from transcripts of court testimony: Webster Millsaps Fitzhugh, Mary Louise Perkins Fitzhugh, Mary Frances Fitzhugh Holmes, Anona Jenkins, John T. Jones, Colonel John Walter Canada, Josephine Naylor Perkins, Gerald FitzGerald.

All quotations from the following people, unless otherwise stated, are from interviews or correspondence with Karen Cook and/or Leslie Brody, and they were compiled from in-person interviews (I), telephone interviews (T), or correspondence (C), either through postal service or email: Sandra Scoppettone, Marijane Meaker, Frederica Leser, Peggy Land Carroll, Ed Thompson, Joan Williams, Jane Wagner, Charlotte Zolotow, Ann DeWar Blecken, Dr. Bertram Slaff, Susanne Singer, George Nicholson, Molly Leeds, Sloane Shelton, Jan Buckaloo, Charles McNutt, Audrey Gonzalez, Mitch Grayson, Ezra Bowen, Lois Morehead, Ross Taylor, Sam Shea, France Burke, Fabio Rieti, Crescent Dragonwagon, Betty Beaird, Barbara Dicks, Michael di Capua, Rachel Chodorov, Joanna Sueno, Glenda McCoy, Nicolas Clarke, Virginia Wolf, Lucille Stoffregen, Ellen Rudin, Cary Ryan, Elizabeth Hearne, Josephine Walt, Betty Prichard Dunn.

NOTES

Introduction: A Nasty Girl and Horrid Example

1. Louise Fitzhugh, *Harriet the Spy*, Special Anniversary Edition (HTS hereafter) (New York: Delacorte, 2014 [1964]), 187.

2. HTS, 83. Allen Ginsberg, *Howl and Other Poems* (San Francisco: City Lights Books, 1955). "Howl" famously begins, "I saw the best minds of my generation destroyed by madness."

3. Betty Friedan, *The Feminine Mystique* (New York: W. W. Norton, 2001 [1963]). Also, Gail Collins's introduction to the 50th Anniversary Edition.

4. Gloria Steinem, "A Bunny's Tale," *Show Magazine*, May 1, 1963, 90.

5. HTS, 29.

6. Friedan, *Feminine Mystique*, 58.

7. HTS, 276.

8. George Nicholson to Karen Cook (KC), interview (I).

9. This description is from her longtime friend, the artist Frederica Leser.

10. Edward Thompson (ET), quoting Louise Fitzhugh to KC (I).

11. Louise Fitzhugh (LF), letter to James Merrill (JM), undated [ca. 1963].

12. "Louise Fitzhugh Is Dead at 46," *New York Times*, November 21, 1974.

13. Jane Wagner to KC (T).

14. Frederica Leser (FL) to Leslie Brody (LB) (T).
15. Lois Morehead to KC (I).
16. Sandra Scoppettone (SS) to LB (I).
17. FL to LB (T).
18. LF, letter to Fabio Rieti, 1969, courtesy of Fabio Rieti.

Prologue

1. Joan Williams (JW) to KC, via correspondence (C).

Chapter One: Classified

1. Josephine was the adopted only child of a New Orleans heiress and a former Confederate officer, Reuben Millsaps, who built his fortune as a cotton factor during Reconstruction-era Mississippi, buying and selling cotton at a profit. Like other white veterans of the war, he owed much of his success to the large, newly emancipated, but still uneducated and piteously low-paid African American workforce. He invested his riches wisely, opened a bank, and later became one of the chief founders of Millsaps College.

2. Millsaps was born in 1903, and his younger brother, Gus Jr., in 1905. Three girls followed: Mary (Mamie) in 1907, Alice in 1909, and Julie in 1912. Alice died in 1911 of "gastroenteritis," just two years old. Julie suffered from a heart condition and died at the age of six.

3. "Separate but equal" was language from Plessy v. Ferguson, 163 U.S. 537 (1896).

4. H. L. Mencken, *A Religious Orgy in Tennessee: A Reporter's Account of the Scope's Monkey Trial* (Hoboken, NJ: Melville House, 2006), 96; Terry Teachout, *The Skeptic: A Life of H. L. Mencken* (New York: HarperCollins, 2002).

5. *Clarksdale Press Register*, February 2, 1926.

6. Peter Taylor, "The Old Forest," *New Yorker*, May 14, 1979, 42. James Conaway supplies a 1950s version of this idea in *Memphis Afternoons: A Memoir* (Boston: Houghton Mifflin, 1996), 92.

7. "Clarksdale Church Scene of Brilliant Wedding," *Memphis Commercial Appeal*, April 29, 1927, 6.

8. "The Wedding March," in C major, was written in 1842 as incidental music for a production of Shakespeare's play.

Chapter Two: Clear and Present Danger

1. Unless otherwise attributed, many of the quotations in this chapter are from court testimony during the divorce trial of Millsaps Fitzhugh and Louise Perkins Fitzhugh.

2. For twenty years, through the 1920s and 1930s, Millsaps's younger brother, Guston Thomas Fitzhugh Jr., wrote and personally published his poetry in small print runs for family and friends. His first book, *Reveries*, published in 1928 (the year Louise was born), was bound in handsomely embossed red leather and dedicated to his mother, Josephine Fitzhugh, his patron and chief enthusiast. In addition to *Reveries*, Gus would publish *Mechanics of the Sun and the Moon*, *The Mechanics of the Stars and Planets*, *The Charmer*, *The Freshman*, *Religious Poems*, and *Collected Poems*.

3. Regina Inez Ragland to LB (C).

4. *Memphis Commercial Appeal*, June 26, 1929; "Fitzhugh Blames Mother-in-Law," *Clarion-Ledger*, June 25, 1929.

5. "Cross Bill Filed in Divorce Suit," *Greenwood Commonwealth*, April 5, 1929.

Chapter Three: Interrogation

1. This was a historic first: no man had before successfully sued for divorce under a statute passed by the Tennessee legislature in 1919 giving husbands the right, previously granted only to wives, to divorce on the grounds of cruel and inhuman treatment.

2. Regina Inez Ragland to LB (C).

3. Transcripts, Chancery Court of Shelby County, Tennessee, No. 36,228 R.D.

4. In later years, this Hollywood sojourn would become mistakenly intertwined with Mary Louise's breakdown in the days after her divorce. Peter Taylor would say that "she went to Hollywood after their divorce and had a nervous breakdown."

5. Regina Inez Ragland to LB (C). The court would give Millsaps discretion to arrange visitation.

6. In the early hours of December 21, 1937, Samarkand burned down. The Captain and Josephine Fitzhugh were home after a Christmas debut ball. Josephine, reading late into the night, heard the crackling of

the blaze. Smoke and fire drove the occupants to a small, icy roof ledge, where they were rescued. "Gus T. Fitzhugh and Wife Have Narrow Escape," *Jackson (TN) Sun*, December 21, 1937, 2. Several weeks later, the couple bought "the palatial Henry Haizlip home on Poplar Avenue, overlooking Overton Park." "Fitzhugh Buys Palatial Home," *Jackson Sun*, February 10, 1938, 1.

7. As Josie Millsaps Fitzhugh, Josephine wrote three books, *Josephine Cook Book* (Memphis: Print Shop, 1936), *Happiness* (Memphis: American Print Company, 1941), and *The International Cook Book* (Memphis: American Print Company, 1941).

8. Fitzhugh, *Josephine Cook Book.*

9. Robert Wilson, "The Forgotten Short Story Master of Memphis," *Daily Beast*, October 8, 2017, www.thedailybeast.com/peter-taylor-the-forgotten-short-story-master-of-memphis.

10. Peter Taylor, "A Long Fourth," in *Complete Stories*, ed. Ann Beattie (New York: Library of America, 2017), 176.

11. LF, letter to Lorraine Hansberry, undated [1963].

12. Alixe Gordin (AG) to LB, in-person interview (I).

Chapter Four: Intelligence

1. Mary Grimes Hutchison, Miss Hutchison's School for Girls materials, circa 1931.

2. Peter Taylor, memorial program, "A Tribute to Louise Fitzhugh, 1928–1974," St. James' Church, December 6, 1974 ("memorial program" hereafter), used with permission of Ross Taylor.

3. SS to LB; AG to LB (I).

4. AG to LB (I).

5. Joan Williams, "Twenty Will Not Come Again," *Atlantic Monthly*, May 1980, 63. Williams mentions it in *The Wintering* (New York: Harcourt Brace Jovanovich, 1971), 379.

6. In 1892, Ida B. Wells was the editor and publisher of her own Memphis newspaper, called *Free Speech*. She was in Philadelphia when an altercation at a Memphis grocery resulted in the brutal lynching by a white mob of three Black men, Tom Moss, Calvin McDowell, and Will Stewart. Wells condemned the atrocities and denounced the kidnappers and murderers in her newspaper. At that time, Carmack was editor of the *Memphis Commercial Appeal* and Louise's grandfather, Captain Fitzhugh, was his protégé and attorney for the newspaper.

Carmack fulminated against Wells as "the Black wench" and mocked her defiance of white supremacy. His columns inflamed the local mania for revenge. Wells was out of town when a white mob burned down the offices of her *Free Speech* newspaper. She moved her base of operations to Chicago, where she continued her work as a journalist, human rights activist, and advocate for universal suffrage. A bronze statue of Carmack has stood on the grounds of the Tennessee State Capitol since 1924, its presence part of a lingering dispute about memorials to Confederate officers and white supremacists of days gone by.

7. Mary Louise married Jake Trevilion on April 8, 1933, six months before Millsaps married Sally Taylor.

8. David M. Tucker, *Memphis Since Crump: Bossism, Blacks, and Civic Reformers, 1948–1968* (Knoxville: University of Tennessee Press, 1979), 33.

9. The Republican Party was considered weak because its predominantly Black membership was confronted by massive resistance to racial equality. The prevailing power of white supremacists made it virtually impossible for Black politicians to expand their base.

10. Her father associated with African Americans and stood up for their civil rights, which made him hated by Democratic Memphis. David Tucker to LB (C).

11. AG to LB (I).

12. Like Louise Fitzhugh, McCullers and their regional counterpart Harper Lee wrote novels featuring child protagonists with supporting casts of misfits and rebels. McCullers and Lee pitched their work to an older audience than Fitzhugh, and their novels are set in the first half of the twentieth century. Fitzhugh did import some characters from Mississippi, and sometimes they employed southernisms in their speech, but all her published books are situated in and near New York City.

13. Carson McCullers, *The Member of the Wedding* (Boston: Houghton Mifflin, 1946), 80.

14. JW to KC (C).

15. Peter Taylor, memorial program.

Chapter Five: Best Assets

1. Peggy Land Carroll to KC (I).

2. Audrey Gonzalez, *South of Everything* (Berkeley, CA: She Writes Press, 2015), 95.

3. Josephine Fitzhugh was eventually permitted an honorary membership, becoming the first woman to achieve that dubious accomplishment.

4. AG to LB (I).

5. Joan Williams, "Twenty Will Not Come Again," *Atlantic Monthly*, May 1980, Kindle loc. 5931.

6. Virginia L. Wolf, *Louise Fitzhugh* (Boston: Twayne, 1991).

7. Wolf, *Louise Fitzhugh*, 15.

8. JW to KC (C).

9. Ann DeWar Blecken (ADB) to LB (I).

10. James Conaway, *Memphis Afternoons: A Memoir* (Boston: Houghton Mifflin, 1996), 4.

11. James Conaway to LB (T).

Chapter Six: Master of Disguise

1. ET to KC (C).

2. ET to KC (C).

3. Charles McNutt to Leslie Brody (I).

Chapter Seven: Private Investigator

1. Arthur Howard Noll, "With Ship and Books I Sail All Seas," Tessa Digital Collections of the Los Angeles Public Library, Bookplate Collection, http://tessa.lapl.org/cdm/ref/collection/bookplates/id/3385.

2. Sally "Soph," "Campus Capers," *Nashville Tennessean*, March 19, 1944. 34.

3. *The Bardian*, ca. 1949.

4. James Merrill, in a 1948 letter to Kimon Friar, quoted in Langdon Hammer, *James Merrill: Life and Art* (New York: Alfred A. Knopf, 2015), 105. Merrill's first three books were *The Black Swan*; *First Poems* (New York: Alfred A. Knopf, 1951); and *The Country of a Thousand Years of Peace and Other Poems* (New York: Alfred A. Knopf, 1959). Many other volumes of poetry followed. Merrill died in 1995.

5. Charles Simic, "Miraculous Mandarin," *New York Review of Books*, April 12, 2001. Meter in poetry means there is a fixed rhythm, such as iambic pentameter; formalists also often employ rhyme schemes. Free verse does not rely on established rhythms or fixed forms and rhyme schemes.

6. Hammer, *James Merrill*, 107.

7. James Merrill, *A Different Person* (New York: Alfred A. Knopf, 1993), 90.

8. Merrill, *Different Person*, 90.

9. Merrill, *Different Person*, 90, 107.

10. Hirsh and his friends Diego Rivera and José Clemente Orozco would influence Louise's future determination to paint frescoes.

11. "5. Painting class, ca. 1949. Fred Segal '49 paints an impression of Louise Fitzhugh '51," on webpage "Bard in Black and White: Selections from the Bard College Archives. Women Arrive," Bard College, www.bard.edu/bardinblackandwhite/page6.

12. Charles McNutt had a long, influential career as an archaeologist and professor emeritus at the University of Memphis.

13. If Louise hadn't been closely following the McCarthy-era Red Scare trials, they would have been brought home to her when the headmaster of Mitch's school, Norman Studer, was called up before the House Un-American Activities Committee (HUAC) for his association with a purportedly left-wing summer camp called Camp Woodland in the Catskill Mountains. Studer pleaded the Fifth Amendment. From Dina Hampton, *Little Red: Three Passionate Lives Through the Sixties and Beyond* (New York: Public Affairs, 2013), 8.

14. William B. Scott and Peter M. Rutkoff, *New York Modern: The Arts and the City* (Baltimore: Johns Hopkins University Press, 1999), 303.

15. James Thurber, *The 13 Clocks*, illustrated by Marc Simont (New York: Simon and Schuster, 1950).

16. Thurber, "Foreword," in *13 Clocks*, xiii. Thanks to Sonja Bolle, "Thurber's World of Wonders," *Los Angeles Times*, July 27, 2001.

17. Robin Jacks to LB (C).

Part Two

1. A fragment of a long sentence in a long letter from Ursula Nordstrom to Meindert DeJong on March 4, 1953, quoted in Ursula Nordstrom, *Dear Genius: The Letters of Ursula Nordstrom*, collected and edited by Leonard S. Marcus (New York: HarperCollins, 1998), 64. Ursula Nordstrom's titles at retirement were senior vice president of Harper and Row and publisher of Harper Junior Books.

Chapter Eight: Clues

1. Temple Fielding, *Fielding's Travel Guide to Europe*, 5th ed. (New York: Sloan, 1952), 298.

2. J. D. Salinger, *The Catcher in the Rye* (Boston: Little, Brown, 1951); Vin Packer [M.J. Meaker], *Spring Fire* (Jersey City, NJ: Cleis Press, 2004; New York: Gold Medal Books, 1952); Hannah Arendt, *The Origins of Totalitarianism* (New York: Harcourt Brace, 1951).

3. Alice Kaplan, *Dreaming in French: The Paris Years of Jacqueline Bouvier Kennedy, Susan Sontag, and Angela Davis* (Chicago: University of Chicago Press, 2013), 99.

4. Elaine Dundy, *The Dud Avocado* (New York: New York Review Books Classics, 2007), 123.

5. Lisa C. Hickman, *William Faulkner and Joan Williams: The Romance of Two Writers* (Jefferson, NC: McFarland and Company, 2006), 70.

6. Joan Williams, "Twenty Will Not Come Again," *Atlantic Monthly*, May 1980, Kindle loc. 6022.

7. Williams, "Twenty Will Not Come Again," Kindle loc. 6018.

8. Williams, "Twenty Will Not Come Again," Kindle loc. 6068; Joan Williams, "The Morning and the Evening," *Atlantic Monthly*, January 1952, 65–69.

9. France Burke, sculpture journal, 1953.

10. Barnes and Abbott were a couple. Their close friendship with France's father splintered when he and Abbott had a brief fling sometime in the 1930s. Barnes never forgave Burke's perfidy, but Abbott remained a friend of the family.

11. Sam Shea and France Burke were married as soon as New York State recognized marriages performed legally outside of the state, but before gay marriage was legal in New York State itself. France suffered cardiac arrest on their forty-eighth anniversary of being a couple.

12. Elspeth Burke's first husband was the musician Jim Chapin, and they were parents of the musician Harry Chapin.

13. Sam Shea to LB (I).

14. In 1970, several years after her father's death, Louise was still interpreting his influence. In one unpublished poem, she imagined "tiny rosebud girls" dancing "furtively" on her "father's coffin."

15. Sam Shea to LB (I); Anatole Broyard, *Kafka Was the Rage: A Greenwich Village Memoir* (New York: Carol Southern Books, 1993).

16. Sam Shea to LB (I).

17. "Louise Fitzhugh," *Memphis Commercial Appeal*, February 22, 1956.

18. Howard Rackliffe, "Village Art Center Review," *Village Voice*, 1956.

19. Virginia L. Wolf, *Louise Fitzhugh* (Boston: Twayne, 1991), xvi.

20. "Louise Fitzhugh Will Exhibit Work in 2 New York Shows," *Memphis Commercial Appeal*, February 22, 1956.

21. New York Public Library, Hudson Park Branch, March 5–31, 1956.

22. France Burke, letter to Kenneth Burke, undated [ca. March 1956], Special Collections Library, Pennsylvania State University.

23. Dundy, *Dud Avocado*, 11–12.

Chapter Nine: Rout

1. "Propeller Kills Vacationer," *New York Times*, August 6, 1956, 30.

2. France Burke, letter to Happy Leacock, August 1956.

3. LF, letter to JM, 1956 (after October 6, when Charles Merrill died).

4. Fabio Rieti to LB (C).

5. France Burke, letter to Happy Leacock, October 1956.

6. Joan Williams, "Twenty Will Not Come Again," *Atlantic Monthly*, May 1980.

7. JW to KC (C).

8. James Merrill, *The Seraglio* (New York: Alfred A. Knopf, 1957).

9. HTS, 299, 106.

10. *Letter from Cairo* is about the disappearance of intelligence officer Steve Spence, after writing a letter to his wife in New York asking for a divorce.

11. AG to LB (I).

12. 1937 Version, with Gaynor and Frederic March, directed by William A. Wellman, written by William A. Wellman, Robert Carson, Dorothy Parker, and Alan Campbell.

13. AG to LB (I).

Chapter Ten: Snoop

1. Ann Aldrich [M.J. Meaker], *We Walk Alone* (New York: Feminist Press at CUNY, 2006; New York: Gold Medal Books, 1955).

2. Thanks to Kelly Hankin, *The Girls in the Back Room* (Minneapolis: University of Minnesota Press, 2002).

3. When Sandy Rapp, a songwriter and activist, was interviewed by Gwen Shockey for her lesbian bar installation and oral history project, Rapp said, "The truth was that bars were our center of gravity and the police were the agents of institutionalized homophobia." See "Addresses Project Oral History Archive," 2019, https://gwen-shockey-rqqr.squarespace.com/oral-history-archive/sandy-rapp?rq=raid.

4. Claire Morgan [Patricia Highsmith], *The Price of Salt* (New York: Coward-McCann, 1952).

5. Donald Webster Cory's book *The Homosexual in America: A Subjective Approach* (London: Peter Nevill, 1953) was a nonfiction book about gay men. Noticing there was nothing similar for lesbians, Meaker used her own observations to write about lesbians and their lives in New York. See Aldrich [Meaker], *We Walk Alone*.

6. Ann Bannon, *Journey to a Woman* (Greenwich, CT: Fawcett, 1960).

7. FL to LB (T).

8. LF, letter to JM, undated.

9. Once at a clambake that Louise hosted for her mother on Long Island, Mary Louise grew ill and came out in a rash. She was later diagnosed as having had an allergic reaction to lobster. Glenda McCoy to LB (C).

10. Kay Thompson and Hilary Knight, *Eloise in Moscow* (New York: Simon and Schuster, 1959).

11. Sandra Scoppettone, *Suzuki Beane*, illustrated by Louise Fitzhugh (Garden City, NY: Doubleday, 1961), 51–52.

Chapter Eleven: Detect

1. Meanwhile, various voting rights lawsuits wound their tortuous way through the courts. In western Tennessee, where white Democratic officials insisted that federal civil rights laws did not apply to the internal rules of their party membership, segregationists continued to refuse to permit African Americans to vote in primary elections. In April 1960, after a federal judge overturned such discriminatory regulations, some local whites retaliated. White landowners abruptly evicted more than four hundred sharecroppers from their homes in Fayette and Haywood Counties. Black landowners gave them sanctuary, and they established

tent cities called Freedom Villages. David M. Tucker, *Memphis Since Crump: Bossism, Blacks, and Civic Reformers, 1948–1968* (Knoxville: University of Tennessee Press, 1979).

2. Scales was arrested under the Smith Act of 1940, which allowed authorities to arrest political organizers across the country for subversive activity and for merely sharing an interest in the theory of communism. Their crime was one of thought, and those arrested were charged with conspiracy. The policy was eventually repudiated and many convictions overturned by the US Supreme Court.

3. Junius Scales and Richard Nickson, *Cause at Heart: A Former Communist Remembers* (Athens: University of Georgia Press, 1987), 61.

4. "The Littlest Beat Has Her Pad in a New Off Beat Booklet," *Santa Cruz Sentinel*, June 22, 1961, 13; "Real Gasser Is Suzuki," *Arizona Republic*, May 7, 1961; "Suzuki Beane Speaks Out," *Pittsburgh Post-Gazette*, April 9, 1961; "Kookie Suzuki," *Miami News*, August 27, 1961; "Beat Book with a Bite: Like, for Youngniks," *Northwest Arkansas Times*, July 28, 1961; "The New Books," *Tampa Bay Times*, May 4, 1961.

5. JM, letter to LF, undated [1961].

6. Andre Gregory, who would have a long and illustrious career in theater (and become well known for his role in the film *My Dinner with Andre*), lost Louise's script and never returned it, according to Alixe Gordin. AG to LB (I).

7. LF, letter to JM, undated [ca. 1961].

8. JM to LF, undated [ca. 1961].

9. LF, letter to Lorraine Hansberry, undated [ca. 1962], New York Public Library, Lorraine Hansberry Papers.

10. LF, letter to Lorraine Hansberry, undated [ca. 1962].

11. FL to KC (T).

12. FL to LB (I).

13. Jane Wagner would become an accomplished and award-winning playwright and the author of *J.T.* (1967), an influential CBS afternoon special, for which she won the Peabody Award. She is married to Lily Tomlin.

14. Ursula Nordstrom (UN), letter to Joan Robins, July 28, 1981, in Ursula Nordstrom, *Dear Genius: The Letters of Ursula Nordstrom*, collected and edited by Leonard S. Marcus (New York: HarperCollins, 1998), 385.

15. LF, letter to David Jackson, 1963.

16. In "Reviews and Previews: New Names This Month," the credited critic, Ti-Grace A. Sharpless, would become better known as the feminist philosopher Ti-Grace Atkinson. *Art News*, May 1963, 19.

17. Virginia L. Wolf, *Louise Fitzhugh* (Boston: Twayne, 1991), 10.

18. LF, letter to JM, undated [ca. 1963].

Chapter Twelve: Agency

1. Deborah Kovacs and James Preller, "Louise Fitzhugh," in *Meet the Authors and Illustrators: 60 Creators of Favorite Children's Books Talk About Their Work* (New York: Scholastic Professional Books, 1991), 96.

2. AG to LB (I). These are questions that Alixe recollected to be like those Ursula and Charlotte asked.

3. Kovacs and Preller, "Louise Fitzhugh," 96.

4. UN, letter to Joan Robins, July 18, 1981, in Ursula Nordstrom, *Dear Genius: The Letters of Ursula Nordstrom*, collected and edited by Leonard S. Marcus (New York: HarperCollins, 1998), 386.

5. UN, letter to LF, November 2, 1964, in Nordstrom, *Dear Genius*, 179.

6. *Julia* was broadcast on NBC from September 17, 1968, to March 23, 1971.

7. Mississippi was where Chicago teenager Emmett Till had been grotesquely murdered on August 28, 1955, because he was not submissive to a white woman. It was also where two people had been killed and dozens injured in rioting on September 30 through October 1, 1962, at the University of Mississippi, with white segregationists protesting the enrollment of a Black student, James Meredith; and where three civil rights workers, James Chaney, Michael Schwerner, and Andrew Goodman, were abducted and murdered on June 21, 1964.

8. Françoise N. Hamlin, *Crossroads at Clarksdale: The Black Freedom Struggle in the Mississippi Delta After World War II* (Chapel Hill: University of North Carolina Press, 2012), 296n82, cites papers reporting "that the library board wanted to close the library, so removing the chairs so that black people could not sit with whites was the concession. The Carnegie Public Library in Clarksdale had allowed black patrons to use a segregated basement room."

9. In 1966, Connie would be "Longhorn Jenny" in the seventeen-episode ABC television network version of *Shane*, with David Carradine

playing the title role. She had some notable villainess roles in movies. In *A Summer Place* (1959), she is Sandra Dee's deranged mom. In 1967, Connie would begin playing the role of Ada Hobson in the daytime NBC soap opera *Another World*, staying on the program for twenty-five years.

10. Read Jacqueline Susann, *Valley of the Dolls* (New York: Bernard Geis Associates, 1966), for an over-the-top evocation of the ubiquitous diet pills. See also Muriel Sparks, *Loitering with Intent* (New York: G. P. Putnam's, 1981).

11. LF, letter to JM, undated [ca. 1965].

Chapter Thirteen: Agent Harriet

1. HTS, 39.

2. HTS, 32.

3. HTS, 276.

4. Elizabeth Hearne first floated the idea as a graduate student in the mid-1960s that *Harriet the Spy* and *Suzuki Beane* reflected a new order. Thanks to her for reflecting on this idea in "Fifty Years of Novel Exploits," *Horn Book Magazine*, May/June 2014, 19.

5. To Holden Caulfield and his acolytes, phoniness is "not only insincerity, but snobbery, injustice, callousness." S. N. Behrman, "The Vision of the Innocent," *New Yorker*, August 4, 1951.

6. Stephen Sondheim, *West Side Story*, used by permission.

7. Athar Yawar, "The Madness of Charlie Brown," *The Lancet* 386, no. 10001 (October 3, 2015): 1332–1333.

8. Behrman, "Vision of the Innocent."

9. Donald Trump called Hillary Clinton a "nasty woman" in the third 2016 presidential debate on October 19, 2016, in Las Vegas.

10. For Harriet, losing Ole Golly also means losing an ally in her struggle to become a spy and a writer. Andi Zeisler, "Harriet the Spy: Teaching to Transgress—Rereading a Feminist Classic of Children's Literature," *Bitch* 1, no. 3 (1996).

11. These directions are from a map by Abigail Dakar included in the fiftieth anniversary edition of *Harriet the Spy*. Other cartographers of the territory include Judith Zuckerman and Leonard Marcus.

12. "All of humanity's problems stem from man's inability to sit quietly in a room alone." Blaise Pascal, *Pensées* (1670).

13. Some of the cats are named after Louise's friends: David (Jackson), Alex (Gordin), Sandra (Scoppettone), Pat (Schartle Myrer), Gloria (Safire), Marijane (Meaker), Francis (Hines), Fred (Leser), and Yvonne (Ray). Jerusalem and Barnaby were the names of Alixe's cats.

14. Although, in the late 1960s, Sally Taylor Fitzhugh did wield some influence as a member of the Memphis Board of Television. *Memphis Press-Scimitar*, June 12, 1956.

15. HTS, 87.

16. FR to LB (C).

17. Harper Lee, *To Kill a Mockingbird*, Harper Perennial Modern Classic (New York: HarperCollins, 2014 [1960]).

18. HTS, 297. Thanks to Ama Holmes for her idea about those socks.

19. HTS, 295.

20. W. B. Yeats, "Fergus and the Druid" (1892), originally published in *The Countess Kathleen and Various Legends and Lyrics* (Boston: Roberts Brothers, 1893).

Chapter Fourteen: Divided Loyalties

1. Geri Trotta, "Not to Be Missed," *Harper's Bazaar* 98, no. 3036 (November 1964): 24–25, 82.

2. Gloria Vanderbilt, "Harriet the Spy, by Louise Fitzhugh," *New York Times Book Review*, November 22, 1964.

3. Ellen Rudin, *School Library Journal* 89 (November 15, 1964): 4638–4638.

4. Jane Adam Smith, "Engines of Mischief," *New York Review of Books*, December 3, 1964.

5. Smith, "Engines of Mischief."

6. "Gracious How These Memphis and Mid-South Authors Do Win Distinction," *Memphis Commercial Appeal*, December 15, 1964.

7. Ann was married by then to Bob Blecken and was an occasional garden columnist for the local papers. This photo may have been taken by an unnamed family friend.

8. HTS, 131.

9. Margaret Libby Sherwood, *Book Week*, January 10, 1965.

10. Ruth Hill Viguers, "On Spies and Applesauce and Such," *The Horn Book*, February 1965, 74–76.

11. Patience M. Daltrey, "The Cold That Came in with the Spy," *Christian Science Monitor*, February 25, 1965.

12. Phyllis Cohen, *Young Readers Review*, February 6, 1965.
13. Crescent Dragonwagon to LB (T).
14. LF, letter to Fabio Rieti, undated (ca. 1965).
15. Boris Kachka, *Hothouse: The Art of Survival and the Survival of Art at America's Most Celebrated Publishing House, Farrar, Straus, and Giroux* (New York: Simon and Schuster, 2013), 127.
16. Boris Kachka to LB (C).
17. Barbara Dicks to LB (I).
18. Leonard S. Marcus, *Minders of Make-Believe: Idealists, Entrepreneurs, and the Shaping of American Children's Literature* (Boston: Houghton Mifflin Harcourt, 2008), 241.
19. Nat Hentoff and George Woods, *New York Times Book Review*, quoted in Michael Cart, *Young Adult Literature: From Romance to Realism*, 3rd ed. (Chicago: American Library Association, 2016), 28.
20. JM, letter to LF, February 11, 1965.
21. UN, letter to LF, February 25, 1965, in Ursula Nordstrom, *Dear Genius: The Letters of Ursula Nordstrom*, collected and edited by Leonard S. Marcus (New York: HarperCollins, 1998), 188.
22. Nordstrom, *Dear Genius*, 189.
23. Nordstrom, *Dear Genius*, 189.
24. Nordstrom, *Dear Genius*, 189.
25. UN, letter to Joan Robins, July 28, 1981, in *Dear Genius*, 383.
26. Charlotte Zolotow to KC (T).
27. AG to LB (I).
28. Ellen Rudin to LB (C).
29. "His Nights Are Filled with Adventure: U.S. DA Dreams About Bull Fighting," *Memphis Press-Scimitar*, January 6, 1958.
30. It's likely that Louise knew of the rumors that her father saw other women. She certainly knew of his violent temper. She may not have known that Sally had once attempted suicide. Hubert M. McAlexander to LB (C) (email, July 10, 2017): "Sally tried to commit suicide while Peter was teaching at Kenyon. I imagine she did that because of Millsaps. He was a notorious womanizer."
31. Emily Maxwell, "Children's Books for Christmas," *New Yorker*, December 4, 1965, 219.
32. "The Long Secret," *Bulletin*, Virginia Kirkus Service, October 1, 1965.
33. Houston L. Maples, "Growing Pains," *Book Week*, October 31, 1965, 41.

34. Carolyn Heilbrun, *New York Times Book Review*, November 21, 1965.

35. The quotation is in a letter from Joan Williams to Virginia L. Wolf, in *Louise Fitzhugh* (Boston: Twayne, 1991), 110.

Part Three

1. Louise Fitzhugh, *Nobody's Family Is Going to Change* (New York: Lizzie Skurnick Books, 2016; New York: Farrar, Straus and Giroux, 1974), 195.

Chapter Fifteen: Luck, Speculation, Windfalls

1. Nat Hentoff, "Among the Wild Things," *New Yorker*, January 22, 1966, 39–73; Maurice Sendak, *Where the Wild Things Are* (New York: Harper and Row, 1963).

2. M.J. Meaker to LB (I).

3. Joan Didion, "On Keeping a Notebook," in *Slouching Towards Bethlehem* (New York: Farrar, Straus and Giroux, 1968). The essay first appeared in *Holiday*, December 1966, 10–12, 19–20.

4. JM, letter to LF, July 14, 1966.

5. LF, letter to JM, undated [summer 1966].

6. All information about unfinished material comes from notes that Cary Ryan made for an inventory after LF's death.

7. Josephine Walt to LB (I).

8. LF, letter to JM, undated [summer 1966].

9. UN, letter to LF, August 8, 1966, in Ursula Nordstrom, *Dear Genius: The Letters of Ursula Nordstrom*, collected and edited by Leonard S. Marcus (New York: HarperCollins, 1998), 225.

10. LF, letter to JM, undated [1966].

11. JW to KC (C).

12. Sally Fitzhugh's last will and testament.

13. AG to LB (I).

14. George Woods and Margaret F. O'Connor, "Best in the Field: For Children," *New York Times Book Review*, February 25, 1968, 18.

15. The quote is from Agnes de Mille, *Martha: The Life and Work of Martha Graham* (New York: Random House, 1991), 264, used by permission.

16. Louise never replied to Charlotte or Ursula directly, and not even Pat Schartle could get Louise to address the issue. Twenty-five years later, Delacorte would apologize for publishing the same text, but attributed to Louise Fitzhugh (with illustrations this time by Lillian Hoban). The manuscript had been in Louise's possession at the time of her death and was sold to Delacorte by the executor of her estate along with other unpublished manuscripts. The book, retitled as *I Know Everything About John and He Knows Everything About Me*, went through production and was published in 1993 without anyone recognizing it. *Publishers Weekly* even reviewed it before a reader identified it and its embarrassed publishers recalled the book. "A Picture Book Mix-Up," *Publishers Weekly*, November 22, 1993, 30.

17. AG to LB (I).

18. UN, letter to Pat Schartle, February 29, 1968, in Nordstrom, *Dear Genius*, 261.

19. AG to LB (I).

20. In a strange convergence of events, Ed Thompson, who had become a public defender in Memphis, found himself briefly assigned by a judge to be counsel of record for James Earl Ray, who was later convicted of the assassination and sent to prison. (He pled guilty to avoid a jury trial and the death penalty.) At the time that Thompson was involved, Ray and his team were arranging for his defense.

21. Louise Fitzhugh and Sandra Scoppettone, *Bang Bang You're Dead*, illustrations by Louise Fitzhugh (New York: Harper and Row, 1969).

22. Karen Cook, "Regarding Harriet: Louise Fitzhugh Comes in from the Cold," *Village Voice, Literary Supplement*, April 11, 1995, SS12.

23. FL to LB (T); AG to LB (I).

24. Pat Hemingway was later co-owner with Francis Carpenter of the Bull's Head Inn, featured in *The Long Secret* as the Shark's Tooth Inn (Harriet and her friends call it "The Evil Hotel").

25. Five years after her summer affair with Louise, Pat Hemingway would try to straighten up. She became a writer of how-to books in some of the many subjects in which was expert. She collaborated on an *Auto Repair Primer* and wrote *The Well-Dressed Woman: A Complete Guide to Creating the Right Look for Yourself and Your Career* and *The Transcendental Meditation Primer: How to Stop Tension and Start Living*. She died in 1978 at the age of fifty-one.

Chapter Sixteen: Tradecraft

1. Leonard S. Marcus, *Minders of Make-Believe: Idealists, Entrepreneurs, and the Shaping of American Children's Literature* (Boston: Houghton Mifflin Harcourt, 2008), 242, 244.

2. Raymond Walters Jr., "Paperback Parcels," *New York Times*, December 1, 1968.

3. Jane K. Hirsch, "The Critical Reception of Three Controversial Children's Books, *Harriet the Spy* by Louise Fitzhugh, *Ring the Judas Bell* by James Foreman, *Drop Dead* by Julia Cunningham" (master's thesis, Catholic University of America, 1966).

4. In the year after *Harriet the Spy*'s publication, Anne Seeley, coordinator of children's services at a library in Montgomery County, Maryland, polled around thirty colleagues and summarized their responses.

5. Harry Gilroy, "Children's Books Move Into Realism," *New York Times Book Review*, April 3, 1969, 49.

6. See Anne Scott MacLeod, "The Transformation of Childhood in Twentieth-Century Children's Literature," in *American Childhood: Essays on Children's Literature of the Nineteenth and Twentieth Centuries* (Athens: University of Georgia Press, 1994).

7. A children's librarian, Frances Clarke Sayers, wrote to John Donovan to state her objections to the "New Realism." A footnote in *Dear Genius* says, "Sayers believed that such books robbed children of the period of innocence to which they were entitled. JD wrote back that innocence was a luxury that most people in contemporary society could ill afford to indulge in." Editor's footnotes on letter from Ursula Nordstrom to John Donovan, September 29, 1969, in Ursula Nordstrom, *Dear Genius: The Letters of Ursula Nordstrom*, collected and edited by Leonard S. Marcus (New York: HarperCollins, 1998), 281n1.

8. See MacLeod, "Transformation of Childhood." MacLeod wrote, "*Harriet* was the breach and after Fitzhugh came the Deluge" (p. 199).

9. Frances FitzGerald, "The Influence of Anxiety: What's the Problem with Young Adult Novels?" *Harper's Magazine*, September 2004, 62. FitzGerald described these mostly formulaic books as having "strong narratives with minimal descriptions of characters or places and little in the way of imagery or metaphor. In them teens speak their own language, often in the immediacy of the present tense. Their voices are sometimes dry and matter-of-fact, sometimes full of emotional

intensity, and sometimes funny, but always they create a world apart from adults."

10. M. E. Kerr, *Dinky Hocker Shoots Smack* (New York: Harper and Row, 1962).

11. Sandra Scoppettone, *Trying Hard to Hear You* (New York: Harper and Row, 1974).

12. Anaïs Nin, *The Diary of Anaïs Nin*, vol. 1, *1931–1934* (New York: Swallow Press/Harcourt, 1966).

13. Elizabeth Winship, "Ask Beth," *Boston Globe*, August 16, 1970.

14. In an interview in Deborah Kovacs and James Preller, *Meet the Authors and Illustrators: 60 Creators of Favorite Children's Books Talk About Their Work* (New York: Scholastic Professional Books, 1991), Charlotte Zolotow says, "I've known dozens of kids who tried to dress like Harriet. After they read it, young people really do run around with their notebook taking notes on things. It's the kids that will make that book last forever."

15. In her book *Blowing My Cover: My Life as a CIA Spy* (New York: G. P. Putnam's Sons, 2006), Lindsay Moran wrote, "I'd always wanted to be a spy and felt as if I'd spent my entire life in training. In childhood, my favorite books, which I would read over and over again, starred Harriet the Spy" (p. 3).

16. Nora L. Magid, "Picture Books," *New York Times*, May 4, 1969.

17. Karen Cook, "Regarding Harriet: Louise Fitzhugh Comes in from the Cold," *Village Voice, Literary Supplement*, April 11, 1995, 15.

18. Cook, "Regarding Harriet."

19. Virginia Woolf, *A Room of One's Own* (London: Hogarth Press, 1929), 63.

20. FL to LB (I); FL to KC (T).

21. FL to LB (T).

22. LF, letter to JM, June 1963.

23. FL to KC (T); FL to LB (T).

24. UN, letter to LF, October 15, 1969, in Nordstrom, *Dear Genius*, 283.

25. Louise had a September 1966 contract deadline for *Sport*, which she did not meet. Afterward they had a more casual agreement.

26. Exchange of letters between LF and JM, undated [ca. 1969].

27. Joanna later said, "They were both cool parents." Joanna Suero to LB (T).

Chapter Seventeen: Survey the Locality

1. Edward Chodorov had been blacklisted in 1953.

2. Rachel Chodorov to LB (C).

3. Louise continued "to refine her highly personal symbolism. Her family of grotesques, of helpless children. These formed a visual iconography which was so emotionally charged that it transcended the personal and communicated to all of us in an almost Jungian dream sense. These visual mythic threads were contained in her earliest work and continued into her last, losing none of their enormous power and immediacy." Louise Fitzhugh memorial program.

4. Probably *The Legend of John Henry* (1974), an eleven-minute short directed by Sam Weiss, featuring Roberta Flack as narrator.

5. Jan Buckaloo (JB) to KC (I); JB to LB (T).

6. In 1973, Sloane was the understudy for Madeline Kahn for the play *In the Boom Boom Room* by David Rabe at the Vivian Beaumont Theater. In 1974, she was in *Felix* by Claude McNeal.

7. *The Brownstone*, a musical, was left unfinished. Cary Ryan inventory.

8. MDC to KC (I).

9. MDC to KC (I); Karen Cook, "Regarding Harriet: Louise Fitzhugh Comes in from the Cold," *Village Voice, Literary Supplement*, April 11, 1995, 40.

10. MDC to KC (I).

11. MDC to KC (I).

12. LF, letters to MDC, January 1974, New York Public Library, Farrar, Straus and Giroux Collection.

13. M.J. Meaker to LB (I).

14. Phyllis Wender to LB (T).

15. AG to LB (I).

16. Mary Louise retired in 1968, after more than thirty years of employment at the library.

17. Louise was satisfied that her mother had a full life in Clarksdale. She and Jake Trevilion were financially sound in retirement. In her late sixties, Mary Louise was healthy. She swam regularly and enjoyed traveling—she and her great niece Glenda explored the Hawaiian reefs together. Mary Louise kept her daughter up to date on other relatives. In 1972, when Mary Louise became a great-great-aunt for the first time, Louise sent Glenda a Tiffany porridge bowl.

18. At the end of her career, Ursula wrote to her friend Katherine S. White, on June 26, 1974, "I've been working for over 40 years and the

worst curse I could put on any man is: In your next life may you be born a talented and creative woman." In Ursula Nordstrom, *Dear Genius: The Letters of Ursula Nordstrom*, collected and edited by Leonard S. Marcus (New York: HarperCollins, 1998), 357. "Mincemeat" quote from Barbara Dicks to LB (I).

19. UN, letter to Joan Robins, July 28, 1981, in Nordstrom, *Dear Genius*, 385.

Chapter Eighteen: Witness

1. Sheridan was Lois's maiden name.

2. Louise Fitzhugh, *Nobody's Family Is Going to Change* (New York: Lizzie Skurnick Books, 2016; New York: Farrar, Straus and Giroux, 1974), 209–210.

3. Coincidentally, Louise shared this philosophy with the boxer Sonny Liston, who died in 1970. The heavyweight champion, who lost his crown to Muhammad Ali in 1964, was wont to say, "People crazy," and "Life a funny thing."

4. *Publishers Weekly*, untitled article, November 4, 1974, 68.

5. MDC to KC (I).

6. JB to LB (T).

7. Alixe was convinced that Louise lived with the fear dating back to a childhood operation that she would die of a brain tumor. She said Louise spoke of this occasionally. In childhood she'd had a mastoidectomy. The doctors had left a piece of a sponge in her head, and this had caused a terribly painful infection, necessitating further surgery. Alixe speculated that the series of paintings Louise had made of a little boy with one portion of his head blurred was related to her fear of pain and death originating in that location. AG to KC and LB (I).

8. JB to LB (T).

9. Louise's death certificate states the cause of death as a ruptured artery in her brain—in technical terms, an "acute subarachnoid aneurysm." Internal hydrocephalus is listed as a significant condition contributing to her death as well, as is hypertension.

10. Fabio Rieti to LB (C). Fabio also said, "What may I add? That I was surprised, and not pleasantly so, that there was a religious service at her death. . . . The Louise I knew was anything but mystical or religious. We deeply agreed on that point. We always regarded religions of any kind as a means of establishing power and keeping people tame. A Marxist view I must own to, but one has to agree from time to time

with the old bearded guy. So what had the church to do with Louise? Would she have approved of the ceremony? I doubt it."

11. Wilde wrote, "To lose one parent may be regarded as a misfortune; to lose both looks like carelessness."

12. Julien Levy, memorial program.

13. Peter Taylor, memorial program, used by permission of Ross Taylor.

14. Hubbell Pierce was a longtime acquaintance of James Merrill and a Connecticut neighbor of Louise and Lois.

15. Frederica Leser, memorial program.

16. FR to LB (C).

17. HTS, 276.

18. Alice Bach to LB, July 24, 2017.

19. Julia Whedon, "Nobody's Family Is Going to Change," *New York Times Book Review*, December 1, 1974.

20. Elizabeth S. Coolidge, "A Trio of Overweight Heroines," *Boston Globe*, December 5, 1974, A16; Mary Somerville, "The Liberation of Children's Books," *Lincoln Journal Star*, February 9, 1975, 63.

21. Sarah Hayes, "Cured Not Changed," *Times Literary Supplement*, April 2, 1976, 375.

22. Adrienne Shirley, "Nobody's Family Is Going to Change," *Off Our Backs* 11, no. 7 (1981): 23. *Nobody's Family Is Going to Change* was awarded *The Guardian*'s 1976 commendation for a children's book that makes a contribution to "the development of a children's literature that reflects our changing society." "National Children's Book Week," *The Guardian*, July 1, 1976, 10.

23. In "'Too Realistic' and 'Too Distorted': The Attack on Louise Fitzhugh's *Harriet the Spy* and the Gaze of the Queer Child," *Critical Matrix* 12, no. 1–2 (2001), Robin Bernstein wrote, "Lying, of course, is part of the arsenal of weapons that the successful trickster heroine uses to survive."

24. Fitzhugh, *Nobody's Family Is Going to Change*, 204

Afterword

1. Kathleen T. Horning, "On Spies and Purple Socks and Such," *The Horn Book*, March 26, 2005, www.hbook.com/?detailStory=on-spies-and-purple-socks-and-such.

2. Jonathan Lethem, "The Insipid Profession of Jonathan Horneboom," in *How We Got Insipid* (Burton, MI: Subterranean Press, 2006).

3. Dahlia Lithwick, "Robert Mueller Needs a New Team," *Slate*, July 17, 2017, https://slate.com/news-and-politics/2017/07/why-robert-mueller-needs-to-hire-harriet-the-spy.html.

4. Bertram Slaff to KC (I).

5. AG to LB (I).

6. Cary Ryan to LB (I).

7. Cary Ryan to LB (I); Cary Ryan, inventory notes.

8. MDC, letters to Roger Straus, New York Public Library, Farrar, Straus and Giroux Collection.

9. Police officers were routinely viewed as "pigs" in the 1960s and 1970s by counterculture youths for their frontline defense of the establishment and the military-industrial complex. The scene illustrates the kind of profiling and bigoted police activity that years later would be exposed and opposed by Black Lives Matter and other social justice movements. As I write this George Floyd's murder has precipitated protests around the world.

10. Jessica Mitford, *The American Way of Death* (New York: Simon and Schuster, 1963).

11. Muriel Cohen, "Study Finds Rise in Attacks on School Books," *Boston Globe*, August 31, 1989, 16. A parent in Sandwich, Massachusetts, asked for the elementary school library to remove *Sport* "because . . . it contained offensive language, racial slurs and sexism." The school's review committee voted to retain the book, and the parent appealed without success.

12. *I Am Five* was one of the unfinished manuscripts found after Louise's death. A complete dummy with black and white sketches was eventually discovered. The book was published by Delacorte in 1978. It was redesigned and hand lettered in a high-quality production by the book artist Lynn Braswell.

13. The musical adaptation was also generally endorsed by the national Black press as a welcome addition to literature about the Black professional class. The fury of the original is diluted in the Broadway version. Emma's story is subordinated to Willie's, and the book's theme of rage at racial inequality is limited to a few powerful moments. In any case, the show mostly delighted audiences. The Reverend Jesse Jackson would embrace a 1986 Washington, DC, production as "heart-warming

family entertainment." "Tap Dance Kid Warner Opening to Benefit Rainbow Coalition," *Washington Informer* 22, no. 18 (1986): 23.

14. Writers are credited as Greg Taylor and Julie Talen for adaptation, and Douglas Petrie and Teresa Rebeck for screenplay. "Harriet the Spy (1996)," IMDB, www.imdb.com/title/tt0116493/fullcredits?ref_=tt_ov_wr#writers.

15. Gregory Maguire, *Wicked: The Life and Times of the Wicked Witch of the West* (New York: HarperCollins, 2004).

16. Amy Biancolli, "Wicked Author Gregory Maguire on Bill at Albany Reading Program Benefit," *Times Union*, October 24, 2019.

17. Alison Bechdel, "By the Book," *New York Times*, July 26, 2012.

18. "Lois A. Morehead," Legacy.com, www.legacy.com/obituaries/name/lois-morehead-obituary?pid=137179128&affiliateid=2715.

19. The plaque in Carl Schurz park was supported by the Empire State Center for the Book, Random House Children's Books, and the Carl Schurz Park Conservancy. Dedicated December 7, 2014.

CREDITS

"Gee, Officer Krupke" by Leonard Bernstein & Stephen Sondheim. Copyright © 1956, 1957, 1958, 1959 by Amberson Holdings LLC and Stephen Sondheim. Copyright renewed. Leonard Bernstein Music Publishing Company LLC, publisher. Boosey and Hawkes, agent for rental. International copyright secured. All rights reserved. Used with permission.

Charlotte Zolotow interview in Deborah Kovacs and James Preller, *Meet the Authors and Illustrators: 60 Creators of Favorite Children's Books Talk About Their Work* (New York: Scholastic Professional Books, 1991), used with permission of Scholastic, Inc.

Excerpt from Agnes de Mille, *Martha: The Life and Work of Martha Graham* (New York: Random House, 1991), courtesy of Penguin Random House.

Excerpt from Joan Didion, *Slouching Towards Bethlehem: Essays* (New York: Farrar, Straus and Giroux, 2008), courtesy of Farrar, Straus and Giroux.

Excerpt from James Merrill, *A Different Person: A Memoir* (New York: Alfred A. Knopf, 1993), courtesy of Alfred A. Knopf. Other James Merrill quotes by permission of his literary executor and the literary estate of James Merrill at Washington University, St. Louis.

Excerpts from Ursula Nordstrom, *Dear Genius: The Letters of Ursula Nordstrom*, collected and edited by Leonard S. Marcus (New York: HarperCollins, 1998), copyright © 1998 by Leonard S. Marcus. Used by permission of HarperCollins.

Excerpt from Kathleen T. Horning, "On Spies and Purple Socks and Such," *The Horn Book*, March 26, 2005, by permission of Kathleen T. Horning.

Sandra Scoppettone, *Suzuki Beane*, illustrated by Louise Fitzhugh (Garden City, NY: Doubleday, 1961), quoted by permission of Sandra Scoppettone.

Excerpt from Peter Taylor, "A Long Fourth," in *The Old Forest and Other Stories* and memorial program, "A Tribute to Louise Fitzhugh, 1928–1974," St. James' Church, December 6, 1974, courtesy of Ross Taylor.

"You Don't Own Me," words and music by John Madara and Dave White. Copyright © 1963 (Renewed) Unichappell Music Inc. All rights reserved. Used by permission of Alfred Music.

"Here's to the State of Mississippi" by permission of the Phil Och's estate, courtesy Meegan Ochs.

Leaflet announcing Louise Fitzhugh art exhibit at New York Public Library, Hudson Branch, by permission of New York Public Library.

Cover photo of Louise Fitzhugh, around twenty-one years old, by Lilyan Chauvin, from the collection of France Burke, by permission of Sam Shea and Julie Ann Johnson.

INDEX

Photo by Emily Tucker

Leslie Brody's books include *Irrepressible: The Life and Times of Jessica Mitford* and *Red Star Sister: Between Madness and Utopia*. She lives in Redlands, California.